PITTSBURGH THEOLOGICAL MONOGRAPHS

New Series

Dikran Y. Hadidian

General Editor

5

STUDIES OF THE CHURCH IN HISTORY

Essays honoring Robert S. Paul
on his Sixty-fifth Birthday

ROBERT S. PAUL

STUDIES OF THE CHURCH IN HISTORY

Essays honoring Robert S. Paul

on his Sixty-fifth Birthday

Edited by

Horton Davies

PICKWICK PUBLICATIONS

Allison Park, Pennsylvania

1983

Copyright © 1983 by **Pickwick Publications**
4137 Timberlane Drive, Allison Park, PA 15101

Printed in the United States of America

Library of Congress Cataloging in Publication Data
Main entry under title:

Studies of the church in history.

    (Pittsburgh theological monographs. New series ; 5)
    1. Theology—Addresses, essays, lectures. 2. Paul, Robert
S.—Addresses, essays, lectures. I. Davies, Horton. II. Paul,
Robert S. III. Title. IV. Series.
BR50.S84 1983 270.8 83-9715
ISBN 0-915138-55-7

CONTENTS

Part One

Introducing Robert S. Paul

Part Two

Essays Honoring Robert S. Paul

PREFACE

This collection of essays is an affectionate salute to Robert S. Paul, minister of the Gospel, ecumenical Churchman, ecclesiastical Historian, artist and caricaturist whose wit is spiced with affection, and its title "Studies of the Church in History" is as broad as his own interests. It is a tribute of admiration from the friends, colleagues, and former students to celebrate his sixty-fifth birthday in June, 1983. Appropriately they come from both sides of the Atlantic, for Robert S. Paul was educated in England, was minister of Christ Church, Leatherhead, and Associate Director of the Ecumenical Institute at Bossey near Geneva before crossing the Atlantic to teach church history at three Seminaries in Hartford, Pittsburgh and, at present, at Austin Seminary in Texas. Two other contributors sent their essays from the Pacific zone, from Australia and Fiji--a further image of Robert's widespread influence.

As a loyal alumnus of Mansfield College, Oxford, he will rejoice in the fact that three successive Principals of Mansfield contribute their essays to this **Festschrift,** as he will lament the death of Erik R. Routley who was to have written on the theme he had made almost exclusively his own--hymnology and Church music--but was prevented by death. Robert's caricatures of some of us while at Mansfield are reproduced as an indication of the wit and humor of the unpretentious man and scholar we honor. We hope these essays on Biblical scholarship, historical traditions, ecumenical concerns, and the contemporary relevance of the Gospel may reflect Robert Paul's profound commitment to the Christian faith and the Body of Christ. We wish him long years of further service beyond his 65th birthday.

April, 1983

Horton Davies
Princeton University

CONTRIBUTORS

Geoffrey Barnes, a student of Robert S. Paul at Hartford Seminary Foundation, Hartford, Connecticut. Formerly Principal of Camden College, Sydney, Australia. He is currently lecturer at the United Theological College in Enfield, Australia.

George B. Caird is Dean Ireland's Professor of the Exegesis of Holy Scripture in Oxford University; fifth Principal of Mansfield College, Oxford and formerly Professor of New Testament Language and Literature at McGill University, Montreal, Canada.

Paul A. Crow, Jr. is President of the Council on Christian Unity of the Christian Church (Disciples of Christ). He was a student of Robert S. Paul at Hartford Seminary Foundation, Hartford, Connecticut. Formerly Professor of Church History, Lexington Theological Seminary, and General Secretary, Consultation on Church Union, Princeton, New Jersey.

Horton Davies is Putnam Professor of the History of Christianity at Princeton University. Formerly Head of the Joint Department of Church History at Mansfield and Regent's Park Colleges, Oxford, and founding Professor of Divinity in Rhodes University, Grahamstown, South Africa.

Robert L. Edwards, an ordained minister of the United Church of Christ, formerly minister of the First Congregational Church of Litchfield, Connecticut where Horace Bushnell was born, and Immanuel Congregational Church, Hartford, Connecticut.

John Garrett, a minister of the Uniting Church in Australia, is Professor of Church History at the regional and ecumenical Pacific Theological College, Suva, Fiji; formerly Director of the World Council of Churches Information Department and Editor of the Ecumenical Press Service.

John W. Grant is Professor of Church History at Emmanuel College, Toronto, Canada. Robert S. Paul met John Grant for the first time in 1981 in Basel, Switzerland at the consultation on "Church History in Ecumenical Perspective" and shared many common interests.

Dikran Y. Hadidian, Librarian of Pittsburgh Theological Seminary. Formerly Librarian of the Hartford Seminary Foundation, Hartford, Connecticut.

John Marsh, formerly Moderator of the Free Church Federal Council, fourth Principal of Mansfield College, Oxford and Professor of Christian Theology at the University of Nottingham.

Jack M. Maxwell is President of Austin Presbyterian Theological Seminary, Austin, Texas; formerly minister of First Presbyterian Church, Sewickley, Pennsylvania.

Donald McKim, a student of Robert S. Paul, is Assistant Professor of Theology at the University of Dubuque Theological Seminary, Dubuque, Iowa.

Donald G. Miller, formerly President, Pittsburgh Theological Seminary, Pittsburgh, Pennsylvania and Walter H. Robertson Professor of New Testament, Union Theological Seminary, Richmond, Virginia.

John I. Morgans, a student of Robert S. Paul at Hartford Seminary Foundation, Hartford, Connecticut, is presently the Provincial Moderator of The United Reformed Church, Province of Wales.

Donald A. Sykes is currently the sixth Principal of Mansfield College, Oxford; former visiting Professor of Religion at St. Olaf College, Northfield, Minnesota.

PART ONE

Introducing Robert S. Paul

A CONVERSATION WITH ROBERT PAUL

Jack M. Maxwell

President of Austin Presbyterian Theological Seminary, Dr. Jack Maxwell, long-time friend and colleague of Robert S. Paul, proposed by a self-denying act—instead of writing an essay—to tape a conversation in which Robert S. Paul could talk about his writings and convictions through the years and plans for the future. Its aim, according to Dr. Maxwell is "an attempt to let those who know him in on the present locus of his pilgrimage, and to introduce a remarkable churchman to those who have never had the privilege of meeting him. It is a candid and casual conversation between friends who know each other rather well; yet he is so engaging that I trust you will quickly enter in and overhear the clear sounds of one whose joy of living and whose commitment to the Church quickly becomes infectious."

Maxwell: Before we get into a more substantive conversation, describe your methods of research and writing. How does a book get written?

Paul: Well, over the years I have kept pretty careful files on any subject that particularly interested me; and insights or ideas I get in the course of my reading go into those files. I am always collecting material on things that I become interested in, and this usually provides me with the basis of any lectures, or any other presentations I am asked to make. When I decide to write on a particular subject, I refer to the file and see what I've got on that subject. It is often quite clear that there are gaps, and I then begin to read into them, using as far as possible original sources, and then the secondary material. And if I get blocks of time when I can work on this, that's how the book gets written. It may start from a lecture series, or it may simply be that I've decided to write on this particular issue which is important to

3

the Church at this time. But it goes back to the accumulated material which I have on file and which I then supplement with additional reading as necessary.

Maxwell: Your file on authority must be a filing cabinet by now.

Paul: It is pretty full. The file on authority actually goes back to the early sixties when I began to study the problem of the Church. What was the authority for saying that the Church should have a certain character or a certain particular form? What is the authority for any denomination claiming to be the Church of Jesus Christ? Once I began to ponder that, I began to see how central the issue of authority is to all Christian theology. As you probably know, I started to deal with it in **Ministry;** and then I went on to pursue the question a little bit further in **The Church In Search of Its Self;** and I intend eventually to write a book on it, because I think it is the ecumenical problem of the time.

Maxwell: What will the shape of that book be? What are the issues in authority? How are you going to go at it?

Paul: Well, it is difficult to say at this moment precisely how I am going to go about it, but the first thing I think we have to see is that the problem of authority not only affects the Church and theology, but it is also one which runs to the very roots of Western society. There is a sense in which what happened from the time of the Reformation onwards has profoundly affected the whole question of authority in society itself. I am not simply talking in terms now of the channels of authority, forms of government and this sort of thing, but how do we arrive at an international ethical consensus able to carry authority, which is self-evident to humankind. That's one thing that needs to be said. It was touched by P. T. Forsyth in **Principle of Authority,** and until the Church gets its signals clear at this level, I don't think we can expect a great deal of respect from the secular world.

Maxwell: Have you seen the bumper stickers that read "Question Authority"?

Paul: No, no I haven't, but I can understand the protest, because there is the problem--the word "authority." I was talking about it in class recently and somebody said, "Your problem is with the word 'authority'." It is, because the word, "authority," implies, first, simply a chain of command rather like from the general going down to the private. We are dealing with something here which is much more fundamental than that, namely, the ground on which we determine that certain things are right and other things are wrong. There is no one word to describe that apart from the word, "authority." When I say, I have authority for doing certain things, or when I quote an "authority", I am not talking about a chain of command, I am talking about ground for my action. That's really what we are concerned with. I am going to try and make it clear; and how to do that will be the trick of that bit of writing. We are not simply concerned with commands as such, but we are talking about the basic grounds for action in personal ethics, in social action, in forms of government, and so on. Does that help at all?

Maxwell: Yes, it does. Do the people with bumper stickers that say, "Question Authority," have a theological problem or some other kind of problem?

Paul: I think that they see the problem of authority simply in terms of a chain of command. Yet each of them, if you press them, would have a reason--their "authority"--for taking the stand that is represented by the bumper sticker. That is the authority under which they themselves are working. So I don't think we avoid the problem by simply shouting, "question authority." By all means question authorities as they have been handed to us, or as imposed on us; but recognize that when you've questioned as far as you can, you've got to have some "authority" for thinking that the questioning is legitimate. What authority have you for that? That's the question that I would put to people with the bumper stickers. I want to press them to the point of seeing that one does not get rid of the authority issue simply by questioning the traditional channels by which authority has come to us.

Maxwell: This may not be the only inference to be drawn from such a bumper-sticker mentality, but I wonder if what they are after is a kind of individualism that would certainly render society, not to mention the Church, utterly chaotic.

Paul: Agreed. If fundamentally they are saying the individual is the only authority we recognize, I would deny that as a church-man. In fact, I would regard it as a fundamental heresy.

As I have already said in **Ministry** and **The Church in Search of Its Self,** there are three fundamental channels of author-ity that come to the Church: namely, the authority that is revealed in the scriptures, the authority that is revealed through the tradition of the Church, and the authority that comes to me as a Christian individual within my own experience. I would point out that the first two are not individualistic, they are corporate. That which comes to me through the testimony of the scriptures comes to me through the testimony which has been itself authorized by the Church, and the authority of the Church is itself a corporate authority, whether I think of the Church in purely contemporary terms or in historic terms. I'll cite Forsyth here when he reminded us that if we are going to put doctrines to the vote, the vote goes with the Christians of the past, because they are always the majority. I think that was a very shrewd comment. I am not simply an individual, I am always an individual within context, whether I regard it as a social context, an ecclesiastical context, or an historical context.

Maxwell: Do you remember how you resolved the matter of authority in **Ministry**?

Paul: I don't know that I can remember the exact quote.

Maxwell: Well, I will quote it to you. You say, "Final authority is to be found in the living Christ (the word of God), as revealed first in the historic record (the Bible), to whom the faithful in all generations (the Church) bear their historic witness, and to whom in the gift of the Holy Spirit the Christian gives the assent of faith." Now, is that just a nifty way of pulling all three together? What have you really said there?

Paul: I have said fundamentally--I am speaking very personally at this point--I have to go to the historic record first of all. I can't ignore that: Christianity is a revealed religion. But it is not a revealed faith which has simply become, as it were, sacrosanct. It is revealed religion as it is seen in relationship to the continuing community of the Church. I think the doctrine of the Holy Spirit forces me to see that Church history is a necessary commentary and exegesis on the Bible. And I have to take into account these corporate testimonies because this community of revealed faith is the one to which I belong. I measure my own ideas in relationship to the corporate witness. There are times when I may want to argue a great deal with scripture or with what Church tradition declares, but always I recognize that my own interpretation and my own understanding to some extent have to come under the judgment of the corporate testimony, if it is to be valid Christian experience, and I hope I would always recognize that. But it is very much a personal approach; it's not simply a piece of theological engineering to bring the different channels of spiritual authority together. I see it very much as being, if you like, that which makes me able to act as a Christian. I don't know if that is a good way of expressing it, but perhaps you can see what I mean.

Maxwell: I can, indeed.

Paul: There is something I want to add to that now, Jack: When I wrote **Ministry** I was very much taken with the three channels of grace which come to us--scriptures, Church tradition, and personal experience. I then began to realize that we are all given a necessary means by which the understanding of these three channels of grace comes to us. I called it "reason". It's not a very good word, because, again, it is a loaded word to which we bring our own theological prejudices, but God gives us the reponsibility of using what we would call our "reason," and this is one of the conditions of being human. It involves, if you like, intuitions, conscience, and all the natural impulses whereby I as a human, whether I happen to be a Russian Communist, Chinese Buddhist, or Japanese Shintoist, exercise this faculty of evaluation and judgment, and I believe it is God-given and needs to be recognized. It is not indeed a theological authority or theological channel like the others I mentioned in **Ministry**, but it is the human filter through which all ideas, insights and revelation come to me.

This means that I have to recognize my theological answers to be tentative. They can never be absolutized in the sense in which sometimes we have absolutized theological answers in the past, to the point where they become virtually Jesus Christ himself to Christians, and I think this should bring a very necessary element of humility to our theological judgments. It is almost as if God is forcing us to go through this channel (reason) so that we may recognize that our theological reconstructions and our ecclesiastical claims can never become absolute. When we do make them absolute, then we put them up as the idol that we worship in place of the God of revelation himself, or herself according to how you want to think of God. It doesn't matter to me which. "You shall have no other gods but me." So we have to wrestle with our need to provide authoritative answers, but our answers are not absolute. One of the great temptations of the Church has always been to set up its theologies as different forms of idolatry--theologies that are based on self-idolatry or ecclesiolotry or bibliolotry. We have absolutized the channels of grace where God demands that we should follow him alone in faith. Our trouble is that we prefer to claim knowledge rather than faith. Trust is a very danger-ous thing because one has to risk one's future destiny to another. But that is what we are called to, and often if we can get rid of the risk by claiming a saving knowledge from a sacrosanct book or a sacrosanct creed or a sacrosanct tradition or a sacrosanct historical succession, then we have got rid of the need for faith: We don't need faith any more, we have knowledge. There is a great temptation not to take God in trust as He is revealed in Jesus Christ. That's where the importance of what I've called "reason" comes in. By our creation as human beings we are forced to go through it. We can't make any theological judgments without it. And therefore I know that my understanding of the basic author-ity I acknowledge is going to be incomplete, tentative; but insofar as we do follow in faith, I think we are not led astray. The point was made by Hans Küng when he made a distinction between infallibility and indefectibility. Our theological answers are not absolute, but the Church is prevented from . . .

Maxwell: Egregious error?

Paul: Egregious error, yes. It is not allowed to go permanently astray; but it is always called to follow in faith without the absolute certainty that really implies a form of idolatry.

Maxwell: But do you honestly believe that? That finally the Church is kept from egregious error? I am not the historian, but I can think of an instance or two . . .

Paul: Right, yes. Let me try to be clearer: I think the Church is able to make shocking, ghastly, damnable errors; but I also believe that there is that within the Church which sooner or later brings it face to face with its own gospel, or to that part of its own gospel which becomes essential for its continued existence as the Church.

As I see it, the two big periods of Church history when the Church was most in danger of wrongly identifying the Kingdom of God with particular cultures were, first, the period just before the Reformation when the Church identified the Kingdom with "Christendom" and was willing to bring it in by force if necessary. The second period was in the Nineteenth Century when the Kingdom was associated with imperialism and we thought we could bring it in by bribing people into the Church. These were two periods of Church history when, if the Kingdom of God could have come in by any other means than the gospel itself, it would certainly have arrived. Think of the immense authority the Church had just before the Reformation. It was a fantastic power--the most powerful and the wealthiest organization in the whole of Western Europe. It could command anything by reason of its power to impose an interdict, for example, on people; and yet the Kingdom did not come in that way.

Something similar may be seen in the Nineteenth Century: Protestant countries had enormous prestige during the Nineteenth Century. We were able to go into places and offer hospitals, social services and education, and the bribery, or the temptation of bribery was there. But the Kingdom didn't arrive. Why? Because God was saying to us, "until you take seriously not only the good news of Jesus Christ, but also the Spirit that is characterized by his love, joy, peace, long-suffering, gentleness, so on--the whole list of spiritual qualities in Galatians 5 or in Philippians 4--until you take that ethical imperative with an ultimate seriousness, you cannot claim the Kingdom. And this is how Church history exegetes the New Testament for me. Does that make any sense at all?

Maxwell: Yes, that helps. I want to raise another matter that I know to be a favorite of yours. Talk to me about Forsyth, whom you have quoted two or three times already. In the Preface to **Kingdom Come** you wrote: "I chose Forsyth deliberately because he speaks to me with a special pertinence at this time." And then you went on to say, "Forsyth spoke out of an Anglo-Saxon context and out of a Free Church experience that gave him a peculiar ability to discern the theological weakness of our time and place." The irreverent part of the question is, Why does an Anglo-Saxon context and a Free Church experience give one distinctive discernment?

Paul: Well, Forsyth grew up in my own Mother Church, and naturally that gives him a certain amount of interest for me. He grew up in that Church very much under the influence of all the liberal presuppositions of that time, particularly the critical presuppositions which were coming into vogue in the last part of the Nineteenth Century, and yet he came through that experience, not to deny those presuppositions, but to modify them to the point where he came to grips with what was essential gospel in the scriptures and also found that he had to deal with Christian experience, and these are evangelical concepts. As a pastor he had to deal with these things, and he recognized that he had to do this in order to be a good pastor. He came to a faith that did not deny the valid critique of scriptural sources, but he was able to reaffirm the gospel through it and with honesty. I think the whole emphasis upon the God of revelation which one meets in Forsyth spoke to me with a particular clarity.

Now about that facetious side of the question. I am living and working at this moment, and have lived and worked for the last twenty-five years or so in America; and I think this Free Church, Anglo-Saxon context is very much the context which has developed out of America's own historic roots. In other words the culture has been essentially Anglo-Saxon up till now in its cultural emphases, and Free Church in its ecclesiastical presuppositions. Forsyth, therefore, speaks very directly to something which lies at the center of the society in which I am engaged at the moment. I think that his words, for example, to the Yale students of 1907 could have been uttered by a modern thinker and that they still speak with some force to us.

That doesn't mean that I think Forsyth is a greater theologian than Barth or Brunner; but I think that continental theologians came to their theological problems out of the context of a Church-State relationship that just doesn't obtain over here, and with a different cultural tradition. Forsyth spoke out of a different context, the context that was brought from old Britain to America with Puritans, Presbyterians, Baptists and even Anglicans to some extent, because after the War of Independence the Anglicans had to accept the Free Church context. Then when you add Methodism, which also came out of Britain, and the Quakers, you have a pretty formidable cultural matrix which is essentially Free Church in its ethos. Forsyth speaks to it. And we should listen to what he had to say, because I think he saw more deeply into the Twentieth Century challenge to this kind of culture than probably any other theologian. He saw where we were likely to go and he raised the flags.

Maxwell: And, we're going there anyway?

Paul: Aren't we, by George!

Maxwell: Bob, your several published volumes form a fascinating constellation. Your first was the religious and political biography of Cromwell, followed by **The Atonement and the Sacraments;** then back to the Seventeenth Century and **The Apologetical Narration.** Next your attention turned to ecclesiology in **Ministry,** which I find to be your most enduring work, **The Church in Search of Its Self** and then, to some extent, **Kingdom Come.** Now you've moved back to the Seventeenth Century with the **Assembly of the Lord,** and from there to theology and detective fiction. What can you possibly say that would make us believe your sanity is still intact. What are you up to? Does this all hang together somehow?

Paul: The first thing is that you cannot remove a writer from the historical context in which he writes. I had certain interests, but they had developed in response to the situation in which I lived. The first interest was the relationship of religion to politics, and for that I chose Cromwell as being, I think, the epitome of the problem

But I was also in a pastorate and took that pastorate with ultimate seriousness, so I was also understandably concerned not only with the problems of religion and politics, but also the problems of the Church as they had to be faced here and now. I was also convinced about the gospel imperative to pursue ecumenical unity in the Church, and this, too, became part of my drive, I suppose, which made me want to work in certain areas. Now as I look back on it, this did have a unity of which I was certainly never conscious at the time. It is really a concern about the testimony of the Church, its gospel and its theology within Western society. There has been a growing recognition, in me at any rate, that until we get our theology straight, until we are clear with respect to our understanding of the gospel, the Church doesn't have a great deal to say to society. I see my books, therefore, while moving on very different planes, as moving towards the same point, which is, how the Church speaks to our society. What do we need to say, and what is our authority for saying it?

Now curiously enough, in dealing with the pastoral problems of people in the parish, as I did with **The Atonement and the Sacraments,** I was pushed at once to consider the ecumenical problem of **Ministry,** and that in turn pushed me to consider the whole nature of the Church in **The Church in Search of Its Self.** That pushes me further to address the question of authority. In other words, starting along a certain line one is impelled to move in directions that are not obvious at first.

You see, Protestantism doesn't work like Catholicism: a Protestant theologian is not in the happy situation of a Catholic who may be directed to go to a monastery for several years and really work on a problem for the sake of the Church. Protestantism relies on individuals who happen to see the point and feel some call to wrestle with the problem it presents. And since nobody else appeared anxious to tackle ordination in the mid-'60's, I then had the responsibility of doing it myself. That's how **Ministry** came to be written, and then there seemed to be an equal reluctance to deal with the problem of the Church. Otherwise I would never have ventured into those fields at all: I would have concentrated on Seventeenth Century studies. I think that if one sees issues that appear to be important, then a member of the Church who has some capacity to address them has the responsibility, not only to see them, but meet the need. That's why those books were written.

Maxwell: I can understand how **The Atonement and the Sacraments** would lead to **Ministry,** which would lead to **The Church in Search of Its Self** and **Kingdom Come** and so on. I gather the **Assembly of the Lord** represents a return to Seventeenth Century research.

Paul: To some extent, and yet at the heart of it there is an ecumenical problem with which we are still wrestling--the problem of authority. Looking back on the acrimonious debate in the Westminster Assembly between the Reformed churchmen who were called Presbyterians and those called Congregationalists or Independents, I couldn't take many of the positions that they took, either one of them. Nor do I think most of the churchmen I know, Congregational or Presbyterian, could accept those positions. Our attitude to the question of authority and how we exegete scripture has entirely changed. This means, first, that a new freedom is offered to us with respect to our traditions, and, second, that we are invited to look at the issues afresh and together. Of course, if one considers oneself 100% bound by either of the Westminster traditions, then one just stands pat. That can be idolatrous. But if we can look at it de novo, then fascinating ecumenical possibilities arise in re-examining the nature of the Church, which didn't obtain in the Seventeenth Century. So, although **Assembly of the Lord** is a continuation of the concern for the relationship of religion and politics, and there is plenty of that in the book, it also provides a significant historical illustration of the authority issue which I am hammering theologically: the importance of it and the necessity to look at it again.

Maxwell: So, authority really is the glue that holds your corpus together--up to this point. But can you explain **Whatever Happened to Sherlock Holmes?**, the book you are writing on theology and detective fiction?

Paul: I would love to do that, but, I am not going to be hypocritical. My early interest in detective fiction was really given to me by Eunice, who decided when I was at Leatherhead, and had to preach morning and evening, that after the evening service, I ought to have some kind of relaxation. She started me on reading Dorothy Sayers, so it began as pure relaxation, and it has continued purely as relaxation; but more and more I became convinced that the basic issues in detective fiction--in its concerns with the question of justice, the distinction of right from wrong, the value of the human personality, the question of retribution, the nature of the truth--were fundamentally theological. Why do the detective writers have to deal with these issues? The best explanation is that their readers expect it of them and probably would not buy their books if they brushed these issues aside as irrelevant. And yet these issues are fundamentally theological questions. So, I became convinced more and more that detective fiction provided us with a very interesting insight into the popular theological presuppositions about life that have been assimilated by the general public, and that if changes have occurred in that "popular theology," they would be reflected in detective fiction sooner than anywhere else, because the author won't sell his books if he doesn't deal with life as the general public expects him, or her, to deal with it. And you have got to say, "her," when you are talking about detective fiction, because you have only got to think of Margery Allingham, Josephine Tey, Dorothy Sayers, Agatha Christie, Patricia Wentworth, Ngaio Marsh, Georgette Heyer, Amanda Cross, Catherine Aird, Emma Lathen, P. D. James, and how many more women can I mention who . . .

Maxwell: Why are there so many women?

Paul: I don't know, but undoubtedly they are the best.

Maxwell: I know very little about most of the names in that list, but did a Dorothy Sayers, for example, in any intentional way use detective fiction to communicate her understanding of the Christian faith . . .

Paul: No.

Maxwell: Or, to what ever extent it may be there at all, did it just seep in through her value system?

Paul: It seeped in through her value system because I think she consciously tried to avoid imposing her own prejudices on her characters. I think Agatha Christie, however, in the Sixties and early Seventies _may_ have been dealing consciously with theological issues; and I would cite as an example of that the very interesting novel called **Endless Night**, which I think is one of the most significant things theologically that she ever wrote. She really deals with the question of heaven and hell in **Endless Night**. It ends with a marvelous descriptive passage about a young man who has murdered his wife, whom he has really loved all the time. But he had been so utterly selfish that he went after other playthings and rejected the love that he had received through her. And at the end he discovered that nothing else mattered, and his last thoughts run like this: It seems odd that nothing matters. Nothing matters at all. Only Ellie, [his wife,] and she can't ever find me again. "Endless night. That's the end of my story."

Very powerful stuff. Wonderfully preachable, if I may say so. What I am saying is that if you have some understanding of what's going on in detective fiction, you may be in a better position to deal with the question of Christian apologetic. That is really what I am interested in, just as I believe that in terms of speculative theology and also in terms of eschatological insights science fiction probably points in a similar direction.

Maxwell: So, the interest in detective fiction is not as a conveyor of the Christian message, but rather as one of those places, and apparently a reliable one, where you can discern where the cultural values are at a given time?

Paul: Exactly--where it is going, what's happening to the culture, because it is quite clear that the whole change in ethics has taken place since the 1950's. We know that, but it is reflected nowhere more clearly than in detective fiction. I am not thinking here about whether the detective hops in and out of bed with lovely young ladies or that sort of thing, but I am talking about the real change in ethics. The whole question of what is truth is much more shadowy than it used to be; the motivation for pursuing the so-called ends of justice is much less clear than it used to be; the identification of the law of the land with justice is much more questionable than it used to be; and ultimately the paradoxical nature of love is more clearly recognized. Agatha Christie provides a case in point.

One of the chapters that I hope to write will be on the Agatha Christie "pilgrimage," because she spanned such a long time and there is evidence of a real pilgrimage in her approach to her work. Some of the characters in two or three of her later novels play on the question of how love can be abused and misused. You can love in the wrong way, and that is a theological issue.

The study really raises very important questions because

as attitudes change, there is no longer any clear cut conception of right and wrong as we assumed before the '50's. Society itself has changed as it has drawn away from the Church, and it may be looking for other spiritual authorities, I don't know. P. D. James is a good example of a woman who sees herself, or rather through her characters she sees herself, in a very ambivalent position to religion. In one way she wants to affirm it . . .

Maxwell: But she certainly didn't affirm it in that scene in **The Skull Beneath the Skin.** She produced an Anglican priest in his dotage, who is the epitome of insignificance and irrelevance.

Paul: Right. In one way she wants to affirm it and yet she finds herself unable to affirm it in that way in which it was often affirmed in the past.

Maxwell: What has happened since 1950 or so which makes that a cut off date for you? You said two or three times that prior to 1950 . . .

Paul: Yes, right. I think that before 1950 we had the pre-War values with very clear-cut concepts of "right" and "wrong," and we identified the law of the land with justice. During the '50's attitudes begin to change, first of all in Western Europe, so that by the time we arrive at the mid-'60's, we can say many writers are struggling with new ideas. Agatha Christie was obviously searching for a new format, and I don't think she ever found it. I've cited **Endless Night,** but you could cite another of her experiments in which she saw the cultural problems very much as a struggle against international principalities and powers in **The Passenger from Frankfurt.** She is fascinating because she spans such a long period of writing. Of course, Dorothy Sayers is interesting from another point of view, in that at the end she gave up detective fiction entirely and turned specifically to theology.

Maxwell: Based upon your reading of detective fiction, could you characterize our society in 1983?

Paul: I think so. There is a pragmatic element which has seemed noticeable in the police procedurals, for example--just doing a job, no need to make any ethical big deal about it, just a job I have to do. There's that, but also I see it very much, too, as a society which is desperately looking for a basic spiritual and ethical "authority" that will exercise its claim on all people. You see this in the ambivalent position of writers such as P. D. James, but not only in her. In several writers you have a similar ambivalence with regard to our society and its ethical standards. They try to affirm the good things of the past but without being able to endorse all the earlier values. Something should fill the ethical gap, and yet they don't know what it should be. If I wanted to comment on where I think most of the detective writers of perception see society and its problems, the quotation, however, would not come from them but from J. B. Priestley, at the end of his book, **Literature and Western Man,** in which he spoke about the need of a new religious base for Western society. He spoke as an agnostic, but he said that until we discover that new spiritual base, we are at sea, unless, of course, we blow ourselves to pieces before it happens. I find that passage one of the most significant and moving passages about our culture in literature at the moment. But its mood is also reflected in detective fiction; and, strangely enough, it is reflected in a rather more positive way in science fiction, because science fiction has to presume there will be a future.

Maxwell: I was going to ask if you think there is any other genre of literature, fiction in particular, that does the same thing as detective fiction.

Paul: I think that science fiction is seriously dealing with the question of apocalyptic and eschatology, and it takes the place of the old speculative theology. Science fiction writers let their minds play and are asking, "Where is the world going?" And when they try to answer that question fictionally, they again have to deal with ethical questions and where our own ethics--social and personal--are driving us. And so science fiction is also very illuminating from the point of view of apologetic.

I want to send people on a little detective hunt of their own. When they read a detective story, they should detect what the detective writer is saying about our society. And what is being said about society now provides me with the most fascinating clues to follow in a detective story.

Maxwell: I find that very insightful. I suspect most of us read detective and science fiction purely for entertainment.

Paul: Well, yes, it always starts that way.

Maxwell: But to sit back and think, maybe this writer is consciously or even unconsciously telling us something that is far more important than "who done it" . . .

Paul: Yes. The readers want to know that everything is going to be all right. That everything can be brought right in the end. And why do they want to know that? Because if all is right with the world, there must be something or Someone good "up there" who is in control.

Maxwell: That desire may be more evident today in certain ways, but what you've just said takes me back to the Western movies

I used to watch as a child. However terrifying they might have been and however nearly the white hats came to losing, you just knew that finally they were going to win . . .

Paul: That's right. It's always been there . . .

Maxwell: That there was some sort of order that was eventually going to prevail.

Paul: There it is, all the way through. There were several writers who tried to romanticize crooks. E. W. Hornung, Conan Doyle's brother-in-law, created the adventurer-crook, "Raffles," but writing about this kind of romanticized crime, E. M. Wrong said that we can never quite accept this kind of character as a "hero," because when it comes down to it, crime is never right. And that's true. And that may be why although that stream of literature makes appearances, it always fades out. People yearn to know that right is going to prevail; we want it to prevail. We know very well that life may be often balanced on a knife's edge as to whether good prevails or not, but at the same time we don't want to live in a world ruled by crooks or one which ends in the ultimate triumph of evil.

Maxwell: Well now, Robert, you speak of Agatha Christie's long career. You've survived a decade or two yourself. What have been the most important theological issues in your own life? You've identified a number of them, but which ones have significantly shaped you?

Paul: I think more than I was ready to understand at the time, I was shaped by my own home background and also by what I received through Mansfield College. That was an extremely fruitful time in the College, although we were only a few students, yet it was marvelous to have the constant debate going on between Nathaniel Micklem, C. J. Cadoux, John Marsh, A. M. Hunter and H. Wheeler Robinson. Each of them was extremely able within his own field, and to observe the way in which these men brought together their theology and their personal faith was something for which I am enormously grateful. At that time, because it was wartime, we were concerned with fundamental questions, and it was a privileged time to be in that particular student body. When I became more knowledgeable, I realized that this was related to what was being done by Barth on the Continent.

I started to read P. T. Forsyth comparatively late--long after I left college. But when I began to read him, I realized that he and Barth were speaking the same language, and in a way they were speaking my language, too, because I had to deal faithfully in a pastorate with the reality of God in Christ. Later, I was also given the benefit of working at Bossey with one of the greatest lay theologians I have ever encountered, Hendrik Kraemer. I learned an enormous amount from him. All these things influenced me, and particularly the fact that my formal education took place in the context of wartime Europe, where social and political issues could never be ignored. That historical context really made the Church and its gospel the primary concern of my life, and I am still wrestling with it, still in it. I don't think I could put it any more simply than that. I have met a lot of interesting people, but I go back to that time to my time in the parish. I was nearly ten years in one church. I learned more from those people than ever I was able to teach them. That is a platitude, I know, but it is true.

Maxwell: What did you learn from your parishioners?

Paul: I learned how a simple faith could live in wartime or in trouble. I learned that the Church is not simply lay people plus minister, or a minister leading lay people. It is total ministry in which the minister's leadership and members' testimony are doing the same thing in different ways, in important different ways, but still united within a total ministry. I also learned that there is no reason for any Christian to retire from learning about the faith. When I saw one of the retired members of my congregation, for example, sitting week by week in the pew with his Greek New Testament--I realized that I had better be faithful in what I was doing; and when another member would question me on something he had read in Brunner, I realized that these people were growing in the faith all the time. That was an enormous testimony to me.

I also learned that economics, whether the economics of poverty or the economics of riches, should never cut anybody off from the gospel, that our Lord is concerned about all of them, everybody, and this was brought home to me by a very wealthy woman. She ministered to me in a way which had nothing to do with wealth. I learned these things in the parish, and I am enormously grateful to that congregation.

Maxwell: You've been teaching Church history, among other things, for twenty-five years. What kind of changes, if any, have you seen in the Church's approach to its own history?

Paul: Oh, Yes. I have been impressed by the fact that there has been on the whole a lessening of interest of churches in their own historical roots. Many of them are no longer interested in how they came to be what they are, they are more interested in asking the pragmatic question, "Where are we going from here?" But I suspect that until we get back to a sense of having roots, we won't get very far on the other question.

I think it is particularly important in America for one basic reason. People who settle in America have to some extent cut their roots in the past. Now, the Church offers a different kind of rootage. Think, for example, of a Central European who has had to come to America because he was kicked out of his own country. He has settled here and made his home here, but he can never go back beyond that date when his people landed and doesn't even want to go back beyond that date in his own family life because it would be too bitter. Well, there is something to be said for exchanging that family tree for one that goes back to Luther or Calvin, to Augustine and to the Apostles. The Church has a very important part to play in giving to that particular American citizen a sense of being rooted in history, of belonging to an historical line that goes beyond any personal family history.

Maxwell: Do you detect any significant difference in the approach to Church history and the appreciation of Church history among, say, Americans vis-à-vis British, vis-à-vis European? Is there even a flavor of a difference among those three?

Paul: Yes, there is a suspicion of a difference. Somebody who was on the Dick Cavett show, a Russian poet, Bronski, said that what struck him about the educational system over here was on the whole its lack of interest in history. I think that America is preoccupied with the present and the future, and that has provided the great drive and incentive in America. I can understand it; but, there is a tendency simply to reduce history to those occasions when it receives public recognition.

I think that just as you are more conscious over here of the ethnic differences of humanity than we are in Europe, so I think the European is more conscious of historical roots than the American, and the reasons are clear. If I go down the streets in my own home town or in the town where I was a minister, I meet every style of architecture back to the Middle Ages. Indeed, the parish churches in both cases are Norman but even go back to Saxon times. There is a pub in Leatherhead that goes back to Chaucer's time, and a restaurant that used to be an inn which has the date, 1384. In other words you are always conscious of history. You imbibe it, you assimilate it. It's done by osmosis. Not that the average Britisher is necessarily more able to understand history, but . . .

Maxwell: Well, he's living in the middle of it . . .

Paul: Living in the middle of it, yes. Now here, you see differences in people. A remark was made to me by a young American who came to us after the war, I think she is entirely right--she said that when she went down a British street, all the people appear the same, but she said, "When I go down a street in America,

I can see black people, white people, Chinese people, Japanese people, Indians and every kind of ethnic background." Here there is much more flavor of the breadth of humanity, but not as much realization of historical depth. And I think this has something to do with the difference of attitudes. You can't say one is right and the other is wrong: it is simply, a difference in the way we look at things.

Maxwell: If you have been teaching Church history for twenty-five years, you have also been in theological education for a quarter-century. Has that changed, or is it fundamentally the same?

Paul: There are some very interesting things that have been happening, and I am not sure that all things are good. I understand, for example, the concern of the Association of Theological Schools for competence in ministry, but I have a feeling that we have become obsessed with trying to measure that, whereas really what you are measuring or trying to measure is ultimately immeasurable, which used to be understood when we talked about the 'sense of call' in a person: you can only recognize it or not recognize it. Only the Church is equipped to give that recognition.

Related to that, I have a feeling that these professional organizations, which have done a necessary job in upgrading the general standard of theological education, may have taken on an ecclesiological significance that is not yet appreciated by the churches. There was a time when the seminaries were under the control of the churches. That had its dangers, but at any rate the Church authority was the authority to which the seminary looked, because it served within the Church. I fear, however, that with the creation of authorizing agencies independent of the churches, a new authority has come into the picture which is not ecclesiastical; and I wonder whether anybody is doing any careful study of the significance of this for our ecclesiology and for our doctrine of the Church. There are other things that I would say. Do you want any more?

Maxwell: Do you have any more?

Paul: Well, I am wondering whether sometime in the future we may have to take another look at the old method of theological education which involved a person's living in as an intern and being taught in part by people who were doing their theology on the job. I have a feeling that something happened when we decided to go the seminary route. I am not talking about our Seminary, I am talking about all seminaries. It has separated the teacher of theology from the practice of ministry. And on the whole I think this is a thing that we have been struggling to get back to, because we recognize that when we are talking about theology, we are essentially talking about something that can only be made real to students as they see it in practice.

Maxwell: As you know, that is why this Seminary, with whatever degree of success, has invested a great deal of time in upgrading the Supervised Practice of Ministry, even giving it academic credit and . . .

Paul: Absolutely. It is one of the places where I would say we can really break--well, I'll say fresh ground, although it is really a return to old ground. Unless students are able to see me exercising ministry, everything that I say will be purely intellectual, of no reality to their vocation. I covet for teachers and for students a situation in which the teachers themselves could be more significantly involved in parish ministry, and obviously so during the course of our teaching, so that what's done on the podium, in the pulpit, and in pastoral counseling is seen as part and parcel of the same ministry.

Another thing I have to say about theological education is this: Because we have gone the route we have, which has really been to follow the university method rather than the old academies and the internship method, we need to demand the very highest standards of intellectual integrity on the part of our teaching faculties and from potential students. People in the pews are certainly not to be confused with the medieval laity who couldn't read or write. These people can demand of a minister the very highest qualities of intellectual integrity, therefore we should demand the very highest standards of teaching. This means, first, that theological teachers ought to be thinking along the edges of the big issues all the time. It should be obvious to the student that the professor is reading everything to be read within his or her field, assimilating everything, trying new ideas, and speculating within the context of a firm church commitment. Unless that happens we are going to have awfully dull ministers, because where on earth is the future young minister to learn how to present the dynamism of the faith to the congregation, inspire church members to speculate, and engage them in thinking theologically what it is to be Christian in the 20th and 21st centuries. Theological education needs teachers who are excited about their subject and are constantly exploring it further.

However, I suggest that theological education needs teachers who are more than simply specialists in their own field. Ministers in parishes cannot allow themselves the luxury of over-specialization, because they are involved with life, and that is liable to demand many avenues of approach. They will therefore not be well served educationally by specialists who are limited to their own specialist jargon. Specialization is inevitable, and probably there can be no excellence without it, but theological education surely demands that a teacher should be able to point out landmarks beyond his or her own frontiers. We need scholars who are prepared to risk themselves by pushing into the subjects that run alongside their own, because only in that way can theology do its own work of reconciliation among the sciences.

Ministers will not stimulate serious intellectual engagement in their congregations unless they have caught the spark from teachers who have it. I fear uninspired teaching for the sake of the Church. And I have had to suffer from it vicariously from many pulpits, where it has been quite obvious that the minister has never had an original idea for years, and has never read beyond the magazines since leaving seminary. Incidentally, I think women students on the whole show, at the present time, more creative insights than do the men.

Maxwell: Certainly one of the major changes in theological education has been in the students themselves. Who they are tends to have an effect on the nature of theological education. They are a different lot than they were in the late '60's and early '70's. As you know, two of the major trends lately have been older students coming into the ministry as a second career and women. Can you speculate about the implications for the Church of these trends?

Paul: I think on the whole they are good. Very good.

Maxwell: Both?

Paul: Yes, both.

Maxwell: You remember, by the way, that in **Ministry** you made a great case for the ordination of women.

Paul: Well, I am absolutely for the ordination of women. But why? Not because I think it is a bright idea or because of Women's Liberation, but because theologically the God who is revealed in the scriptures reveals a concern for all his people and shows that he is willing to use all his people, irrespective of sex. I think that too often the question of the ordination of women is put as if it is simply in line with what happens to be the fashion at the moment. That's not the point. The fundamental argument is concerned with the essential nature of the God we worship: What would such a God want for the Church? We are not going back to proof-text here and there and everywhere; the whole scriptures tell the story.

The new trends are good, because it means that the Church is using all God's people. It would be a bad thing, however, if because women now seek ordination, young men get their nose put out of joint and now dismiss the ministry as only a woman's job. In other words, it will be sad if they can't take equality in ministry.

I think that older people coming in can be a tremendous help to the Church not only because of their experience, but also often because of a pension or other resources, many may be in a position to serve the Church in places where ministry is needed, but not economically viable. I can see older persons being able to give of their experience in such situations without putting the churches under a tremendous economic pressure. I tried to get leading qualified laypeople to take ordination examinations before their retirement when I was in England because of the post-war economic situation. I've always been convinced that older people, as long as they are people who are still prepared to learn, can be of enormous importance to the Church in the future.

Maxwell: At least two areas of the Robert Paul that I know haven't been touched on. One is the ecumenical area. You've been known internationally for a number of years as an ecumenist. What is still at stake for us in the ecumenical movement, and how much damage have the World Council and the National Council sustained lately? Can you still affirm those two organizations?

Paul: I still affirm them. I think that they have had a bad press, but that also, on occasion, they have done unwise things. One has to distinguish between an ecumenical commitment--which to me is simply the imperative of the gospel to see that the Church shall be visibly one--and support for any particular organization in the ecumenical movement. That distinction needs to be made very clear. There have been occasions and there will doubtless be other occasions when I and others have had to criticize what is done by a particular agency, but that does not take away one bit from the conviction that Christ wants his people to be visibly one.

I am always impressed by the passage in the 17th chapter of John, verses 20-23. Our Lord says two things: "that they may be one even as we are one," and "that the world may believe." That speaks directly to the question of evangelism. I am more and more impressed by the fact that until the visible unity of the Church is made clear, we can't expect the rest of the world to take us with the seriousness with which we want to be taken. If we are to proclaim reconciliation, it must start with the churches.

Maxwell: How can a broken world believe in a divided church?

Paul: Right. I am also impressed by the fact that we are to be one as visibly as the unity between our Lord and the One he called Father. That means to say I can't treat the visibility of unity as an incidental. That doesn't mean, however, that I have to endorse every movement for unity that comes down the pike. One has to examine each proposal to see that it is true to the gospel and that it will enhance the characteristics of the Church that are essential to Christian faith and practice: its ability to adapt, for example, flexibility in being able to re-organize itself in accordance with the needs of the gospel at any particular moment.

Looking back on it, we were very disappointed when the Plan of Union didn't go through for COCU; yet what would we have been involved in now if it had? We would have been committed to a form of the Church that would have been well on the way to creating its own tradition in structure and without any real possibility of change. Now the new basis on which unity is being considered in COCU, the basis of a covenant, is far more healthy from the point of view of the Church, because it means that we understand the Church as evolving and not simply as a static, fixed institution with an unchangeable structure. We will be able to change in accordance with the needs of the gospel. This is what I mean by making a distinction between commitment to the ecumenical cause, which must remain unchanged, and the need to look critically at particular proposals offered in the name of ecumenism.

Maxwell: Let's push that on into another interesting area. You have taken your ecumenicity into places where some might not go. You have been a minister through the years of a Church that is generally regarded as liberal, but you have deep interest in the sacramental questions and liturgical reform, and yet you have not hidden your interest in evangelical elements in the Church, for which some of your liberal friends, I am sure, are suspicious. Are you working to be all things to all people?

Paul: It is Pauline! But, it gets back to that authority question again, Jack, doesn't it? I have been an inheritor of several Christian traditions--I have been a legatee of the great tradition of liturgically structured ways of worship, and I have benefited enormously from the kind of liturgical interests which were alive in Mansfield College when I was there and which . . .

Maxwell: Particularly Micklem, I suppose.

Paul: Micklem, but not only Micklem. It was Micklem, of course, who was the great inspirer of that, but I remember attending lectures by the Catholic, Gervase Matthews, and Father D'Arcy, who was then the Master of Campion Hall. I inherit that, too; that's part of the Western tradition which we've got to affirm: the fact that liturgy just didn't happen haphazardly, but evolved according to certain basic theological principles. There's that.

There is also the liberalism of my own Church with its strong emphasis upon social action, on the gospel being translated into ethical terms. That is another thing I have to affirm.

And then there are the evangelicals. I have found that the evangelicals are saying something to me that I need to listen to. Namely, that although there is more to Christianity than a personal affirmation of faith, yet certainly there is a personal affirmation of faith in Christianity, if it is to be Christianity. And I think this is something that some branches of the Church, particularly the more liberal, have tended to forget. I also believe the evangelicals are right to remind us--again without affirming it in the literal way in which many conservatives have often affirmed it--that our faith has its center in a revelation, a recorded revelation, and that we have to treat this with ultimate seriousness.

All I am trying to do is to keep the conversation going between all these elements in the Church. I would be untrue to the catholicity of the Church if I were to deny any of them. And I see as one of the great ecumenical questions of the future not only the question of the Catholic branches and Protestantism, but also the debate going on within Protestantism itself: How far have orthodoxy in belief and orthodoxy in ethics and practice to be held together? How far must they be held together in order to have a viable gospel? In that, perceptive evangelicals stand for something we have to listen to, and I would hope to keep the conversation going with them.

Maxwell: Following up on that, those of us who know you well are very aware of your personal piety and your commitment to regular corporate worship. Is it inappropriate to ask a distinguished theologian and Church historian why he is so committed to weekly corporate worship in a local congregation?

Paul: I couldn't function without it, Jack. If I miss a Sunday, I know it. Now there may be something psychologically wrong with me, I don't know. All I am saying is that whether I agree with any particular minister or not, whether I like what is being done in worship or not, I have to join myself to those who have also assembled to worship God, and to emphasize my corporate oneness and need with them. As I listen to God's Word, irrespective of whether the sermon is good, bad or indifferent--I prefer a good sermon, of course, and I like good music--but irrespective of what is being done in that way--to come and to listen and to pray, and to be there with those who, in whatever faltering way, are still affirming that they, too, have the same need, that is something I need to engage in regularly. That, I think, is where the support of the Church comes in. I couldn't function without it. Of course I was brought up to have that need, and maybe it was a conditioned reflex, I don't know; but I can't conceive of being able to dispense with public worship and make piety simply a private affair. If it were a private affair for too long, I suspect it would soon cease to be even a private affair. I could function far better without books than without worship!

Maxwell: It's an expected question in such a conversation, but if you had it to do over are there things you would do differently?

Paul: I don't think so. But I just don't know. I would have gone into the ministry, I am quite convinced of that. You know, when I started out there were three or four things I could have done. My art teacher wanted me to do art, and my headmaster wanted me to go into dramatic art, because I did a great deal of acting and loved it. But I don't think I could have escaped the ministry. Having started out in that way I can't conceive of it being very much different from what it was. There was a time when I was being pushed to concentrate on preaching, and I was approached by several distinguished churches in England. I love the preaching ministry: but there were intellectual questions nagging in the back of my mind, and there was the teaching need. It so happened that I had the qualifications to do the teaching, and therefore got drawn more and more into concentrating on that ministry, but I have never seen it as separate from what I would have done in the parish. As far as I am concerned, it is all part and parcel of one ministry. In a way I would have preferred to stay in the parish, if I had my druthers, but there were these other things that needed attention--the problem of the nature of ministry, the problem of the relationship of the sacraments to the work of Christ, and intellectual issues that nobody seemed to be doing anything about; and therefore, who was talking to me at that point, telling me to do it? That's where the evangelical piety, I suppose, comes out; but I really feel that was a "call" to do these things.

Maxwell: Talk to me about the way in which Eunice has contributed to your work.

Paul: I couldn't have done it without her. You know us. We support each other. Certainly, she has genuinely supported me in everything that I have done. We are complementary. Thank God, she's not like me. I mean I would have had an insufferable time if she were.

Maxwell: Wouldn't we all?

Paul: Well, maybe you're right. Eunice adds that streak of practicality to our corporate efforts that I just haven't got. She also brings a very good critical mind to bear on anything I write, although she doesn't necessarily have my own consuming interest in the subjects I write about; but her contribution has been absolutely essential.

I remember in the early 60's when we were getting called to do a lot of speaking to Roman Catholics who were rapidly coming under the impact of the Second Vatican Council. They got interested in Protestants and what we thought, and when I was in Hartford I seemed to be called out to do a lot of speaking all round the State to Roman Catholic groups on Protestantism. Time and time again I would be asked by Catholic priests how I saw my marriage and how it affected my ministry, because to many of them it looked as if it were something that would prevent them from doing what they needed to do. I could only say that I could not conceive of performing my ministry without Eunice beside me. There is a passage in **The Church in Search of Its Self** (350 f.) on what ministry really is that I put in because of Eunice. Service is what ministry is about, and that is what has been shown to me in my own marriage.

And that's what the Church is about. Marriage is a very natural relationship, but at its best that service which is shared in marriage, that service which is being shown in the ministry of the Church is also that which the Church is to show to the world. They are all part and parcel of the same image, the same picture--that which I also believe to be true to the very heart of God Himself. Now I don't think I can say much more. It sounds very highfalutin' that, but it is not intended to be--it is no more than simple truth.

BIBLIOGRAPHY OF ROBERT S. PAUL

1. Books

The Lord Protector: Religion and Politics in the Life of Oliver Cromwell. London, The Lutterworth Press, 1955. American Edition with Preface for American Readers. Grand Rapids, William. B. Eerdmans, 1964; 412 pp. plus bibliography and index.

The Atonement and the Sacraments: The Relation of the Atonement to the Sacraments of Baptism and the Lord's Supper. New York and Nashville, Abingdon Press, 1960. 387 pp. plus index.

An Apologeticall Narration: (Editor) a Facsimile edition of the 1643 pamphlet, edited with historical Introduction, and critical notes on the text. Philadelphia and Boston, The United Church Press, 1963. 130 pp. plus index.

Ministry: the meaning of Ministry and Ordination. Grand Rapids, William B. Eerdmans, 1965. 142 pp. plus index.

The Church in Search of Its Self: theological principles behind an ecumenical approach to ecclesiology. Grand Rapids, William B. Eerdmans, 1972. 375 pp. plus indexes.

Kingdom Come! A tract on eschatology. Grand Rapids, William B. Eerdmans, 1974. 88 pp.

Awaiting Publication:

The Assembly of the Lord: Politics and Religion in the Westminster Assembly and the 'Grand Debate.'

In Preparation:

Whatever Happened to Sherlock Holmes? Detective Fiction, popular theology and society.

The Quest for Authority.

2. **Contributions to Symposia, Encyclopaedias, etc.**

'The Historical Background' in **The Free Churches and the State,** London, The Federal Free Church Council, 1953.

'The Cinderellas of the Movement' in **Unity in Mid-Career,** edited by Keith Bridston and Walter D. Wagoner, New York, Macmillan, 1963.

'The Deacon in Protestantism' in **The Diaconate Now,** edited by Richard T. Nolan, Washington and Cleveland, Corpus Books, 1967.

'Theology in Connecticut, 1860-1960' in **Contributions to the Ecclesiastical History of Connecticut,** Vol. II, Hartford, Conn., Conference of the U.C.C., 1967.

'Protestantism and Monasticism' in **The Encyclopaedia Britannica,** 1965 edn.

'Puritanism' in **Weltkirchenlexikon,** Stuttgart, Kreuz-Verlag.

'The Lord's Supper' in **An Encyclopaedia of Religious Education,** edited by Kendig B. Culley.

'The Work of Christ' in **Christian Confidence,** (Essays presented to Nathaniel Micklem by some of his former students on his 80th birthday,) edited by Roger Tomes, London, S.P.C.K., 1970.

Five brief biographies for a **Biographical Dictionary of British Radicals in the Seventeenth Century** (John Davenport, Obadiah Sedgwick, Herbert Palmer, William Spurstowe, Sidrach Simpson), (edited by Richard Greaves), Harvester Press, 1982.

'Ecclesiology in Richard Baxter's "Autobiography" ' in **From Faith to Faith,** (edited by Dikran Y. Hadidian), a Festschrift in honor of Dr. Donald G. Miller, Pickwick Press, Pittsburgh, 1979.

' "A Way to Wyn Them": Ecclesiology and Religion in the English Reformation', in **Reformatio Perennis** (edited by B. A. Gerrish), a Memorial Volume in honor of the late Ford Lewis Battles, Pickwick Press, Pittsburgh, 1981.

'Social Justice and the Puritan "Dual Ethic" ' in **Intergerini Parietis Septum** (Eph. 2:14) (edited by Dikran Y. Hadidian), a

Festschrift in honor of Professor Markus Barth of Basel, Pickwick Press, Pittsburgh, 1981.

'P. T. Forsyth: Prophet for the Twentieth Century?' in **P. T. Forsyth: The Man, The Preacher's Theologian, Prophet for the 20th Century** (with Donald G. Miller and Browne Barr, and including a reprint of Forsyth's **Positive Preaching and Modern Mind)**, Pickwick Press, Pittsburgh, 1981.

'The Cost of Covenant: Studies in the New Covenant' (Three Bible Studies presented at the 15th Plenary of the Consultation on Church Union, in Digest of the Proceedings of the Fifteenth Meeting of the Consultation on Church Union, edited by Gerald F. Moede, Princeton, N.J., C.O.C.U., 1982.

Contributed to:

The World Council of Churches Faith and Order Department Study on 'Christ, the Holy Spirit and the Ministry,' 1966: Contributed 'The Messianic Ministry of Jesus and Ordination.'

The National Council of Churches Study on Baptism and Confirmation: 'The place of Faith in Baptism--the Individual and the Community,' in **Baptism Confirmation**, n.d. (1966).

Shorter Writings:

About the Congregational Churches: a booklet published privately by Christ Church (Congregational), Leatherhead, Surrey, n.d. (c. 1949); republished for general distribution by Independent Press for the Life and Work department of the Congregational Union of England and Wales.

Congregationalism and the Ecumenical Movement, London, Independent Press, n.d. (Life and Work pamphlet of the C.U.E.W.).

Oliver Cromwell (1599-1658), London, Independent Press, n.d. (Life and Work pamphlet of the C.U.E.W.).

Oliver Cromwell (1599-1658), London, Independent Press, 1961.

'Defenders of the Faith,' light-hearted verses on British

ecumenical affairs which appeared in The British Weekly, 1955.

3. Articles

"The Lord Protector: a study in personal religion and public action." Congregational Historical Society, Transactions, September, 1950, (Vol. XVI, No. 3).

'Congregationalism'--a series of 10 articles in a debate with the Presbyterian historian, Prof. Basil Hall, during the union discussions of 1949-1951. The Christian World, 1950.

"The Writings of Richard Bancroft and the Brownists." Congregational Historical Society, Transactions, August, 1954, (Vol. XVII, No. 3).

"Shall we rewrite our History?" The Congregational Quarterly, July, 1954, (Vol. XXXII, No. 3).

"Oliver Cromwell and the Jews," Tercentenary Supplement to The Jewish Chronicle, January 27, 1956.

"British Churches and the Ecumenical Future," The Ecumenical Review, Vol. VIII, No. 2, January, 1956.

"Sacrifice and Sacrament," The Chaplain, April, 1956. (The same article was translated into French and reappeared in Verbum Caro, 43, Vol. XI, 1957, published by Delachaux and Niestle of Neuchatel, Switzerland).

"Confessions and the Covenant," The Christian Century, August 6, 1958.

"Church History and Ecumenicl Problems in Theology," Inaugural Lecture. The Bulletin of the Hartford Seminary Foundation, No. 26, February, 1959.

"The Seminary and Its Research," The Hartford Quarterly, Vol. 1, No. 1, Fall, 1960.

"Teaching Church History in an Ecumenical Perspective," The Ecumenical Review, Vol. XIV, No. 1, October, 1961.

"Theology and Detective Fiction," in "The Image of Man in Contemporary Literature," The Student World, Geneva, Switzerland, Vol. LV, No. 2, 1962. (This article was re-published in an abridged form in World Christian Digest, November 1962, and in a revised and slightly expanded form in The Hartford Quarterly, Spring 1966).

"The Word 'Congregational': an Historical Footnote," The Hartford Quarterly, Vol. IV, No. 1, Fall, 1963.

"Theology and the Technological Revolution," The Hartford Quarterly, Vol. IV, No. 4, Summer 1964.

"Connecticut and the New Dialogue," The Hartford Quarterly, Vol. V, No. 1, Fall, 1964.

"Weber and Calvinism: the Effects of a 'Calling,' " The Canadian Journal of Theology, Vol. XI, No. 1, 1965.

"Henry Jacob and Seventeenth-Century Puritanism," The Hartford Quarterly, Vol. VII, No. 3, Spring, 1967.

"Hooker: Puritanism: Democracy," The Hartford Quarterly, Vol. VII, No. 4, Summer, 1967.

"New England Contributions to the Ecumenical Church of the Future," **Centennial Addresses**, 1967.

"Violent Revolution is Obsolete," Presbyterian Life, January 1, 1970.

"The Unity of the Church--Quo Vadis?" Mid-Stream, Vol. XIV, No. 1, January, 1975.

" 'An Asylum for the Virtuous and the Oppressed,' " The Presbyterian Outlook, September 27, 1976.

"Ecumenical Vision in the 1970's," Mid-Stream, Vol. XVI, No. 2, April, 1977.

"The Accidence and the Essence of Puritan Piety," Austin Seminary Bulletin (Faculty Edition), Vol. XCIII, No. 8, May 1978.

"Where we begin: Freedom and Responsibility in the United Church of Christ," Polity and Practise, New Conversations, Fall, 1979.

"The Case Against . . . Children and the Supper," Austin Seminary Bulletin (Faculty Edition), Vol. XCV, No. 3, October, 1979.

'The Covenant Theme in Church History,' in COCU and Covenant, Austin Seminary Bulletin (Faculty Edition), Vol. XCVI (Special Issue), March, 1981.

4. Reviews

Reviews on Historical and Theological books have been contributed to the following journals:

The Christian World (London)
The British Weekly (London)
The Congregational Quarterly (London)
The Congregational Monthly (London)
The Ecumenical Review (Geneva)
Church History (Chicago)
Encounter (Indianapolis)
The United Church Herald (St. Louis and New York)
The Union Seminary Quarterly (New York)
The Hartford Quarterly (Hartford)
Religion in Life (Nashville)
The Scroll (Lexington)
The Christian (St. Louis)
The Pittsburgh Perspective (Pittsburgh)
Journal of Presbyterian History (Philadelphia)
The Review of Books and Religion (Springhill, Vt., and
    later Lexington, Ky.)
The Christian Century (Chicago)
The Western Humanities Review (Lake City, Utah)
The Journal of Religion (Chicago)
Mid-Stream (Indianapolis)
Interpretation (Richmond, VA.)
The Journal of Religion (Chicago)
The Journal of Ecumenical Studies (Philadelphia)

5. Other Literary Activities

Joint-Editor: The Transactions of the Congregational Historical
        Society, London, 1951-1954.
Editor: The Hartford Quarterly, 1961-1967.
Member: Editorial Council of Encounter (Indianapolis) 1956-1965.
        Editorial Board, The Pittsburgh Perspective, 1970-1973.
        Editorial Board, Mid-Stream (Indianapolis) 1975-1977.
A 'Bicentenial Editor' of The Presbyterian Outlook, 1976.
Chairman of the Editorial Committee of the Austin Seminary
        Bulletin, 1978-.

EUNICE M. PAUL

MANSFIELD COLLEGE, OXFORD: FACULTY, 1942

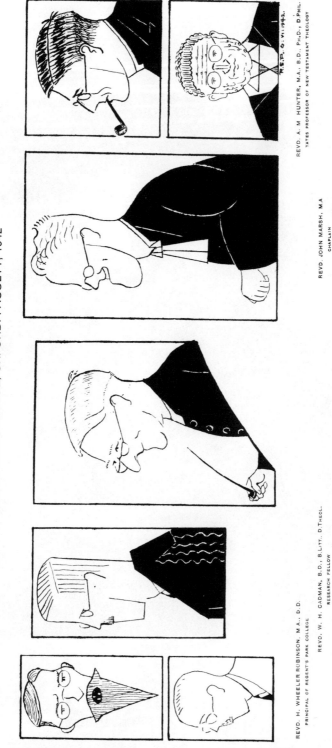

REVD. A. M. HUNTER, M.A., B.D., Ph.D., D.PHIL.
YATES PROFESSOR OF NEW TESTAMENT THEOLOGY

REVD. C. J. CADOUX, M.A., D.D., D.LITT.
MACKENNAL PROFESSOR OF CHURCH HISTORY

REVD. JOHN MARSH, M.A
CHAPLAIN

REVD. NATHANIEL MICKLEM, M.A., D.D., LL.D
THE PRINCIPAL

REVD. H. WHEELER ROBINSON, M.A., D.D.
PRINCIPAL OF REGENT'S PARK COLLEGE

REVD. W. H. CADMAN, B.D., B.LITT., D.THEOL.
RESEARCH FELLOW

REV. J. H. MILNES, M.A.
BURSAR

MANSFIELD COLLEGE, OXFORD: STUDENTS, 1942

GEORGE WILLIAMS   PETER SCOTT   'PETER' BROOKS   GEORGE CAIRD   CYRIL LLOYD   BILL DAVIES

BASIL SIMS   ERIK ROUTLEY   TONY HALL   PHILIP LEE WOOLF

EDGAR YOUDELL   HORTON DAVIES   'AL' BEEZLEY   DR. HIRSCHWALD   G. D. BOAZ   TOM HAWTHORN   JIM HARDIMAN   BOB PAUL

PART TWO

Essays Honoring Robert S. Paul

THE ONE AND THE MANY IN MARK AND JOHN

George B. Caird

More than forty years have passed since my friendship with Robert Paul began in the Junior Common Room of Mansfield College, Oxford. We were a small company, preparing in war-time for ordination to the ministry of the Congregational Church, but a company which was to make its mark in many fields of enterprise. When I look at the framed copy of the caricature that Robert drew of us all, which still hangs in my study, and reflect on that part which the friendships of those days had in the molding of my own destiny, I cannot but be grateful for having been one of that number. So I welcome this opportunity to pay tribute to a member of that small circle whose distinction has lain in the study of historical theology. His varied interests have included Christology and churchmanship, and I have therefore chosen to offer in his honor a New Testament investigation in which those two interests meet.

I

The course of any enquiry is largely determined by the question with which it begins. There are those, of a dogmatic turn of mind, who assume that the all-embracing Christological question is "Cur Deus homo?" They take the incarnation to be a datum, guaranteed by the word of scripture and the creeds of the church, and ask why it had to happen and how the early Christians came to believe in it. This is the line adopted, for example, by Donald Guthrie in his **New Testament Theology**, in which the chapter on the person of Christ occupies 188 pages, and the chapter on his saving work 78 pages, largely devoted to a defense of the words "substitution" and "propitiation" as tools of interpretation. Atonement is thus treated as a corollary to belief in the divinity of Christ: "the early Christians were not merely interested in who Jesus was, but also in his activity" (p. 431).

Robert and I, by contrast, were brought up in the evangelical persuasion, that the center of New Testament theology is the cross, and that any convictions about the person of Christ which may have emerged in the early church were inferences from the experience of atonement. The question from which we were taught to start was accordingly quite different: granted that the one has done for the many that which they could not do for themselves, what is it that he has done, and by what right has he done it? Any attempt to expound the New Testament answers to the first part of this question would require a book of its own. The purpose of this essay is to explore the contribution which two of the evangelists make to the second part.

In his profound and illuminating book, **The Origin of Christology,** to which it will be obvious that I am much indebted, Professor Moule has given us a precise and sensitive exposition of what he calls Paul's "corporative" view of the relation between the one and the many, the view that the many benefit from the act of the one because, through the corporate and representative nature of his person, they were included in the doing of it. Paul's old life had died on the cross with Christ (Rom 6:6; Gal 2:19). "The love of Christ constrains us, once we have reached the conclusion that one man died for all, and therefore all died" (2 Cor 5:14-15). Moule goes on to argue that this incorporative view is nowhere fully worked out except in the letters of Paul, that it is not present in John, since he uses the preposition en to denote a mutuality of relationship which, in comparison with Pauline ideas, is more individualist in emphasis, but that what is explicit in Paul is implicit elsewhere, both in the primitive use of huper and anti, and in the claim that the life, death and resurrection of Jesus were "according to the scriptures". In agreement with Dodd, Moule takes this to mean that "Jesus, in an extraordinary way, turned out to be occupying the position that, according to the Scriptures, had always been intended for Israel, and through Israel, for all mankind" (p. 129). I propose to examine two points at which, in my opinion, this statement of the case needs to be modified, amplified, or perhaps even simplified.

II

I begin by doing what Moule admits he has not done, that is, by examining the theology of Mark; and I open my case with the verse which, by common consent, comes nearer than any other to justifying the term "substitution": "the Son of man came not to be served but to serve, and to give his life as a ransom for many" (Mk 10:45). Let me in passing remark that the notorious difficulties of this verse arise almost entirely out of the practice of treating the Synoptic Gospels as a quarry for material to be used in the reconstruction of the teaching of Jesus, or of primitive Christianity, or of the history of the gospel tradition, instead of dealing with it first as part of the theology of the writer, as we automatically do with any verse from Paul or John. Rather than treat Mark as an incompetent botcher together of diverse traditions which he imperfectly understood, let us do him the courtesy of regarding him as an intelligent writer who means and understands what he has written, even when, or perhaps I should say particularly when, as occasionally happens, he appears to us to contradict himself.

The first point to note is that the verse under consideration is the conclusion of a discussion about kingship. James and John ask a favor which assumes that Jesus is a king, shortly to enter upon royal dignity; and Mark has no quarrel with their assumption. For the answer to their request turns on the way rulers behave towards their subjects. Jesus is indeed a king, but he and those associated with him in the exercise of kingly power are not to behave like rulers of gentile nations. This leads to the provisional hypothesis that, in Mark's estimation at least, the Son of man is related to the many as king to subjects.

The one point about which Mark leaves no room for doubt, since it is the one piece of information which he conveys propria persona, is that he believed Jesus to be Messiah. I should like to add "and Son of God", since I firmly adhere to the longer text of Mk 1:1, but this is not germane to my present case. Mark is not one of those who believe that Jesus' command of silence at Caesarea Philippi was tantamount to rejection of the title Peter accorded him. But the Messiah, the Lord's Anointed, is by definition the King of Israel, and it is as claimant to the throne of Israel that Jesus is arraigned, condemned and crucified. The Roman soldiers salute him sarcastically as "King of the Jews", and the Roman governor causes that title to be nailed to the cross. But this is an alien form of address, such as only a gentile would use. The Jewish crowd, even though it is in mockery and rejection, use his correct style: "Let the Messiah, the King of Israel, come down from the cross" (Mk 15:32). Mark is as sensitive to irony as is John, though he does not find it so necessary to rub it in. For him, Jesus is the King of Israel, and therefore Son of God, precisely because he does not come down, and he allows the gentile centurion to be spokesman for all who share his faith.

To this we must add that the King of Israel is also Son of David. It is true that Mark appears to call this equation in question. "How can the scribes maintain that the Messiah is Son of David?" (Mk 12:35). The simple answer of course is that the scribes are right to maintain this, and that they could cite pages of Old Testament quotations to prove it: they say that the Messiah is Son of David because that is what "Messiah" means. It is true that the prophecies of Zechariah speak of two "sons of oil", the anointed king and the anointed priest (4:14), and that these two figures appear side by side not only in the documents of Qumran, but also in the imagery of Revelation (11:4). It is true also that it has been fashionable to talk loosely of Jewish expectations of a variety of "messianic figures" or even "quasi-messianic figures." But for this there is not a shadow of linguistic warrant. Certainly to the writers of the New Testament "Messiah" and "Son of David" were synonyms. The Davidic descent of Jesus is widely attested, and the attestation can have had no other function than to support his claim to Messiahship. Moreover, Mark can hardly be deemed to deny it. For the Markan Jesus cites David's appropriation of the shewbread as precedent for his own sovereign freedom, accepts the title of "Son of David" from Bartimaeus by commending his faith, and makes no objection to the hosannas of the pilgrims, "Blessings on the coming kingdom of our father David" (Mk 2:25-26; 10:46-52; 11:10). What he rejects, therefore, with the hyperbole characteristic of Semitic debate, is the notion that "Son of David" is all the Old Testament has to say on the subject.

But the "Son of David" pericope contains a further contradiction which is not as easily resolved. Jesus appears to be laying claim to a royal status higher than that of David. "David himself calls him 'Lord' (Kyrios); how can he also be his son?" Yet in the pericope with which we started Jesus refuses to construe his kingly role in terms of lordship. It is the rulers of the gentiles who lord it (katakyrieuousi) over their subjects. In such a monarchy the king is lord and all his subjects from the least to the greatest, from slave to minister of state, are servants. But Jesus and his associates are not to be the recipients but the givers of service. Here then is a paradox, that he whom David (and therefore scripture) hails as lord, he whom God enthrones at his own right hand, himself abjures any such dignities.

There are two ways of resolving this paradox, one wrong and the other right. The wrong way is to see lordship at the right hand of God as a promotion achieved through humble service, much as the boss might start life on the factory floor, the theater director work his way up from being assistant to the stage carpenter, or the marshal's baton be found in the private soldier's knapsack. The right way is to see that the career of service chosen by Jesus is the only greatness recognized in the sight of God. At this point there is a close affinity between Mark and the so-called hymn of Phil 2:6ff., where the exaltation of Jesus and the bestowal of the name of Lord are not the reversal of earthly humility and servanthood but the enthronement of them.

If kingship is to be so drastically reinterpreted, however, does it make sense to go on harping on the title as Mark does? This is a question which Moule himself asks. "The crucifixion must once and for all have extinguished absolutely any literal hopes that Jesus might become the King of Israel" (p. 33). Because his interest is in origins, he concludes, quoting Cullmann, that "the early church believed in Christ's Messiahship because they believed that Jesus believed himself to be Messiah" (p. 34). Without wishing to disagree with this conclusion, I am uneasy about the way it is reached, because there seems to be a suggestion that Jesus in his lifetime was content to abandon to the Zealots any literal idea of kingship and to interpret his own role in some non-political, etiolated and pietistic sense. This, I am convinced, was not the view of Mark; and I am strengthened in this conviction by the contention of Martin Hengel in his recent work on the Atonement that the Synoptists were deliberately trying to reproduce a pre-Easter point of view.

For any Jew the archetypal kingship was the reign of David, and the story of that reign points to a function of kingship other than the exercise of autocratic power which Jesus renounced. The king did not merely rule Israel; he <u>was</u> Israel. In the studies of sacral kingship in the Old Testament and the Ancient Near East, which we associate with the "Myth and Ritual" school, all the emphasis was placed on the position of the king as the agent or representative of God. But sacral kingship had another side to it, which was no less prominent in Old Testament thought. As R. de Vaux has put it (**Ancient Israel,** p. 110): "It is a common idea among primitive peoples that the king embodies the good estate of his subjects: the country's prosperity depends on him, and he insures the welfare of his people." A. S. Tritton (**Encyclopaedia of Religion and Ethics** VII, p. 726f.) speaks of "the national significance of the king's person." A calamity to the king was a national disaster; and he accordingly draws the conclusion that "the question whether certain of the penitential psalms are individual or national is beside the point; it is the king, the people's representative, who speaks for the nation." Pharaoh exemplifies this solidarity between king and people when he confesses to Moses, "I and my people are in the wrong" (Exod 9:27), when the people had done nothing except what was included in the act of their royal representative. It is exemplified further by Jehoiada's covenant (2 Kgs 11:17), and by many of the royal psalms (see esp. Ps 18:50; 20:7-9; 63:11). Davidson has remarked that "in Zech 9:9 Zion's king shares the character of the saved people" (Hastings' **Dictionary of the Bible** IV, p. 123) and H. Wheeler Robinson has said of the same passage that the king is not so much the bringer of salvation as the recipient of it on behalf of the nation.

I have recently been greatly impressed to find that this aspect of kingship, which has received all too little notice from

Old Testament scholars and been totally ignored by students of the New Testament, is taken to be self-evident by one of our great literary critics. In **The Great Code** Northrop Frye first distinguishes and then reunites two types of identification, identifying <u>with</u> and identifying <u>as</u>: "When we combine these two forms of identification, and identify an individual <u>with</u> its class, we get an extremely powerful and subtle form of metaphor, which I sometimes call the royal metaphor, because it underlies one of the most symbolically pervasive of institutions, that of kingship." (p. 87). In illustration of this theme he cites the lament over the death of the king, which is seen at the same time as the death of the nation: "the breath of our nostrils, the anointed of the Lord was taken in their pits, of whom we said, 'Under his shadow we shall live among the heathen' " (Lam 4:20).

A king, then, is a man whose actions are such that his subjects are included in the doing of them, and his calamities such that his subjects are included in the suffering of them. To believe in the Messiahship of Jesus is to claim that he has the right to stand before God and say, "I and my people". But for the full implications of this we must examine the story of David in greater detail, beginning with his installation.

> Now all the tribes of Israel came to David at Hebron and said to him, "We are your own flesh and blood (Heb. 'bone and flesh') . . . " And the Lord said to you, "You shall be shepherd of my people Israel; you shall be their prince." All the elders of Israel came to the king at Hebron; there David made a covenant with them before the Lord, and they anointed David king over Israel. (2 Sam. 5:1-2)

The solidarity of prince with people, of shepherd with flock, is grounded on divine appointment, on the bond of kinship, and on the reinforcing bond of covenant; and in the ensuing wars with the Philistines, when his life has been in danger, "his officers took an oath that he should never again go out with them to war, for fear that the lamp of Israel might be extinguished" (2 Sam 21:17). Before long the further bond of loyalty is invoked. For in opposition to David Absalom is anointed king; and a messenger reports that "the hearts of the men of Israel are after Absalom" (<u>opiso</u> Abessalom), or as the New English Bible has it, "The men of Israel had transferred their allegiance to Absalom" (2 Sam 15:13). As soon as the rebellion has been suppressed, a quarrel arises between Israel and Judah over the right to escort the king home. To the claim of Judah that the king is their near kinsman, the men of Israel reply: "We have ten shares in the king; and, what is more, in David we are senior to you" (2 Sam 19:43). This retort appears absurd until we recognize that "in David" was to the speakers interchangeable with "in Israel", and that in Israel Judah was only the fourth of the sons of Jacob. Almost at once, however, Sheba ben Bichri is calling them to renounce their loyalty in a new rebellion:

> What share have we in David?
> We have no lot in the son of Jesse. (2 Sam 20:1)

And the death of David is not the end of the story; for a generation later the cry of Sheba is renewed by the ten tribes in their rebellion under Jeroboam ben Nebat (1 Kgs 16:12).

All this might seem remote from Mark, were it not that the unity of the nation and the embodiment of its welfare and salvation in David's anointed person imprinted itself on the Jewish mind as an abiding ideal and remained throughout the centuries their living hope.

> It shall no longer be said, "They are not my people",
> they shall be called Sons of the Living God.
> Then the people of Judah and of Israel shall be
>   reunited
> and shall choose for themselves a single head. . . .
> For the Israelites shall live many a long day
>   without king or prince . . .
> but after that they will again seek
> the Lord their God and David their king.
>   (Hos 1:10-11; 3:4-5)

> As a shepherd goes in search of his sheep when his flock is dispersed all around him, so I will go in search of my sheep and rescue them, no matter where they are scattered in dark and cloudy days. I will bring them out from every nation, gather them in from other lands, and lead them home to their own soil . . . I will save my flock . . . Then I will set over them one shepherd to take care of them, my servant David.
>   (Ezek 34:12-13, 22-23)

Above all, there is the promise of Isa 55:4-5, where the royal covenant once made with David is renewed with the nation as a whole.

> I made him a witness to all races,
> a prince and instructor of peoples;
> and you in turn shall summon nations you do not know,
> and nations that do not know you shall come
>   running to you.

It is well known that the intertestamental literature shows a bewildering variety and even a discrepancy of belief about almost every aspect of the Jewish eschatological hope; but the one element which appears with remarkable constancy is the gathering of the scattered people of God into a single united nation, as in the time of David.

It follows from this that to acclaim Jesus as Messiah is to make an affirmation not merely about him, but also about the Israel he embodies; and in a divided Israel it is also to raise the question of loyalty. Every Israelite must decide whether he has a share in the king, a lot in the Son of David. This is precisely what the Markan conversation at Caesarea Philippi is about.

> Anyone who chooses to give me his allegiance (opiso mou elthein) must set self aside; he must take up his cross and come with me. Anyone who chooses to save his life shall lose it. But anyone who will lose his life for me and for the gospel shall save it. What can anyone gain by winning the whole world and forfeiting his life? What can he give to buy his life back? If anyone disowns me and my teaching in this treacherous and sinful age, the Son of man will disown him when he comes in the glory of his Father with the holy angels. (Mk 8:34-38)

Peter has hailed Jesus as Messiah, though he does not yet understand the term as Jesus understands it and God intends it. Of course Jesus could save his life if like David he withdrew from the battle into obscurity, but that would be to lose his life as Messiah, the life which God promises here and hereafter to those who obey him. He could fall in with popular expectation and pursue the course of world dominion, but that also would be to lose his life, to quench the lamp of Israel. And what holds for him holds for his followers. The prospect is forbidding, but the alternative is more forbidding, for it is to forfeit a place in the Israel of God. When the king renders his account to God, justice requires that he should disown those who on earth have disowned him. The Son of man must be able to vouch for the saints of the Most High.

Here, however, we face the second of Mark's apparent self-contradictions. Mark knows and his readers know that even Peter in the end disowned his king. If those who have disowned Jesus on earth are to be disowned before the judgment seat of God, who then can be saved? What can even Peter give to buy back his forfeited life? We appear to be confronted by a shepherd in danger of losing not one sheep out of a hundred, but the whole flock, by a king whose subjects have to a man renounced their allegiance, by a Son of man without saints to represent. What a pyrrhic victory is this for the justice of God! Thus it is that Mark brings his readers to that further function of kingship indicated in the text from which we began: the king must redeem.

> He shall have compassion on the needy and the poor;
> he shall save the lives of the poor;
> from oppression and violence he shall redeem their lives
> and precious shall their blood be in his eyes.
> (Ps 72:13-14)   (Ps 72:13-14)

It is important to recall that in Israel's code of civil law the right and duty of redemption, whether from slavery, debt or the alienation of property, lies with the next of kin; the one word goel means both kinsman and redeemer. Because he is bound to them by ties of kinship, the king has the responsibility of redeeming any among his people who have no other legal recourse and are in need of redemption. But where can there be greater need than when the whole nation has forfeited its life in rebellion against their king? Mark has already told us that Jesus had compassion on the crowd because they were like sheep without a shepherd (6:34). Divine justice demands that he should disown those who have disowned him, but divine compassion demands that he accept the duty of redemption, even at the cost of his own life.

The dilemma which faces the Markan Jesus is precisely that which the prophets attribute to God himself.

> Back they shall go to Egypt,
> the Assyrian shall be their king:
> for they have refused to return to me . . .
> bent on rebellion as they are.
> Though they call on their High God
> even then he 'will not reinstate them.
> How can I give you up, Ephraim,
> how surrender you, Israel?
> (Hos 11:5-8)

It is also the dilemma that Paul expounds and resolves in Rom 1:3. The whole world is reduced to silence under the judgment of God, and justice requires the sentence of condemnation; but that would be a defeat for the gracious purpose and promise of God. In the hilasterion of the cross the righteousness of God is demonstrated, because there justice and mercy are reconciled and proof is given that God is "both just and the justifier of anyone who has faith in Jesus."

When we see that the Markan Jesus gives his life as a ransom, not merely for those who are unable to redeem themselves, but for those whose lives are forfeit because, whether by rejection, by denial or by desertion, they have declared that they have no share in the king, then it may appear that "substitution" is the most adequate descriptive term. Its inadequacy becomes apparent only when we recognize that he who thus gives his life as a ransom for the many is the king of Israel, who by divine appointment, by kinship and by covenant is entitled to act as the embodiment of his people, and who by his share in the divine compassion refuses to disown even those who have disowned him. Whatever he does is a corporate act, so that they are included in the doing of it. If then we find Jesus, in Moule's words "occupying the position that, according to the Scriptures, had always been intended for Israel", this need occasion no surprise, since this was the role which the king of Israel could be expected to discharge.

It is not the purpose of this paper to enlarge on Paul's doctrine of the corporate Christ, but in passing let us note that at many points he shows himself well aware that the possibility of a new solidarity "in Christ" rests on the historic fact of his solidarity with the old Israel. In the midst of a passionate assertion that in Christ there is neither Jew nor Gentile, he reminds his readers that Christ was "born under the law to redeem those under law" (Gal 4:4). He opens his most systematic exposition of the gospel by declaring that Jesus was born of David's line kata sarka; and lest we should be beguiled into dismissing this as pre-Pauline Christianity to which he pays a merely tactical lip-service, he later resumes the theme with a reminder that his kinsmen kata sarka are Israelites "from whom comes the Messiah kata sarka" (Rom 1:4; 9:4-5). The gospel is "for the Jew first" (Rom 1:16); and although in Christ there is neither Jew nor Gentile, it is into a Jewish olive tree that the branches of the Gentile wild olive are grafted (Rom 11:17). In short, when Paul depicts the relationship between Christ and believers by the use of the simile of the body, when he speaks of the Christian life as being "in Christ", when he claims to have died with Christ on the cross, he never intends his vivid language to signify a union which is either more corporate or less personal than that which subsists between a king and his subjects.

III

I turn in the second place to the Fourth Gospel, and to the contention that John's Christology is more individualistic than Paul's and lacks the Pauline emphasis on the corporate Christ. I do not for a moment dispute Moule's interpretation of the evidence he has cited, that John uses the preposition en to denote a relationship of mutuality in a way subtly different from the usage of Paul; but I have four reasons for questioning the conclusion he has drawn from it.

1. It does not appear to me that mutuality and individualism are inseparable bedfellows. If in the thinking of John the person of Christ was such that a multiplicity of individuals could have a mutual relationship with him, and thereby be drawn into unity not only with him but with God and with one another, can we seriously suppose that John thought of that person in individualistic terms?

2. The match which Moule has arranged between Paul and John is played on Paul's home ground, and to be sure of a fair result we need to arrange a return fixture. No doubt the phrase en Christo is a peculiarly Pauline form of shorthand by which the apostle refers to his belief in the corporate Christ, but that is not to say that John does not have quite different ways of expressing what is substantially the same belief. Indeed, by a different selection of evidence we might even turn the tables and claim that Paul is the individualist; for, whereas in the Fourth Gospel Jesus is the Savior of the world, to Paul he is the one "who loved me and gave himself for me" (Gal 2:20). The truth is that Paul and John are individualistic at exactly the same point, in their insistence that the relationship of Christ to the Christian becomes real, operative and effective in faith, which is an individual act of acceptance, loyalty and obedience. The many have not in advance authorized the one to act as their representative; their part is to recognize in retrospect that what he has done was done in their name, so as to include them in the doing of it.

3. John has been at some pains in the compilation of his Gospel to show an interest in the same themes as we have found in the theology of Mark, and I propose to draw attention to five of them.

(a) Much of John's Gospel is concerned with the controversy between God and the world, but he never leaves us in doubt that in the drama of redemption the part of the world is played by Jewish actors. "He was in the world; but the world, though it owed its existence to him, did not recognize him. He entered his own realm, and his own did not receive him" (1:10-11). "His own" are the Jewish nation, and we need to remember this when later Jesus, as shepherd, repeatedly refers to "his own sheep" (10:3, 4, 11), and when in the upper room, having loved his own, he loved them to the last (13:1).

(b) John tells us explicitly that he wrote "in order that you may believe that Jesus is the Christ, the Son of God" (20:31); and, lest we should suppose that he intended the word Christos in some purely Christian, or even quasi-Gnostic, sense divorced from its Jewish origins, he uses at the first appearance of Jesus the Hebrew form Messias, and follows it immediately with the declaration of that "true Israelite" Nathanael, "You are the Son of God, you are the king of Israel" (1:41, 49). Whatever extra sense the phrase "Son of God" may have in this Gospel, it is first and foremost a title of royalty. The strong emphasis on the kingship of Jesus which Dodd discovered in this book, and which he believed to be bedrock tradition, is not for that reason to be excluded from John's own theology.

(c) John believed that "salvation is of the Jews" (4:22). In The Journal of Theological Studies (1981, N.S. XXXII pp. 341-368) there is an article by Raphael Loewe entitled "Salvation is not of the Jews." He argues that in John salvation is the release of the individual from sin and his consequent attainment of eternal life; whereas in the Jewish tradition salvation is always the rescue of the nation from external threat. The case is powerfully presented and carefully documented, and I should want to dissent from it at only two points. The first is that in the prophetic and apocalyptic tradition the external threat from which the Jewish nation needs to be rescued is uniformly seen as divine judgment for national sin; and the second is that, with that proviso, I believe that John stood firmly in the very Jewish tradition Loewe has so fully and brilliantly expounded.

(d) John believed that Jesus died for the nation (11:51). With his celebrated irony he records as a prophetic utterance the verdict of Caiaphas that "it is in your interest that one man should die for the people and not the whole nation be destroyed." It is the nature of irony that a statement should mean one thing to the speaker and another to the writer and his readers, but the force of the irony is blunted if the two senses are so far apart as to be equivocation. John no doubt saw universal implications in the death of Christ, but those implications arose out of its primary significance: he died for the nation.

(e) John, like Mark, portrays the coming of the Messiah as a crisis of loyalty for Israel. The purpose of his coming is salvation, but the consequence of his coming is judgment. He is the light of the world, and the coming of that light divides the world into believers and unbelievers, those who come to the light and those who flee from it. If the world will not have him as its Savior, it shall have him as its Judge. But as the story proceeds, the ranks of believers grow thinner, until Jesus is left alone with the Twelve, questioning even their loyalty: "Do you also want to leave me?" (6:67). Finally, in the upper room, when the disciples say, "We believe that you have come from God", Jesus replies, "Do you now believe? Look, the hour is coming, has indeed already come, when you are all to be scattered, each to his home, leaving me alone" (16:30-32). The judgment by light leaves us with no gospel, for it leaves Jesus alone in the light, alone in the bosom of the Father, and all the world in darkness under God's judgment. It leaves Jesus alone--unless the cross is the point at which he ceases to be alone; and this is exactly what John has to say about it. "Unless a grain of wheat falls into the ground and dies, it remains by itself alone; but if it dies, it bears much fruit" (12:24). The cross is the point at which Jesus, out of loyalty to the disloyal, puts himself where the world is, in the darkness and under judgment; he outfaces Satan in his claim to be prince of this world by proving that Satan has no claim over him and therefore no claim over those with whom he makes common cause, and so draws all men to himself (12:32, 14:30).

4. At this point, however, I have begun to anticipate the fourth and weightiest of my arguments. If it be true, as I have claimed--and I do not think Moule would disagree--that the starting point for New Testament Christology is the cross, then the question whether John, like Paul, believed in a corporate Christ needs to be reframed. The fundamental question is whether John believed that in the cross the salvation of the world has been achieved, in such a way that believers could subsequently acknowledge that they had been included in Christ's vicarious death. A prima facie case for this is provided by the claim of the Johannine Christ that he has finished the work God has given him to do (17:4), a claim repeated in the final word from the cross (19:30). Bultmann, it is true, has argued that this work was wholly a work of revelation: the purpose of the incarnation was that the Son should reveal the unseen Father, and the cross is nothing more than the supreme example of what had been going on all the time in the ministry. But this reading of John scarcely requires refutation. The first twelve chapters of John's Gospel, even more explicitly than the first thirteen chapters of Mark, are a prelude to the passion story. Through them the references to the coming hour of Jesus reverberate like the tolling of a great bell, and they are reinforced by many incidental premonitions--the destruction of the temple which is Jesus' body, the lifting up of the Son of man as Moses lifted up the serpent in the wilderness, the need to eat the flesh and drink the blood of the Son of man, the mysterious allusions to Jesus' going away, the coming of the night when no man can work, the good shepherd laying down his life for the sheep, the prophecy of Caiaphas. Above all, by restricting the reference of the very doxazo to the crucifixion, John draws a distinction between the glory which Jesus displays during his ministry and the glory which accrues to him through his death.

For all these reasons it must be maintained that for John as for other New Testament writers something decisive happens in the cross. If it were not so, as I have already argued, there would be no gospel, since the coming of the light into the world leaves Jesus in the end alone and the world in darkness. But how exactly does John envisage this decisive event?

The key, as Robert Paul and I learnt forty years ago in the lectures of W. H. Cadman, is to be found in the opening petition of Jesus' prayer: "Glorify your Son". Why does Jesus on the eve of his passion pray for what he already possesses? John has told us that in the incarnation the glory of the logos, the glory which the logos had with God before the world began, has been imparted to the man Jesus (1:14; cf. 17:5), and that in his first sign, and by implication in all the signs, Jesus has manifested it (2:11). At no point is there a suggestion that in this glory there is anything incomplete or defective. What Cadman taught us was to define doxa, as any good linguist ought, by the substitution of Johannine synonyms, and to identify the synonyms by observing what in the Gospel the words and works of Jesus are said to reveal, and what the disciples are said to believe in. Not only the glory, but the life, the light and the truth are incarnate in Jesus; and the Father loves him, has sent him, abides in him. "Believe the works, that you may recognize and know that the Father is in me and I in the Father" (10:38; cf. 14:10). The glory of Jesus is one word used to describe his relationship of mutual inbeing with the Father. Why then does he pray for that which he has already so fully enjoyed and manifested?

The great prayer of chapter 17 has traditionally been known as the high-priestly prayer, and it is an apt description. It is true that only at one point in it does John use priestly language, but that is enough. "For their sake I consecrate myself, that they too may be consecrated by the truth" (17:19). Like the king, the high priest stands before God as the representative of his people, and his consecration embodies, symbolizes and guarantees theirs. Even so, in Zechariah's vision the high priest Joshua stands before God "wearing filthy clothes", which the prophet expressly identifies as "the guilt of the land"; and God's command that he be reclothed in clean garments is the prophetic symbol and guarantee of a national deliverance (Zech. 3:1-10). As the author of Hebrews reminds us, "every high priest is taken from among men and appointed their representative before God . . . and so it is with Christ" (Heb 5:1, 5). The Johannine Jesus, then, prays for glory, not for himself, but because he prays as the royal and priestly representative of the people of God.

It is important to note, however, that Jesus does not pray, or at least does not pray directly, that glory, the glory of the eternal logos which he has possessed and manifested, should now be bestowed on his disciples. He asks that it be bestowed on him. Only when he has received it on their behalf, as their inclusive representative, can he then impart it severally to them. "The glory which you have given to me I have given to them" (17:22). The prayer of Jesus to be glorified in his representative role is answered in the cross. Already in the incarnation manhood has been taken into unity with the logos, but it is an individual manhood which, like the grain of wheat, abides by itself alone. Only in the cross does it become inclusive of others; only by being lifted up from the earth does Jesus draw all mankind to himself (12:32).

What then are we to say about the element of mutuality which Moule has rightly detected in John's use of the preposition en? I do not dispute, indeed I have in this essay myself asserted, that John portrays the incarnation in terms of the reciprocal inbeing of Jesus and the Father. It is also true that through the cross he sees the possibility offered to believers that they too may enjoy just such a reciprocal relationship. But this possibility depends on their being taken up, objectively in the death of Jesus and subjectively in their own response of faith, into his inclusive manhood.

IV

In the introduction to his treatment of the corporate Christ Moule cites a number of theologians who have professed to find the notion mystifying, and there is no doubt that they speak for large numbers of our contemporaries who would not think of themselves as theologians. New Testament scholars are bound to take such puzzlement seriously, and I should like in conclusion briefly to suggest three ways in which scholars may have contributed to the mystification, thereby incidentally misrepresenting the very authors they purport to expound.

1. It is possible to present the corporate and inclusive nature of Christ's person as though it were a fact. I have been arguing that it is not a fact but an interpretation of the cross. "The love of Christ constrains us, once we have reached the conclusion that one man died for all and therefore all mankind has died" (2 Cor 5:14). No doubt Paul believed that this conclusion was valid long before he personally became convinced by it, but that does not make it any the less a conclusion, nor is it valid independently of any conviction. An objective atonement is incredible if it is presented independently of the power of Christ, through the Holy Spirit, to elicit the faith that it is so. Salvation may be conceived as a free gift of God, but it is not a thing, an object to be transferred from donor to recipient; it is a life to be lived, a right of access to a presence, a relationship with God.

2. A doctrine of the corporate Christ becomes incredible if it is cut off from its roots in the solidarity of family and nation which is the common experience of mankind. I have been trying to show that in Mark and John at least these roots are intact,

and I believe that the same can be shown for other New Testament writers also. The notion of group solidarity, symbolized and embodied in a representative head, whose actions may be deemed to be those of the whole, surely ought not to lay too severe a strain on modern credence.

3. We may still misconstrue the New Testament if we suggest that solidarity is in itself redemptive. Even in its widest and most universal aspect the contrary may be the case. Nothing could be more universal than the solidarity of mankind in Adam. If Paul, Mark and John, to say nothing of other New Testament writers, believed that the death of Christ had brought them into a redeeming solidarity, this was because they also believed that in his act of self-giving, the one for the many, Christ was not alone. "God was in Christ, reconciling the world to himself" (2 Cor 5:19). "It is the Father who dwells in me doing his own work" (John 14:10).

HISTORY IS MORE! or YOU CAN HAVE IT BOTH WAYS!

<u>Yet another look at Eschatology</u>

John Marsh

The exponents of the Hebrew-Christian tradition have always been ready to ask, and to attempt to answer, a question about the historical order: "How and when will history end?" Theologians have discussed the issues under the title of "eschatology", while Biblical scholars have approached the question largely in a study of "The Kingdom of God." The issues are complex and manifold, and considerable differences in both analysis and solutions remain. This essay is intended to assist the attainment of a common judgment on these important matters, for they are not simply academic: every human being faces the question of the "end" of his own history.

*   *   *   *   *   *   *

THE OLD TESTAMENT

The Old Testament offers some conclusions about an "end" to the historical order that gives, or will give, from within or from without, a meaning to it. The Israelite nation, the "people of God" traced its origin to a number of Semitic tribes that were brought into a federal relationship largely under the leadership of Moses, who led them out of their slavery in Egypt, and brought them to the very border of the Promised Land. As they entered upon their new home it seemed that in more senses than one they had come to the end of their journey. Now at last the divine providence that had brought them to their promised settlement would ensure for them a permanent, peaceful and prosperous future. They had come to the "last days" of their history as the people of God.

But they had not. In their transition from a nomadic to a settled way of life, the Israelites were much affected by two factors which they observed in the neighboring states. First, the profitable agricultural propriety of placating the local deities alleged to affect the harvest of the land. Second, that monarchical government seemed to be acknowledged as the most successful instrument of social and political administration. A positive reaction to these two factors remained in the eyes of the "orthodox" a trouble to Israel throughout the period of the monarchy. To the end of the period the prophets enveighed against the "whoredom" of forsaking Israel's true "husband" Yahweh for the passing fancies of local baalim or deities of other states (e.g. Jer 13:27; Hos 4:12ff). That was not all: just as Yahweh was Israel's true husband, and Israel his true bride, so, in the brave imagery of the prophets Yahweh was declared to be Israel's true king, and Israel his kingdom of subjects (Isa 44:6; Ps 149:2).

God was Israel's true king; but his sovereign sway extended far beyond that small nation. It came to be recognized that even before the entry into Canaan his reign was exercised beyond the wandering tribes in the wilderness. "The Lord your God will himself go over before you; he will destroy these nations before you, so that you shall dispossess them" (Deut 31:3). In the end the sovereign rule of Yahweh was believed to be universal and ever-lasting, a theme frequently expressed in the Psalms. "The Lord has established his throne in the heavens, and his kingdom rules over all" (Ps 103:19), and "Thy kingdom is an everlasting kingdom, and thy dominion endures throughout all generations" (Ps 145:13).

It is interesting and important to note that though God's sovereign sway was universal and constant, it becomes manifest in particular historical occasions. Thus Isaiah: "On that day the Lord will punish the host of heaven and the kings of the earth . . . for he will reign on Mount Zion and in Jerusalem, and before his elders he will manifest his glory" (Isa 24:21ff). Events have no "halo" which marks them as divine actions; but to those with eyes to see [his elders] the divine activity in history is manifest.

The divine providence established the monarchy in a remarkable way. First, the king was in a special way the representa-tive of God's own sovereignty over his people. Thus it could be said to David: "I will raise up your offspring . . . and I will estab-lish his kingdom . . . I will be his father, and he shall be my son" (2 Sam 7:12ff). But the monarchy did not stand alone. For second, it was established and accompanied by the activity of the prophets, to whom God spoke his word to his people and his king alike. Third, although the king represented the authority of God to his people, the duty of preserving the proper obedience to, and worship of God was laid upon the priesthood. It was in this threefold strand of exercising his wise dominion that God sought to have a people through whom he could achieve his gracious purposes for the world.

Such a triple safeguard was adequate in design, but proved inadequate in practice. Human nature could not consistently respond sufficiently to its demands. Among kings, priests and prophets were many who failed. Many kings, despite, or even because of, cultural achievements, "did that which was evil in the sight of the Lord" (1 Kgs 11:6, etc.). The priesthood was equally liable to serious shortcomings: and many prophets failed to declare the true word of the Lord (1 Kgs 22:5; Jer 14:14; 23:32; 1 Kgs 22:13-23).

Monarchical government thus proved a failure, and the settlement in the Land of Promise did not turn out to be the end of Israel's pilgrimage, but rather the beginning of another cycle of exile and exodus to a re-entered Promised Land. Faced with this prospect of an endless stultifying cycle of disobedience and retribution the prophets of Israel articulated two different but positive responses. First, it was affirmed that a real "end" to history would come within the historical order itself (Isa 4:2-6; 9:2-7; 14:1f). Second it was proclaimed that the present order would be done away: there would be, and have to be, a "new heaven and a new earth" to accord with the final and perfect "reign of God" (Isa 65:17; 66:22).

Israel thus became an expectant people, looking with hope to a future when God's sovereignty would be fully implemented, not only in Israel, but in all the nations of the earth; and not only among human beings on earth, but among all animate and inanimate creatures as well (Isa 40:9-11; 49:6f; Isa 35:6-10; 41:18f). Israel articulated that hope in images drawn from her own history of her dealings with God, or rather of God's dealings with her: the people looked for a new leader like Moses (Deut 18:15-18), for a new king like David (Jer 23:5; 30:9), and for a new prophet like Elijah (Mal 4:5f). The advent of one who could thus be deemed to be "God's anointed" (= Messiah) would constitute the recognizable sign that the "end" of Israel's history had begun in unmistakable actuality. It is interesting to reflect that in the early years of Jesus' life there was one messianic excitement in the revolt of Judah of Galilee, with its watchword that only God should be king of Israel.

The Old Testament thus shows God's rule (= kingdom) as one constant factor in the world's history, whatever be the inconstancy and inconsistency of men. He controls all history, and Jeremiah gives a good picture of him as a potter, able to throw an unpromisingly developing lump of clay back to its shapelessness, in order that he may make of it either the beautiful thing or the useful vessel he originally intended. So God can accept the foibles and sins of men into his sovereign rule, and bring history to his desired end. Events have no "halo" to proclaim their divine quality, but at times, as Isaiah saw, God's rule becomes particularly evident, and the eye of faith observes it in action (Isa 24:21-23).

* * * * * * *

THE NEW TESTAMENT

The New Testament inherits the understandings of the Old. It continues to speak of the kingdom of God, though the word "kingdom" comes from the Greek rather than from the Hebrew tongue. It is better to speak of the "reign" or "rule" or "sovereignty" of God, avoiding any reference to a geographical entity. But the New Testament speaks to a very differently organized community of Israelites from that in the Old Testament. The monarchy, in any Davidic sense, has vanished; the Herodian "kings" were Roman Tetrarchs, not Davidic sovereigns and "God's anointed." Prophecy had ceased, though the populace waited for "the prophet who was to come" (Deut 18:15-18) or for the reappearance of Elijah (Mal 4:5f). The Priesthood survived, its life centered on the Temple, and assuming some king-like functions in negotiation with Rome concerning certain Jewish liberties. But the subject status of a Roman-occupied country could not quench the confident hopes of the Jews that God would soon make his reign manifest.

Into this expectant situation John the Baptist appeared from the desert, where he had been for a considerable time (Luke 1:80), more than probably in close contact with if not actual membership of, one of the desert communities such as the Essenes or that whose writings have recently been recovered from Qumran. He came with a sharp critique of contemporary Jewish life, religious, social, economic and political (Mark 6:17f). It would have included a "puritan" morality, a repudiation of animal sacrifices, the practice of "daily baptisms" to preserve "cleanness" before God, a communal meal where bread and wine were consumed, and the rejection of any compromise with Rome, even to secure the preservation of some Jewish "right." Luke reports (in the **New English Bible** translation) that the people "were on the tiptoe of expectation, all wondering whether perhaps he was the Messiah" (Luke 3:15). John called his fellow countrymen to a baptism of repentance for the forgiveness of sins, thus becoming part of a new Israel or people of God (Mark 1:4). In the desert sects baptisms were part of the daily ritual, self administered, by which each sectary could daily keep himself "clean" before God. But John now offered his fellow-countrymen a once-for-all baptism, like that which, as Paul also saw, was parallel to that which the Israelites had undergone as they went by dry land through the waters of the Red Sea, leaving behind their old life, and coming to a new life, as yet uncharted in which they would be guided by the hand of God. Those responding to John's call for a repentance, a turning away from the life they had been living, would become part of the new "Israel" or people of God, committed as such to establish a just and righteous society, to worship God with integrity, and above all, to become what they had for long failed to be, a missionary agency to proclaim God's gracious rule to the Gentiles.

Jesus came to accept that baptism, and so offered repentance with and for his people for their failure to be a true people of God. John deemed it unfitting that he should baptize his kinsman, but Jesus protested that to do so would simply be in accordance with the righteous purposes of God (Matt 3:13ff). He was, after all, a member of the old, rebellious, disobedient people of God. So Jesus was baptized by John (Mark 1:11), and as the ceremony took place he heard a voice which said: "You are my son; my favour rests on you" (Mark 1:10). He also saw a vision of a dove (the Hebrew word for which is "Jonah") descending on him, signifying that, like Jonah, he was to be the means of the Gentiles hearing of the goodness of God.

"You are my son" . . . In this context the word "son" has no filial content drawn from human parentage, though that has been drawn into a good deal of Christian thinking since. What could have been brought to Jesus' mind by the quotation from the Old Testament (Ps 2:7)? In the Old Testament the title indicated some part of the close relationship between God and his people. Moses was directed to visit Pharaoh and say to him "Israel is my first-born son . . . let my son go" (Exod 4:22). Much later Hosea looked back on the great Exodus from Egypt, and said "When Israel was a child, I loved him; and out of Egypt I called my son" (Hos 11:1). But "son of God" also meant the king as representing the whole body of the people. So God promised David: "I will raise up your offspring . . . I will establish his kingdom . . . I will be his father, and he shall be my son" (2 Sam 7:12f). Jesus heard the words "You are my son", and they would convey to him "You now constitute my people Israel"; and "You are Israel's true king really incorporating the body of my people." This sheds new light upon the temptations in the desert following the baptism, and forms an understandable basis for Jesus' proclamation as his message for his time that "The kingdom of God is upon you" (Mark 1:15).

"The kingdom of God is upon you!" . . . So the New English Bible renders the good news Jesus proclaimed. Other translations offer a more modest rendering: "The kingdom of God is near" or "at hand." If this arises from a sense of contradiction between any real presence of the kingdom and the manifest evils in the world, the hesitation is unwarranted. The Old Testament exposes God's age-long and universal rule as a constant magnitude in history. Yet though constant, it is not always manifest. What Jesus proclaims in his life and message is that in his person and work the present exercise of God's sovereignty will once more, and finally be manifest.

Both John and Jesus realized that time was not on their side. Many were seeking to establish the reality of a new people of God by force, and Galilee had for some time been a breeding ground for revolt by those who sought to re-establish the old empire of David. (Matt 11:12; Luke 16:16). But John and Jesus saw that unless contemporary Jewish attitudes radically changed (= repentance) to Gentiles in general, to Romans in particular, and to the despised Semitic Samaritans, national calamity lay ahead. The calamity came in 70 AD. So when Jesus began his mission in Galilee and gathered disciples to send out on his mission, he understandably enjoined them not to waste time in fruitless arguments with Gentiles or Samaritans, but to concentrate on "the lost sheep of the house of Israel" (Matt 10:5f). For, as Paul observed: "They have the sonship, the glory, the covenants, the giving of the law, the worship and the promises; to them belong the patriarchs, and of their race, according to the flesh, is the Messiah" (Rom 9:4f).

God's rule, or sovereignty, was made manifest in the life and ministry of Jesus and his followers. They lived "in the kingdom." They were not thereby shielded from the "slings and arrows of outrageous fortune"; contrariwise, it could bring additional cares, sufferings and persecution: but it did give them, and gives their successors, a peace and serenity that is invincible. Jesus made the benefits of the kingdom available--bodily, mental and spiritual health--among Gentiles and Samaritans as well as Jews. This brought him a considerable following, as it aroused some passionate opposition. Not all his followers understood his message. Some wanted to make him take office as the new Davidic king (John 6:15). His opponents thought that his activity, if not his actual spoken claims, was "blasphemous" (Mark 2:3ff; 11:27).

Jesus' Galilean ministry ended in a communal meal where some five thousand people were miraculously fed. The excited crowd saw in him the "prophet who was to come" (Deut 18:15-18), and sought to make him king. But he slipped away from them; and on the morrow tried to convince them of the real nature of his ministry and God's reign.

On his last visit to Jerusalem Jesus made a fresh proclamation of the kingdom of God and of himself as that kingdom's king. His "sermon" was not however in words, but in a recognized prophetic language of an "acted prophecy." He rode into Jerusalem on an ass in precise and conscious enactment of Zechariah's pacific prophecy (Zech 9:9f). He entered "his" city as its true king, and as such cleansed the temple that had been defiled, not by unwanted Gentile feet treading its courts, but by the Jewish-enforced absence of Gentile footsteps in the holy places. "My house shall be a house of prayer for all nations; but you have turned it into a robbers' den" (Mark 11:17).

So the kingdom of God which Jesus proclaimed and incorporated was "manifested" in Jerusalem, though it was not acknowledged, but rather opposed, by the authorities and powers of other "kingdoms" operative in Jerusalem at the time. The Jewish "kingdom" saw the kingdom proclaimed by Jesus as a very real threat to its own peace and even its existence: it could all too easily provoke a riot incurring retributive destruction for the Jewish state. (Mark 14:2; John 11:47-53, 57). The Roman imperial power was understandably anxious about the activity of Jesus (Mark 15:2), who had entered the city in a strange but unmistakably "kingly" fashion; measures had to be taken to deal swiftly and effectively with any possibility of riot during the Passover festival time. Even those who had so far appeared to share Jesus' conviction that the kingdom of God had now become manifest found his actions during the course of the week so incomprehensible that towards the end of it they "all forsook him, and fled" (Mark 14:50).

It is impossible within the brief limits of this paper to review all that took place during the last week of the life of Jesus. Suffice it to say that at his trial before the Jewish and the Roman authorities the two crucial points by which Jesus brought condemnation upon himself were secured by questions as to whether he was "the son of the Blessed" (in the Jewish court) (Mark 14:61) and as to whether he was a "king" (in the Roman court) (Mark 15:2; John 18:33-37). The record leaves it plain that in neither court did his judges really understand Jesus' claim.

In the end the "king" was enthroned, but upon a cross; and he was crowned--but with a crown of thorns. The power of temporal kingdoms had proved too much for the power of the kingdom of God which Jesus claimed to possess and incorporate in himself. Or so it seemed, and must still seem. For though the power behind the throne of Jesus was omnipotent, it was the omnipotence of love, which will always appear to be weak against other authorities and powers in a world where sin has disturbed and corrupted the divinely created order. But the omnipotence of love did not remain without its own manifestation: on Easter Day the risen Jesus returned to the defeated, disheartened and fearful citizens of the kingdom of heaven, and changed their whole experience of the world for ever. The "kingdom" had not only been made manifest; it had been shown to be manifestly indestructible. At last the words of Isaiah became actuality:

How beautiful upon the mountains are the feet of
him who brings good tidings, who publishes peace,
who brings good tidings of good, who publishes salvation,
who says to Zion, "Your God reigns". Hark, your watch-
men lift up their voice, together they sing for joy;
for eye to eye they see the return of the Lord to
Zion. Break forth together into singing, you waste
places of Jerusalem; for the Lord has comforted his
people, he has redeemed Jerusalem. The Lord has
bared his holy arm before the eyes of all the nations;
and all the ends of the earth shall see the salvation
of our God.   (Isa 52:7ff)

*   *   *   *   *   *   *

ESCHATOLOGIES - IMPOSSIBLE, POSSIBLE AND PROBABLE

The Jewish religion, like the Christian, has had important
things to say about "the end of the world" and of its history,
about "the last things", the "eschata", hence the world "eschatology",
the study of the last things. By the time that Jesus was born
eschatology had become one great concern for Jewish theologians
and teachers, a strong stimulus to activist groups seeking a renewed
Jewish independence, and a comforting mythology for the ordinary
quiet citizen who had to endure a period of national adversity
and a much resented occupation of Palestine by the power of
Rome. In brief, the Jews believed that the "present age" would
be brought to an end in and through a great cosmic "day of the
Lord", heralded by signs and portents, both heavenly and terrestrial,
and accompanied by the appearance of a heavenly being, a "son
of man", a "messiah" or "king", who would deliver a "final" or
"last judgment" on all evil, which would from thence forward
be destroyed (Isa 2:12; 13:6; Joel 3:14; 2 Cor 1:14). A new age
would thus be inaugurated, either by life continuing within the
present created order, or by the appearance of some new creation,
"a new heaven and a new earth", where God's reign or kingdom
would prevail permanent and unchallenged (Isa 65:17; 66:2; 2 Pet
3:13; Rev 21:1).

It is idle to suppose that Jesus' teaching about the kingdom of God can be properly understood save as against such an
environment of expectant belief. There seem to be five possible
assessments available:

1. "Consistent Eschatology"

After Peter had confessed that Jesus was "Messiah" (Mark 8:29), Jesus spoke of his approaching suffering and death, and told his disciples that they must "deny themselves, and take up their cross" as they followed him (cf. Mark 8:34). He then added: "Truly, I say to you, there are some standing here who will not taste death before they have seen that the kingdom of God has come with power" (Mark 9:1). It is clear in the context that Jesus envisaged the circumstances of his own death as that historical crisis in which it would be possible to see "the kingdom of God come with power." If "coming with power" be understood in terms of current Jewish belief, the crucifixion would somehow be or become an historical event unmistakably constituting a divine intervention, with an appearance of Jesus himself as the heavenly "son of Man', or as "Messiah", together with the enactment of a final judgment of the world, when all evil would be done away, and God's reign (or kingdom) established in full and final authority. But, so the argument ran, the Gospel narratives of the crucifixion (and resurrection) cannot yield to such an interpretative scheme, and it must be admitted that Jesus was mistaken in his expectations.

Yet it would be unwise to discount his eschatology altogether. The kingdom which Jesus proclaimed was simply not as imminent as he had thought. So the Christian Church has had to wrestle, early and late, with the question of its arrival time. Meanwhile Jesus' ethical teaching is best understood, according to "consistent eschatologists" as directed to the "interim" period between his own historical ministry and his "coming again" in an end that lies still in the future.

2. "Futurist Eschatology"

Despite the plea that Jesus had erred about the arrival of the Kingdom at the time of his crucifixion, it remained (and remains) clear that the error had not eliminated eschatology from Christian thought and practice. Jesus' own teaching, and the substantial concern of the rest of the New Testament were sufficient to ensure that a future coming of the Kingdom was still to be expected. Through the centuries there have been many erroneous identifications of the time of "the end", just as throughout almost two millenia there has been a considerable theological elaboration of what the study of "the last things" could mean. Many believers have looked, and many still look for a future coming of the Kingdom at some as yet unspecified time, when there will be a "second coming" of Jesus "in power and great glory" (Mark 13:26).

Such a futurist eschatology is certainly able to relate itself satisfactorily to a great deal of the biblical material: the "present age" will end in a great cosmic "day of the Lord", which will be heralded by "signs and portents", and accompanied by the appearance and activity of Jesus as the "Son of Man", who will deliver a final judgment on the world. Nevertheless it seems to fail on at least two important counts. As simply "futurist" in its eschatology, it has taken inadequate recognition of Dr. Dodd's well-documented presentation of Jesus claiming that in his own person and activity the kingdom of God had already arrived. Second, it shows some lack of a necessary "poetic" understanding of the figurative presentation of the various phenomena with which any description of "the last things" is given.

3. "Realized Eschatology"

Dr. Dodd takes with full seriousness the indications in the Gospels that Jesus himself saw his ministry as an effective appearance of the kingdom of God: "If it is by the Spirit of God that I cast out demons, then the kingdom of God has come upon you" (Matt 12:28; cf. Luke 11:20). As for any "future" implied in Mark 9:1 (Dodd, **Parables** . . . p. 37n), he insists that a correct translation should read "Some of those standing here will not taste death until they have seen that the Kingdom of God has come with power". The Christian Church does not look simply toward the future in contemplating the "end", but views "the end" through what has already taken place. "At a particular point in time and space" he claims "the eternal entered decisively into history. An historic crisis occurred by which the whole world of man's spiritual experience is controlled. To that moment in history our faith always looks back. The Gospel is not a statement of general truths of religion, but an interpretation of that which once happened" (Dodd, **Parables** . . . p. 163-164.

Dodd has been held to deal satisfactorily with the indubitable eschatological reality of the kingdom of God as present in Jesus Christ and his mission; but can he be deemed to deal as satisfactorily with other elements of contemporary Jewish expectation about the "end of the age"? Dodd is certainly aware of the problem. He writes:

> The ancient images of the heavenly feast; of Doomsday, of the Son of Man at the right hand of power, are not only symbols of supra-sensible, supra-historical realities; they have also their corresponding reality within history . . . The historical order however cannot contain the whole meaning of the absolute . . . The Son of Man has come, but also He will come; the

> sin of men is judged, but also it will be judged. But these future tenses are only an accommodation of language . . . The Kingdom of God in its full reality is not something which will happen after other things have happened. It is that to which men awake when this order of time and space no longer limits their vision . . . "The Day of the Son of Man" stands for the timeless fact . . . That which cannot be experienced in history is symbolized by the picture of a coming event, and its timeless quality is expressed as pure simultaneity in time--"as the lightning flashes" [Luke 17:24; Matt 24:27] (Dodd, **Parables** . . . p. 82-83).

Dodd says of Jesus that "He points His hearers directly from the historic crisis in which they were involved to the eternal order of which that crisis was a mirror" (Dodd, **Parables** . . . p. 84).

4. "Inaugurated Eschatology"

Despite Dodd's persuasive presentation of his case, many scholars found his thesis unacceptable unless modified. Dodd may have established satisfactorily that Jesus taught that the Kingdom of God had arrived as an historical reality in his own person and work; but though actually present, that Kingdom can hardly be deemed, either then or now, to have come in its fulness. The continuing potency of evil in the world prohibits that thought, as do the references to the future in Jesus' own eschatological teaching, and the expectancy of the early Church, which undoubtedly looked forward to a "second coming" or "parousia." In short, a futurist, as well as a realized element is indispensable to a satisfactory eschatology. So if the understanding of the person and work of Jesus as a present reality of the Kingdom of God were joined with taking the "future tenses" of Jesus' eschatological utterances not as "only an accommodation of language" but as true "future indicatives", a more acceptable and understandable eschatology would be possible. Jesus could be seen as "inaugurating" the Kingdom in history, though at the same time anticipating its development and completion in the future. But that would prove to be basically a restatement of one strain of Old Testament prophecy, in which the "day of the Lord" would usher in a new and final historical order of universal peace and prosperity. (e.g. Isa 11:1-12:6)

But such an eschatology would fail to recognize the significance of the other strain of Old Testament eschatology, in which the day of the Lord would usher in a "new heaven and a new earth", a kingdom which is clearly "not of this world" (Isa 65:17ff; 66:22f). It thus appears that a fully satisfactory eschatology must relate to the Johannine report of Jesus' statement that "my Kingdom is not of this world" (John 18:36). An inaugural eschatology fails because whatever is "inaugurated" in history must find its development and conclusion in history: John 18:36 makes that quite clear. It is also significant that the New Testament speaks of life after death not in terms like "survival" or "immortality" which suggest some sort of continuance of the life of this world, but instead characteristically talks of "resurrection", a state of being radically different from the spatio-temporal existence of earth-born humanity. (cf. 1 Cor 15:35-50).

5. "Manifested Eschatology"

Can a satisfactory eschatology be devised, to comprise both the historical reality of the Kingdom of God in Jesus, and the indispensable necessity of awaiting its future coming? Can any eschatology "have it both ways"? The answer can be affirmative by adopting what is now proposed: a "manifest eschatology."

The term derives from, and carries forward, an Old Testament understanding of eschatology: "the Lord of hosts will reign on Mount Zion, and in Jerusalem and before his elders he will manifest his glory" (Isa 24:23 **RSV**).

The Old Testament came to realize that God's reign was not confined to those occasions when it was manifested: it was rather one permanent factor in history. That view was reached only after periods when it seemed that the Lord's "hand was shortened that it could not save" (Isa 50:2; 59:1; 42:18-22; Num 11:23; Exod 14:18). But Israel's "discipline" eventually brought the conviction that "the Lord will reign for ever and ever"--the conclusion of the hymn of praise and thanks to God for his miraculous deliverance at the Red Sea (Ps 10:16). "The Lord is king for ever and ever" is the confidence of the Psalmist that God will deliver his people from all their afflictions. The historical order with its succession of events is the area where man can learn of the sovereignty or kingdom of God, and eternity is the sphere from which God manifests himself in and through his sovereignty (or Kingdom) to his own people, and to mankind at large.

Manifest Eschatology in the Ministry of Jesus

The Gospels make it clear that there were occasions in the life of Jesus when the Kingdom of God was specially manifest--and that he knew it! Such was his exorcism of demons. "If it is by the finger of God that I drive out the devils, then be sure the Kingdom of God has already come upon you" (Luke 11:20; Matt 12:28). Again, when the Baptist sent a deputation to ask Jesus if he were the one who was to come, or not, Jesus told the delegates "Go and tell John what you have seen and heard; how the blind recover their sight, the lame walk, the lepers are made clean, the deaf hear, the dead are raised to life, the poor are hearing the good news" (Luke 7:22; Matt 11:4. For all this as an eschatological fulfillment see Isa 35:5f).

It is also clear that Jesus saw the arrival of the Kingdom of God as manifested in and constituting a drama of history, beginning with his baptism and ending with his death and whatever victory lay beyond it.

John baptized Jesus, and not long after was arrested and imprisoned. Jesus went to Galilee, with his own formulation of John's message: "the time has come; the Kingdom of God is upon you; repent and believe the good news" (Mark 1:15). The presence of the Kingdom was publicly manifested in the various "messianic" signs.

But the "realized" elements in the eschatology of Jesus were not confined to such "signs and wonders." The Kingdom was also being manifested in a dramatic course of historic events in which Jesus was actively and willingly implicated. When he heard Peter confess his Messiahship, he began to indicate what sort of Messiah he would be: not a "Davidic" Messiah, a king to lead his loyal subjects in a successful rebellion against Rome (cf. John 6:15; though Jesus claimed to be Israel's true king: cf. Matt 21:5); not an awesome apocalyptic figure, descending from heaven with supernatural power and great glory to establish his sovereignty on earth; rather would he be a "suffering servant" of God such as Isaiah had conceived (Mark 10:45; Isa 53), a Son of Man such as Daniel had dreamed of (Dan 7:13f; Mark 14:62), one who by his vicarious suffering from and for the wrongs of others would die, but on his death ascend to the "Ancient of Days", there to receive for the people of the saints of the Most High a universal and imperishable kingdom (Dan 7:27; it is regretfully impossible in the space of this essay to justify every such use of scripture).

It was evidently some such course of events that Jesus had in mind when after Peter's confession he spoke of "having a baptism to be baptized with", adding "what constraint I am under until the ordeal is over" (Luke 12:50)--a saying which intensifies the use of the same idea when Jesus asked James and John whether they were able to drink his cup or to be baptized with his baptism (Mark 10:38). Long ago, at the time of the Exodus from Egypt, the people of God (Israel) was historically, and therefore provisionally constituted by undergoing a "baptism" of passing

68

through the waters of the Red Sea (1 Cor 10:1f). God held the waters back, and the people of God survived: but their enemies drowned in the flood. The baptism of Jesus was an historical fulfillment or re-manifestation of the baptism at the Red Sea, the authentic historical constitution of the final people or Israel of God (Mark 1:11 where "Son" = "people" [cf. Hosea 11:1]). Yet even that manifestation awaited a further enactment, a final historical fulfillment in the baptism of Jesus' death. When he went, as he saw he must, into the deep waters of death, and the flood swept over him, what would be the outcome? (Ps 69:2, 14b, 15). Would there be a final "manifestation" of God's power to constitute a people for himself? Would he thus survive? The answer could be obtained only by dying: "What constraint I am under until the ordeal is over!" (Luke 12:50 **NEB**).

Jesus approached the final days of his ministry in such understandable tension (cf. Mark 14:36 and Mark 15:34 with Luke 23:46; John 19:30). He tried to restate his message in quite unambiguous ways. He rode into Jerusalem as its one true king, forswearing war's weapons and proclaiming peace to the nations, to establish a universal and imperishable kingdom (Zech 9:9f). How then can the words of Mark 9:1 be understood in such a context of events?

Two points: first, to restate the decisive lesson of Dr. Dodd when he affirmed that, as was known to every schoolboy, the translation of the verse should be: "There are some of those standing here who will not taste death until they have seen that the Kingdom of God has come with power" (Dodd, **Parables**, 37). "The bystanders" he claims "are not promised that they shall see the Kingdom of God coming but that they shall come to see that the Kingdom of God has already come, at some point before they became aware of it" (Dodd, **Parables**, 37n). The Kingdom will not come with whatever may happen at a crucifixion or parousia; they can be but instrumental in "making the penny drop", so that they shall see that indeed the Kingdom of God had come upon them in his ministry. Second, the phrase "with power" cannot now be taken as so often it has, to mean "with power and great glory", an impressive display of political, judicial and military force; it must be understood as used in Romans 1:4, where Jesus was said to be "declared according to the Holy Spirit to be Son of God with power." That cannot mean great political, judicial or military power; but only the power of humility and love which alone could "save" men, "make them whole", and bring them into right relationships with God and their neighbors. So Mark 9:1 means "Some of you who are here will, before you die, come to realize that my claim is true, that in my coming among you the Kingdom of God verily came upon you."

Jesus taught and believed that in his life and work the Kingdom of God was a reality in history, and so manifest to men.

But much more than that is attested in the Gospels: the nature and quality of life in the Kingdom; the coming of the end of the world in the coming of the Kingdom; and the relation of the crisis produced by the Kingdom to the crises precipitated by men themselves.

Life in the Kingdom of God is described in the Sermon on the Mount. The citizen of the Kingdom has, like Jesus himself, God's favor resting on him, though that does not save him from "the slings and arrows of outrageous fortune"; on the contrary, he may suffer more just because he is a heavenly citizen. Yet he will know that he is always under God's providential love and care, and so may be "congratulated" even in his misfortunes on having compensations beyond value and compare. His life is lived with God and in the fellowship of his people, and all share with their heavenly Father a divine life that here before death and thereafter beyond death is indestructible and, in Johannine terms "eternal."

To proclaim the presence of the Kingdom of God is to face men with a crisis, with the crisis of all crises, for this crisis has eternal dimensions, while others have historical and temporal dimensions. Yet the response of men to the crisis of the Kingdom inevitably affects the crises they themselves precipitate, and affects their actions. The Gospels take care to indicate that the crisis which Judaism found itself in at the time of Jesus could not be other than deeply affected by the crisis which Jesus precipitated with the Kingdom of God. Thus Jesus claimed to be Jerusalem's true king (Matt 21:1-5), but foreswore the armed revolt against Rome which many would have liked him to lead (John 6:15). Jesus realized that, if the present attitudes of Jewish people remained unchanged, then the "Roman crisis" would end—as it did—in calamity for Jewry. It is perhaps no matter for surprise or complaint that the two crises of the Kingdom of God and of Roman dominion somehow got intermixed in the "apocalypses" of the Synoptic Gospels.

The evangelists try to make one more thing plain, difficult then as now, for the mind to grasp and understand. Using their own historiographical device they took the popular apocalyptic imagery of contemporary Judaism to tell their readers that what the Jews were looking forward to at the "end of the world" had already taken place when Jesus died and rose again. This is the almost unimaginable but quite inescapable peak of realized eschatology. In the apocalypses of Matthew, Mark and Luke reference is made to that last day when the Son of Man shall come, in terms such as:

> . . . in those days . . . the sun will be darkened,
> and the moon will not give its light, and the stars

> will be falling from heaven, and the powers in the
> heavens will be shaken. And then they will see the
> Son of man coming in clouds with great power and
> glory. And then he will send out the angels, and gather
> his elect from the four winds, from the ends of the
> earth to the ends of heaven.   Mark 13:24-27

The "last day" phenomena are therefore used by the evangelists to give their narrative of the crucifixion and resurrection some explicit references of meaning. "The sun will be darkened"--from the sixth hour "there was darkness over the whole land until the ninth hour" (Mark 15:33): "the powers in the heavens will be shaken"--"the curtain of the temple was torn in two, from top to bottom"--impossible for any human hand!: "they will see the Son of man coming in clouds" (Mark 13:26)--Jesus told the High Priest that "you will see the Son of man sitting on the right hand of power, and coming with the clouds of heaven" (Matt 26:64), which shows Jesus as accepting the role of Daniel's Son of Man who goes to the Ancient of days to receive his universal and everlasting kingdom: "the Son of man with great power and glory"--John penetratingly tells how Jesus spoke of his approaching death: "Now is the Son of man glorified, and in him God is glorified": "the Son of man will send out the angels (or "messengers")--And Matthew relates how Jesus came as Son of man to the eleven and commissioned them to teach, baptize and found his living community throughout the world.

Manifest Eschatology in Man's Experience and Understanding of the World

The most interesting implication of the New Testament teaching that the end of the world happened when Jesus died and rose again is probably the inference that whenever finite man meets the infinite God he is in the presence of one in whom and for whom there is no future, no past, and therefore strictly no present, but whose being holds all historical successions of events together in his one eternal being. It is some such basic insight that makes the seer of the Apocalypse write of the lamb "slain from the foundation of the world" (Rev 13:8--so according to R. H. Charles should the verse be translated.): Matthew to speak of the Kingdom prepared for the "sheep" from the foundation of the world" (Matt 25:33-34): Jesus himself to give thanks for the glory which the Father's love has given him "before the foundation of the world" (John 17:24): Paul to confess that God had chosen his people in Christ "before the foundation of the world" (Eph 1:4) and Peter to say, very much in the language of this essay, that Christ, the lamb without blemish and without spot, was "destined before the foundation of the world but was made manifest at the end of the times for your sake" (1 Pet 1:19f).

The lamb, Jesus Christ, was of course slain in history at a particular moment of time "under Pontius Pilate"; but in the non-temporal realm of divine being the slaying of the lamb can be only one element in one eternal nature, neither "before" nor "after", but just "there." Thus it is that whenever the Kingdom of God (which means God, for God is always the one who reigns over all) is manifested in history the actuality of the manifestation is always fuller than itself. Thus the Exodus from Egypt was not simply one event in the series of events that befell the Jews; it was a moment of that history when the event manifested, or was made to manifest the sovereignty of God, and so brought the reality of the divine kingdom within reach of human experience. So it was an event of "promise", sharing a number of features with a later "Exodus" from Babylon, as well as with the coming of Christ, his suffering, death and resurrection. So the return from Babylon was both descried and described in terms of the Exodus from Egypt (cf. Isa 48:20f; 51:9ff). Similarly Paul could say that "Christ died for our sins according to the scriptures", and "rose again according to the scriptures", not because he had in mind some Old Testament reference to a rising on the third day, but because the past manifestations of God's sovereignty could not but reveal a like pattern of his activity. It is an impropriety to search the Old Testament for prophecies of a rising on the third day: rather is Christ's resurrection better prefigured in the birth of a nation as Hebrew tribes find a new life in an escape from bondage in Egypt to a new life of unity under Moses dedicated to the service of one God; or in the death of a nation carried into exile in Babylon and its rebirth ("resurrection") in the return under Cyrus; and all such events can be seen in their fulness in the manifestation of the Kingdom in the life of Jesus Christ, the true King of God's people, living, dying, rising, eternally regnant, bringing eternal life to men.

The manifestations of eschatological realities admittedly bring an experience of God. But that experience cannot be classed as "mystical", for mystical experience retreats from the historical, and is by nature and intention "timeless." But manifested eschatological realities are disclosures of the very stuff of history, and convey reliable insights into its depth and meaning. When such realities are manifested, God is manifested, and where God is thus manifested in history, Jesus Christ is manifested, for he is the one being who spans both the eternal and the temporal, both God and man in the one Kingdom where God alone is king.

Where do all these considerations leave us? Is the Kingdom of God still to come, or has it come already? Can we both pray "Thy kingdom come" and in the same prayer say that "Thine is the kingdom . . . for ever and ever"? Even more difficult is the question whether the end of the world has already come, or has it still to come. Is it possible to think in terms of a "realized" (or "manifested") apocalyptic?

The contribution of this paper is to affirm that we "can have it both ways." The Kingdom of God has already come, and it is still to come: the end of the world has come upon us, and it still has to reach us. The inescapable linguistic and substantial difficulties can be met once the true nature of Christian eschatology and apocalyptic are recognized. For in the divine realm the "end" which is the "last thing" in the historical order, and the "beginning" which is there the "first", are both part of an "unsuccessional" whole. In the order of historical succession, however, the eternal reign, sovereignty or Kingdom of God becomes manifest in and through certain occasions. But in that historical order there was one occasion when the full nature and reality of the divine sovereignty was made manifest, in the life of the historically incarnate divine king. Similarly it can be affirmed that the "end of the world" has come, made symbolically manifest (whether really or literary) in the crisis of Jesus' historical death and resurrection. Thus a Christian apocalyptic is able to assure believers that whenever and however the end of the world comes, it will come in the "pattern" of Jesus Christ (Mark 15:33), whose death brought great darkness on the world and whose resurrection heralded a new day (Mark 16:2f).

Finally, there is need to note that the issues about the Kingdom of God are neither simply exegetical or philosophical, but finally and inevitably personal. God reigns for ever and ever. Of his kingdom there is no end. But, as with earthly kingdoms, there are, as well as true subjects of the king, some who are disloyal, disobedient, rebellious and even treacherous. The good news of the eternal reality and indefectibility of God's kingdom is addressed to all his subjects. God "has the whole world in his hands", from beginning to end, from south to north, from east to west, from farthest galaxy to farthest galaxy. None can avoid being in his kingdom; but each subject can avoid, as each can come to enjoy the privileges and blessedness of those who acknowledge their loyalty to the true and heavenly king. To pray "Thy Kingdom come" is much more to ask that humanity shall acknowledge the sovereignty of God that is real, rather than to ask God to make his kingdom real.

UNDERSTANDINGS OF THE CHURCH
IN THE CAPPADOCIANS

Donald A. Sykes

The Cappadocians form a significant group among 4th century Greek theologians, regarding themselves as legitimate successors of Athanasius. Basil of Caesarea was acknowledged as leader by the other two major writers, Gregory of Nazianzus and Gregory of Nyssa, developing as he did a churchmanship which was to prove very influential. [1]

In one aspect **Basil** may be represented as the straightforward man of affairs, whether ecclesiastical or secular. Yet another side of him wants to withdraw, physically and mentally, from the active world. This is why one of the most energetic bishops of his century is a pioneer of monastic practice. The ways in which Basil attempted to resolve this tension cannot here be explored, [2] beyond my remarking that a passion for order is fundamental to both sides of his life. Absorbed as he was to become in the maintenance of the visible structure of the church, Basil would never have considered himself at variance with what he wrote in his celebrated **Address to Young Men:** [3] "We, my children, in no wise conceive this life of ours to be an object of value in any respect, nor do we consider anything good at all, or so designate it, which makes its contribution to this life of ours only." The "other life" is what matters and the present is no more than preparation. [4] For some people, or for particular periods in individual people's lives, the preparation is best undertaken in isolation. It is fairly clear that Basil was sometimes inclined to find in this life the ideal way, [5] and this might seem to undervalue the Christian profession of ordinary members of congregations, business men, say, and the priests whose lives are taken up with them. Are they less "real" Christians than those whose withdrawn lives might seem to bring them closer to the "real" world beyond this? (Cf. Basil's contrast of "shadows and dreams" with "reality." [6]) For Basil however any such absolute

73

restriction of pure apprehension to particular groups or individuals could not be conceived without irreparable loss to the church. It is within the church that this purity must find its context. If it is not present as an interacting, rather than an isolated element, there can be no meaning in the unity which was for Basil an overwhelming concern.

A glance at Basil's life discloses that a great deal of his attention was taken up with the condition of the visible church as expressed through its structure. He defended its tangible unity extensively and passionately against the splits of doctrinal dissension, being deeply affected by the prospect of churches "constantly drifting into a worse condition." [7] Basil had a clear enough idea of what the church should be like. For one thing, he believed it had a recognizably continuous tradition, given sharp formulation by the Council of Nicaea [8] and open to further limited clarification by such people as himself. But clarification is not to be confused with innovation. Nothing which Nicaea laid down and nothing which its defenders maintained was new. When unity is destroyed (torn like an old cloak [9]), reconciliation can be effected only if the full implication of the tradition is drawn out. It is, he claims, on the basis of a Nicene Creed, which in turn rests on tradition stretching back to scripture, that he is able to call for acknowledgment that the Holy Spirit is not a creature and to make this a test of correct belief. The orthodox church consists of those who accept Nicea in its expanded or clarified form. [10] Within this pattern the bishop has a primary responsibility to preserve the truth within his own church and thus to contribute to the homonoia and semphonia of the whole church. The Church at large had a corresponding duty to support individual communities and bishops. One reason for Basil's great respect for Athanasius arises from the Alexandrian bishop's part in the interplay of individual and great church. Basil praises him as exercising a responsibility for all churches [11] and would wish to emulate him in his own vast correspondence. Convinced, for instance, that the true church at Antioch is represented by Meletius, Basil seeks to uphold him by a network of orthodox connections. He writes to Athanasius, hoping to use his reputation in the West to commend the cause of Meletius to Rome. [12] But when, in a situation of intricate exchange and elaborate misunderstanding, Pope Damasus supported the rival candidate Paulinus, Basil stuck to his understanding and continued to see in it the true center of unity for the church at Antioch. He can ignore the disdainful attitude of Damasus. "If the Lord has been reconciled to us, what further assistance do we need?" [13] Such an outburst, understandable as an expression of frustration, and of the autocratic side of his nature, is not wholly typical of Basil's way. It may be necessary to act uncompromisingly against what is seen as outright error. But it is no less essential to the church that its unity should be maintained by conciliation and the progressive removal of misunderstanding. It was natural for Basil to hope for solidarity with Rome which had a good record in remaining firm against Arianism. We may assume some reluctance on Basil's part in rejecting an opinion emanating from its bishop. Yet ultimately Basil felt compelled to stand by the authority he derived from his own development of Nicene orthodoxy. In some ways his appeal to the Roman bishop is parallel to his appeal to the Emperor Valentinian: he would welcome the support of both, but would not change his view if he failed to secure it.

The energy Basil showed in church affairs extended beyond what many churchmen would have regarded as their proper sphere of duty. Particularly after he became Bishop of Caesarea in 370, he defended both the involvement of the church in the life of the empire and its independence of the empire. The church has a right to its own organization, he wrote, defending himself to a provincial governor, [14] and this in no way infringes the prerogatives of the state. When a complex agency of social services (accommodation, medical care and the like) is set up through Basil's initiative--a whole New Caesarea--this is justified as an intrinsically Christian, properly ecclesiastical enterprise. At the same time, Basil wishes for a definable connection with the state. He can claim protection, calling on officials for favorable consideration, applauding the attitude of an administrator of whom he could write: "[He] is a true guardian of justice, easy of access for the victims of injustice, terrible to lawbreakers, fair to both poor and rich, and, greatest of all, [he] was for restoring Christianity to its ancient honour." [15] Having seen the effect of an Arian sympathizer in the person of the Emperor Valens, he might consider the advantage of securing Valentinian's adhesion to the orthodox side. But the emphasis would fall on the responsibility of an emperor before God to uphold the true faith, the determination of which lies within the church.

In all this there is a recurrent stress on active responsibility. Basil clearly felt that he and others were constantly called to act for the preservation of the church and this accounts for his periods of despondency when he feels the inadequacy of what has been done in the face of heretical opposition. But there is another side to Basil's understanding of the place of the church in the pattern of providence. The determination of events is not ultimately governed by his and other people's energy: Basil is not prepared to abandon history to purely human agency. The struggle for truth within the church has to be seen within a pattern in which the devil is the promoter of discord [16] within the overall structure of divine providence. His confidence in the church as a community with a destiny beyond vicissitude is expressed in hex.4.7. [17] Like the ocean, "the church enjoys a profound calm and the malicious spirits cannot trouble it with the breath of heresy." This confidence fits well with his contemplative, monastic bent, in tension with the energetic activist life of the bishop and man of affairs. The Holy Spirit then becomes not merely an object of correct belief to be campaigned for by the defenders of the true faith. It is the Spirit who, within the dispensation of the Trinity, gives life and energy to the church; the Spirit is the structure of the church. "Is it not plain and incontestable that the ordering of the church is effected through the Spirit?" [18] This is the counter-balance to the vigor of human activity, the union of the Spirit with human purpose [19] which gives authenticity in the present life and continuity with the eternal world.

Basil went a long way toward resolving the tension between the active life of the church leader and social improver and the contemplative, ascetic way. His friend Gregory Nazianzen found resolution far more difficult. Though he briefly held one of the highest positions in the church, as Bishop of Constantinople at the time when the city was host to one of the most important of church councils in 381, all his ecclesiastical offices were reluctantly accepted, uneasily held, abandoned at the earliest opportunity. He was a man of curious contrasts, taking obvious delight in the attention attracted by his carefully-wrought sermons before crowded congregations in the eastern capital, yet longing for seclusion and frequently finding it. But all the time he was very much a churchman. Despite the self-absorbed musings in verse which often occupied his periods of withdrawal, he never allowed his solitariness, physical or mental, to block his awareness of belonging to the whole church, indeed to the whole of humanity.

His thought often turns to the question of salvation. The work of Christ was directed to all men. When Gregory writes in or.30.6 "He takes me wholly, with all my infirmities" [20] he considers himself primarily as a representative human being. This sense of the universal man lies behind what he has to say about the universal church. In his personal relationships Gregory can show great respect for non-Christians, [21] so long as they are prepared to live peaceably alongside the church. Conversely, the attacks he made upon the memory of the Emperor Julian who had attempted to subvert Christianity are among the bitterest ever made on an enemy of the faith. [22] For the place of the church is unique in world history, unique in the history of salvation. It is the sole focus of the faith. If all men are saved in Christ, they can come to know it only if the church faithfully communicates the truth of Christian theology. To do this, it must in some real sense be the truth. This is strikingly expressed in language which relates the church directly to the divine being and functions. The church is to be a harmonious whole, not simply because this is humanly desirable, but because the church must actively represent to the world the harmony of the Trinity and the harmony of creation. [23] The doctrine of the Trinity is frequently to be found as the animating point of Gregory's theology. To maintain its very identity, the church must maintain the unity in trinity of the Godhead.

Gregory had then a very powerful sense of the unity of the church, based as it was upon theological rather than practical necessity. The present church is united with the heavenly in the praise of God; [24] his hearers are to think of themselves as citizens of the heavenly Jerusalem. [25] For all the rhetorical effect of these and similar passages, they refer to a dimension of reality in his thinking. But the primary area in which unity has to be sought is in the church existing on earth. Here there ought to be a coincidence of unity in teaching and in church office, [26] with an integrated structure of church life guaranteed by the acceptance of a single system of doctrine. As we have seen, Gregory is prepared to act towards people outside the church in a fairly open, amenable way. But churchmen he regards as under strict obligation and he feels justified in demanding absolute conformity. It is into a faith that Christians have been baptized and this faith can and must be given demonstrable shape. This, he believes, is to be found in the legitimate interpretation of the faith formulated at Nicaea. Arians of whatever brand break the unity, despising the one narrow way, [27] by violating the central faith, and all other heretical teachers follow them. It is tragic, Gregory believes, that a community which, more than any other, has broken the barriers of race and class, should invent new ones. [28] Dissension cuts like a plough. [29] Time and again, the argument comes back to the unity of God. There must be semphonia or homonoia in the church to correspond with the divine harmony. [30] Or the imagery of the Body of Christ is used to the same effect.

Unity for Gregory could be maintained only through the acceptance of authority. In one sense this was the creed of the Nicene Council taken as a summary of true apostolic faith. But in another way this answer seemed to him insufficiently concrete and it is here that the priest in the local congregation finds his place. For it is noticeable that, whereas the Nicene faith itself issued from an assembly of bishops, Gregory is very uncertain about the function of subsequent assemblies in defending it. Though for a time he attempted to guide the Council of Constantinople which came to be thought of as continuing the work of Nicaea, generally his point of unity is to be sought in the individual church, specifically in its bishop. In him is found a concentration of authority in precise proportion to his doctrinal fidelity. The figure of the Body is developed: the true bishop is the soul of his church, according to divine ordinance. [31] He should be a many-sided man, answering the needs of a variety of people. But primarily he should be a ruler [32] by whom baptism is administered and the faith preserved. Though Gregory is at some pains to emphasize the responsibility of the whole Christian people for the deposit of true faith, [33] there is still a distinct teaching office, essential to the existence of the church and fundamentally belonging to the bishop. Without this, the flock will disintegrate. [34]

Gregory had frequent experience, he felt, of the failure of the true faith, when bishops abandoned orthodoxy for heretical lines of thought. His easily disturbed temperament could be brought almost to the point of despair, as he wonders whether God had abandoned his providential care of the church, [35] as Macedonian and Apollinarian calamities assail it. Gregory may fall back upon his vision of the heavenly church as the ultimate comfort, but he still has recourse to more immediate help. Distrusting a proliferation of councils ("I never have and can never honour anything above the Nicene faith," [36]) he was prepared to accept Constantinople, with its firm exclusions, as providing a necessary protection for the earlier council. He was also prepared to accept the backing of the Empire in upholding its provisions [37] and defending the orthodox church. Yet he is still eager to assert the church's independence in other ways. The church should have separate jurisdiction in ecclesiastical affairs. He argues for powers parallel to those of the state. In another mood he can yearn for an ideal Christian life entirely separate from the everyday political and economic world. "What concern have you with Caesar and his affairs?" [38]

It is not difficult to find in Nazianzen vacillations. He believed deeply in the church's unity in doctrine and practice and was nonplussed and distressed by shortcomings. Yet for all his vagaries and uncertainties about how the oneness of the church should be maintained, he held firmly to the belief that unity was essential to its being.

Gregory of Nyssa, Basil's younger brother, was even less inclined than his friend Nazianzen to participate as a bishop in the active life of the church and certainly had no more obvious talents for this work, in which he none the less became involved. Though a talented writer, trained in oratory, he gained less satisfaction than Nazianzen from public preaching and showed greater capacity for the speculative exploratory probing of the Christian mystery in a life of solitude. On the other hand, he did not disdain political influence on behalf of orthodoxy and was prepared to write panegyrics on the death of members of the royal house. [39] Nor is he lacking in awareness of the corporate being of the church.

There is a good deal in Gregory's writing which supports a straightforward understanding of the church as an institution with definable parameters and recognizable ways of proceeding. He is clear that the faith is central to the church's existence. When he writes against Eunomius, he emerges not as a remote theologian, concerned to ascertain the truth on a christological point, but as an ecclesiastical writer fearing for the very identity of the church. Equally, when he deals with baptism and eucharist, he emphasizes the church context of all his teaching. The "affinity and likeness" between disciple and master which is expressed in baptism is integral with the three fold immersion traditionally practiced by all orthodox Christians. [40] (The Eunomians were accused of abandoning the practice, exposing their inadequate theology. It is essential for Gregory that the church is the teacher of belief in the Trinity. [41]) The Christian is thus incorporated into the Body of Christ and enters an area of shared responsibility. The Catechetical Oration is written to assist Christian teachers in the vital duty of building up the church by presenting the faith as at once reasonable and based upon the authority of tradition. It is within the church that scripture can be claimed to hold an unassailable place as the guide and arbiter of Christian doctrine. [42]

A tension however may be detected in Gregory's thought. For it undoubtedly contains a strong individualist element which might seem to go against the corporate understanding of the Christian community. As in Origen, so in Gregory, the Bride in the Song of Songs may be either the individual soul or the church. It may be argued that Gregory places such weight on the first that the second interpretation is attenuated. [43] He writes with great intensity of the knowledge of God to be gained by the soul as it ascends in purity and persistence. Yet the individual vocation is not meant to displace the corporate: the vision of God as he is, in so far as it is granted to an individual, need not be divisive. Such a vision, for all its intensely individual character, will be in accord with the God-given revelation of his nature which is open, at varying levels, to all Christians. It may be that Gregory does not do enough to integrate into the life of the church the experience of the Christian who, while remaining within the present life, is privileged to ascend to something of the condition of the next. There is no theoretical antithesis, no avowal of Christian gnosticism. But as Gregory writes of the ascent of the soul, he seems not to see how this solitary and ultimately incommunicable journey may isolate from the community which shares a different degree of understanding. On the other side, it may be said that passages which equate the Bride with the church, while not co-ordinated with the interpretation of the soul, do speak strongly for instance of the church's unity with Christ, [44] of a close link between knowledge of God and the church, [45] and Gregory applies the imagery of crowning to the church. [46]

There is however another tension in Gregory's thought, not between corporate and individual, but between two ways of understanding the corporate. If all men are joined to Christ through the deification of human nature which results from the Incarnation, [47] how does Gregory see the specific place of the church? His answer tends to stress the sacraments of baptism and eucharist

80

as the ways Christ has appointed for the continuation of his work: these make effective the union of God and man.

Finally, we must see the ultimate context of Nyssen's writings on the church in his Origenistic belief in the final consummation in which all will be saved, albeit after long pains. Here will be the final harmony with God in which all shall share, [49] the true goal of divine willed unity in which the church has through the ages had its part.

In their writings on the church, the Cappadocians show a pattern familiar in other parts of their theological work, in that we find sufficient unity of conception and detail to make it reasonable to consider them as a group, while at the same time evincing sufficient independence and diversity as to call for differentiation in understanding.

NOTES

1. Basil of Caesarea, c. 330 - 379; Gregory of Nazianzus, c. 330 - c. 390; Gregory of Nyssa, c. 330 - c. 395.

2. Cf. H. von Campenhausen, **The Fathers of the Greek Church** (ET 1963), 84-100. Nazianzen is dealt with on 101-114 and Nyssen on 115-125. See also Quasten, **Patrology** Vol. 3, (ET 1960), 203-296, together with P. F. Fedwick, **The Church and the Charisma of Leadership in Basil of Caesarea** (1979), E. Bellini, **La Chiesa nel Mistero della Salvezza in San Gregorio Nazianzeno** (1970)., F. Trisoglio, **San Gregorio di Nazianzo in un quarantennio di studi** (1925-1965) (Rivista lasalliana 1973), c. XXIV 'Ecclesiologia', 367-377 and c. XXV 'Sacerdozio', 379-383, R. M. Hübner, **Die Einheit des Leibes Christi bei Gregor von Nyssa** (1974).

3. Migne, **Patrologia Graeca** (hereafter referred to as 'M') 31, 565B. This work is translated in the Loeb series by R. J. Deferrari, **St. Basil: the Letters** (1934), Vol. IV. Translations are taken from this version. It has also been edited by N. G. Wilson under the title **Saint Basil on the Value of Greek Literature** (1975).

The text reads: hēmeis hō paides ouden einai chrēma pantapasi ton anthrōpon bion touton hupolambanomen, out agathon ti nomizomen hoiōs, out onomazomen, ho ten synteleian ēmin achri toutou parachetai. (Loeb 380; Wilson 20f.)

4. Ibid., 565 B-C; Loeb 380-2; Wilson 20, line 10. . . . kai pros heterou biou paraskeuēn hapanta prattomen.

5 ep. 22, M. 32.288B ff.; ed. Courtonne (1957), Vol. I, 52ff.; Loeb Vol. I, 128ff.

6. Address II. M. 31.565C; Loeb 382ff.; Wilson 20, lines 20ff.

7. ep. 30, M. 32.513B; Courtonne, Vol. I, 72, lines 17ff.; Loeb 176f.
. . . dei de pro to cheiron ton pragmatōn huperreontōn.

8. ep. 113, M. 32.528A; Courtonne Vol. II, 17, lines 32ff.; Loeb Vol. II, 224, lines 1ff.

9. Ibid., 525C; Courtonne 16, lines 16f.; Loeb 222, lines 12f.

10. ep. 125, M. 32.545B ff.; Courtonne Vol. II, 30ff.; Loeb Vol. II, 258ff. Note especially 545C (31, lines 16-19; 260, lines 18-21): . . . kata ta rēmata ta hupo tōn paterōn hemon ektesthenta en tē Nikaia kai kata tēn ygios hypo tōn rēmatōn toutōn emphainomenēn dianoian.

11. ep. 69, M. 32.429B ff.; Courtonne Vol. I, 161ff.; Loeb Vol. II, 38ff.

12. ep. 66, M. 32.424A ff.; Courtonne Vol. I, 156ff.; Loeb Vol. II, 26ff.

13. ep. 239, M. 32.893B; Courtonne Vol. III, 60 line 12 - 61 line 2; Loeb Vol. III, 418, lines 14-16: kai gar ean men hilasthē hēmin ho kyrios, poias heteras prosthēkēs deometha.

14. ep. 94, M. 32.485B ff; Courtonne Vol I, 204ff.; Loeb Vol. II, 148ff.

15. ep. 96, M. 32.492B; Courtonne, Vol. I, 209, lines 15ff.; Loeb Vol. I, 158, lines 11ff.

16. ep. 99, M. 32.504B; Courtonne Vol. I, 218, lines 25ff.; Loeb Vol. II, 182, lines 9f.

17. M. 29.93C; ed. Giet (1949) 274ff. The words apply to his own church but may well be turned to the wider community.

18. De Spiritu Sancto 16.39, M. 32.141B; Garnier and Maran, 2 ed. Gaume (1739), 3.34; ed. G. F. H. Johnston (1892), 84, lines 2f. hē de tēs ekklēsias daakosmēsis ouchi saphos kai anantirrētōs dia tou Pneumatos energeitai.

19. ep. 227, M. 32.852C; Courtonne Vol. III, 30, lines 17ff.; Loeb Vol. III, 344, lines 14ff.

20. or. 30.6, M. 36.109C; ed. Mason (1899), 116, lines 1ff.; ed. Gallay (Discours 27-31, 1978), 236.

For Gregory's doctrine of salvation, see H. Althaus, Die Heilslehre des Heiligen Gregor von Nazianz (1972) and D. F. Winslow, The Dynamics of Salvation: A Study in Gregory of Nazianzus (1979).

21. One such was probably Nemesius to whom he addresses one of his poems (carm. 2.2.7, M. 27.1551A-1577A) and epistles 198-201 (M. 37.324C-329A;

82

ed. Gallay (Budé, 1967) Vol. II, 90-93; ed. Gallay (**Die Griechischen Christlichen Schriftsteller der ersten drei Jahrhunderte,** 1969) 143-146.

22. Cf. or. 4 and 5, passim (M. 35.532A-720A). Other references are given in M.-M. Hauser-Meury, **Prosopographie zu den Schriften Gregors von Nazianz** (1960) 101-9.

23. Cf. Bellini, op. cit. 75f.

24. or. 39.11, M. 36.345B ff.

25. or. 45.23, M. 36.653C ff.

26. or. 21.8, M. 35.1089B ff.

27. or. 27.8, M. 36.21C; Mason 14, lines 14ff.; Gallay 90.

28. or. 6.8, M. 35.732A f. Cf. especially: to mesotoichon tou phragmou.

29. Ibid., 1, 721A.

30. Ibid. 12, 737A ff.

31. or. 2.3, M. 35.409B.

32. Ibid., 44f., 452B ff.

33. or. 40.41, M. 36.417A ff.

34. or. 42.2, M. 36.460A.

35. ep. 202.1, M. 37.329B; ed. Gallay, Jourgon **Lettres Théologiques** (1974) 87.

36. ep. 102.1, M. 37.193C; Gallay, Jourgon, 70.

37. ep. 125, M. 37.217C ff.; GCS 92 f.; Budé Vol. II, 15f.

38. or. 40.19, M. 36.384A. Cf. ep. 185, M.37.304B; GCS 134, line 15, Budé 76, line 11: ti koinon ziphei kai pneumati.

39. E.g., The Empress Placilla. oratio funebris de Placilla M. 46.864C ff. Cf. Campenhausen op. cit., 119.

40. oratio catechetica 35, M. 45.85D ff.; ed. Srawley (1903) 129, lines 9ff. Note the expressions to suggenes and homophulon (88A; 130, line 5).

41. Eun. 1.19, M. 45.520D; ed. W. Jaeger I (1960) 94, lines 1ff.

42. anim. et res. M. 46.49C f.

43. Cf. Quasten **Patrology** Vol. 3, 266.

44. <u>hom. 4 in Cant.</u>, M. 44.836D; Jaeger VI (1960) 108f.

45. <u>hom. 7 in Cant.</u>, M. 44.908B; Jaeger 205, lines 6ff.

46. <u>Ibid.</u>, 916C ff.; 213f.

47. <u>or. catech.</u> 27, M. 45.69C f.; Srawley, 101, line 10ff. – 102, line
10.

48. <u>Ibid.</u>, 26.68D ff.; 99 lines 4ff.

49. <u>or. catech.</u> 26, M. 45.68D ff.; Srawley 99, lines 4ff.

WILLIAM PERKINS AND THE THEOLOGY
OF THE COVENANT

Donald K. McKim

Robert Paul's interests are wide-ranging. His writings on Puritanism, the Covenant and the developments of doctrinal understandings, however, would suggest that a study of "William Perkins and the Theology of the Covenant" would be a fitting way to pay tribute in a small way to this remarkable Christian scholar to whom I owe so much. [1]

I. PERKINS ON THE COVENANT

After thoroughly discussing the "foundation" of Election as Jesus Christ in **A Golden Chaine** (Chs. XV-XVIII), Perkins turned to dealing with the "Ovtward meanes of executing the decree of Election" (Ch. XIX). [2] These means are "Gods couenant, and the seale thereof" (I, 31). Perkins defined God's Covenant as "his contract with man, concerning the obtaining of life eternall, vpon a certen condition." This Covenant

> consists of two parts: Gods promise to man, Mans promise to God.
>
> Gods promise to man, is that, whereby he bindeth himselfe to man to be his God, if he performe the condition.
>
> Mans promise to God, is that, whereby he voweth his allegeance vnto his Lord, and to performe the condition betweene them.
>
> Againe, there are two kinds of this couenant. The couenant of workes, and the couenant of grace.
> Ieremie 31.31, 32, 33. (I, 32)

For Perkins, the Covenant of Works was found chiefly in the Old Testament, the Covenant of Grace in the New (II, 647-48). "Law" belonged to the Covenant of Works and had the function of preparing humans to appropriate the benefits of the Covenant of Grace wrought through the death of Christ (II, 250). The Covenant of Works was "Gods couenant, made with condition of perfect obedience, and is expressed in the morall law" (I, 32). This Moral Law finds its "abridgement" in the Ten Commandments. Then, in **A Golden Chaine**, Perkins gave a detailed exposition of the Decalogue with each Commandment being dealt with in turn (I, 32-69). From there the "Use of the Law" is discussed (ch. XXX), then "Of the Couenant of Grace" (ch XXXI). Baptism and the Lord's Supper each have a chapter devoted to them (Chs. XXXIII and XXXIV) after one on the nature of the Sacraments in general as "appendants" to the Preaching of the Word (I, 71).

Perkins' discussions of the "Covenant of Works" always referred to the Covenant as the Moral Law found in the Ten Commandments rather than as a Covenant made for all humanity with Adam in the Garden. [3] He did believe that all were under the Covenant of Works but it served the purpose of humbling humans, driving them to the Gospel and rendering them inexcusable before God. The Law has two parts: "The Edict, commanding obedience, and the condition binding to obedience. The condition is eternall life to such as fulfill the law, but to transgressours, euerlasting death" (I, 32). Thus the Covenant is the way in which God binds Himself to His people.

But no one can keep the Law. So another Covenant was needed. [4] This is the "Euangelicall couenant" or the Covenant of Grace. As he wrote:

> In the legall couenant, the promise of eternall life is made vnto workes. Doe this and liue. If thou wilt enter into life, keepe the commandements. But thus no man can merit, because none can fulfill the law. In the Euangelicall couenant, the promise is not made to the worke, but to the worker; and to the worker, not for the merit of his worke, but for the merit of Christ, as Apoc. 2.20. Bee faithfull vnto the end, and I will giue thee the crowne of life, the promise is not made to fidelity, but to the faithfull person, whose fidelitie is a signe that he is in Christ, In whome all the promises of God are yea, and Amen, that is, most certaine and infallible (II, 392-93).

This Covenant of Grace "which is nothing else, but a compact made betweene God & man touching reconciliation and life euerlasting by Christ" (I, 164) again has two parties--God and humans. God is the "principall, and he promiseth righteousnes and life eternal in Christ: Man againe bindes himselfe by Gods grace to beleeue and to rest vpon the promise" (I, 164). This Covenant was "first of all revealed and delivered to our first parents in the garden of Eden" and after the Fall by the promise of the woman's seed bruising the serpent's head (Gen. 3:14). It was "continued & renewed with a part of <u>Adams</u> posteritie, as with <u>Abraham,</u> <u>Isaac, Iacob, Dauid,</u> &c. but it was most fully reuealed and accomplished at the comming of Christ" (I, 164). This Covenant of Grace is "absolutely necessary to saluation: for of necessitie a man must be within the couenant, and receiue Christ Iesus the very substance thereof; or perish eternally" (I, 72).

That not all people were elected to salvation expressed itself in that not all people were thus included in the Covenant of Grace:

> Now Gods practise and dealing with <u>Isaac</u> and <u>Ismael</u> is this: <u>Ismaell</u> is vouchsafed to bee made partaker of temporall blessings; but yet he is cut off from the spirituall couenant of grace, and <u>Isaac</u> is the man that must receiue the couenant, and by vertue thereof be made partaker of life euerlasting. And so accordingly it is with others; God hath decreed to chuse some men to saluation, and these are admitted into the Couenant: others he hath decred to reiect, and they are cut off from the Couenant, and from life euerlasting. (III, 118; cf. I, 164).

The "contract" nature of the Covenant is seen in Perkins' descriptions of each party's vows and promises:

> Some thinke, that men may bee brought within the Couenant, by the doctrine of Vniversall grace and redemption. But this way perswading a man that hee hath title in the Couenant of grace, is both false, and vnfit. False it is, because all the promises of the Gospel, are limited with the condition of Faith and Repentance, not beeing vniuersall to all, but made onely to such persons as repent and beleeue: therefore they are indefinite in regard of whole mankind, and to beleeuers onely they are vniuersall (II, 23).

For those who repent and believe,

> God in mercie on his part promiseth to men the remission of sinnes and life euerlasting: and man againe for his part promiseth to beleeue in Christ, and to obey God in all his commandments . . . This vow is necessarie, and must be kept as a part of the true worship of God; because it is a promise wherein

88

> we vow to performe all duties commanded of God,
> either in the law, or in the Gospel (I, 583-84). [5]

The promises of God fully received in the Covenant of Grace are, according to Perkins, "the foundation of all true comfort" since this means that "God is our God" (III, 520). Not only in this life but in the life after death these Covenant promises are the source of "all our happiness." They form the very ground of

> those two maine Articles of our faith, the resurrection
> of the bodie, and the immortalitie of the soule: for
> by vertue of this Couenant alone shall we rise againe
> after death to life, glory, and immortalitie; as Christ
> himselfe disputing against the Sadduces, from hence
> proveth the resurrection, in that, God is the God
> of Abraham, Isaac, and Jaacob. (III, 520).

But also, the nature of this Covenant of Grace is "the ground of all obedience." Since God is the Lord, His people must obey (Psalm 95:7) argued Perkins. And "the Preface of the morall law enforcing obedience laieth the same ground . . . and whosoeuer is truely perswaded that God is his God, cannot but obey him?" (III, 520). Thus the "third use of the Law" is present in Perkins' thought. [6] He stated: "The use of the Law in such as are regenerate, is farre otherwise: for it guideth them to new obedience in the whole course of their life, which obedience is acceptable to God by Christ" (I, 70). Not only individuals, but also the Church is to be obedient since God's Covenant with the body of believers is the same:

> God had made a couenant with his Church, the tenour
> whereof is this, I will bee thy God, and thou shalt
> bee my people. This couenant is not for a day or
> an age, or for a thousand yeares or ages, but is euer-
> lasting and without end, so as Gods people may say
> of God for euer, God is our God: and likewise God
> will say of his Church for euermore, this people is
> my people (I, 314).

II. PERKINS' THOUGHT IN PERSPECTIVE

The prominence of the so-called "Federal Theology" or "Covenant Theology" as a distinguishing feature of both English and American Puritanism has been well-documented. [7] In England William Ames (1576-1633) is often cited as "the leading British exponent of federal theology." [8] By 1623 in his **Medulla theologiae**

(English translation: **The Marrow of Sacred Divinity**) Ames has developed his thought on the Covenant to such an extent that it can be said that "no previous thinker in the Calvinist-Puritan tradition analyzed the covenant of grace with an acuteness comparable to that of the Franeker professor." (Ames had been forced to leave England because of his Puritan sympathies. He became Professor of Theology at Franeker in 1622). [9] Ames was a student of Perkins at Christ's College, Cambridge, serving there as a Fellow from 1601 till his expulsion in 1610.

But Covenant Theology had Continental roots as well. Rhineland theologians such as Kaspar Olevianus (1536-1587) of Heidelberg used the theme as a way to clarify the nature of grace and moral obligation while his colleague Francis Junius (1545-1602) made a distinction between Covenants of works and grace, but used it in discussing Justification rather than Election. [10] Yet because the Covenant doctrine was not yet firmly developed as an organizing principle of theology in these theologians, "it is probably wisest to speak of a theology of covenant rather than covenant theology, so far as the sixteenth century is concerned." [11]

What has been done, however, is to examine the various flows and streams of influence on early English Covenant Thought. [12] Two major sources of traditions have been identified as having significance for the development of the theology of the covenant in England. One came through William Tyndale (1494?-1536). It is found also in Heinrich Bullinger (1504-1575) and Ulrich Zwingli (1484-1531). This line stressed the Covenant as an agreement with attendant responsibilities on humans by virtue of their baptismal vows to God. The other stream, with a greater distinction between Law and Grace and a heavier emphasis on the promissory nature of the Covenant, flowed more directly from the thought of John Calvin (1509-1564). [13]

Contractual Covenant

In examining these two currents, it has been noted that in the works of Zwingli, the covenant idea itself is not prominent. In his early period, Zwingli stressed the differences between the "two covenants," the Old and New Testaments. In his 1523 "Commentary on the Sixty-two Articles," Zwingli argued that among the Biblical terms used interchangeably, testamentum, pactum, and foedus, testamentum is most frequent and points to the idea of one entering freely into a relationship with another. [14] The term foedus for Zwingli, as he explained in his 1525 "Commentary on True and False Religion," is seen also in terms of a bilateral commitment. [15]

Zwingli appealed to these understandings in his May, 1525 piece "On Baptism" written against the Anabaptists. There he argued in favor of infant baptism on the basis of his view of sacraments as initiatory rites indicating a covenant pledge. He wrote: "Baptism is an initiatory sign or pledge with which we bind ourselves to God." [16] The sign signifies one's willingness "to hear what God says to him, to learn the divine precepts, and to live his life in accordance with them." [17] Consequently, "They who do not keep the covenant glory in the symbols [the Sacraments] in vain . . ." [18]

This line indicates Zwingli's stress on the human obligation in the covenant, the "contractual elements" or mutual nature of the covenant. The human obligations must be carried out for the covenant to have effect. Zwingli did not develop fully his views on this in relation to the doctrine of election. Nor did he delve into the implications of stressing the bilateral nature of the covenant. [19] For, while it is the free mercy of God that initiates the covenant, and not human merits or work, still God will be our God in Zwingli's mind if "we walk wholly according to his will." [20] Yet the place of human obligation is plain.

Zwingli's successor as leader of the Zurich church was Heinrich Bullinger. Bullinger's teachings on the covenant go beyond Zwingli's at several points. Bullinger more strongly than Zwingli stressed the unity of the Old and New Testaments. This meant that hermeneutically he could base his theology of the covenant on both Old and New Testament examples. [21]

Also in Bullinger, the bilateral nature of the covenant was developed more definitely and clearly than in Zwingli. When Bullinger wrote of the Covenant in discussing infant baptism, he termed the sacraments "signs and seals" (zeichen und sigel) of the Covenant in which one is received and enrolled when baptized. [22] He wrote: "By our sacraments, especially by baptism, we are received and enrolled in the military service of Christ, and by taking the sacraments we profess and bear witness that we are soldiers of Christ . . . " [23] In his definitive work on the Covenant, **De testemento sev foedere dei unico & aeterno** (1534), Bullinger stressed the Scriptural use of testamentum as pact (pactum) or covenant (foedus) as particularly used in Genesis 15 and 17. He thus gave primacy to the conditional nature of it by appealing to the rules, stipulations and obligations found in these Biblical covenants. [24] In God's Covenant with Abraham, there was the duty given: "to adhere firmly to the one God through faith and to walk in innocence of life for His pleasure." [25] For the Christian who has accepted the covenant sign of baptism as the initiation into Christian community (the church) by God's election or predestination, there was also the reminder that this covenant obligated the Christian to live a holy life of love, have faith in God and give service to neighbors. These were human conditions of the covenant. If one met them it meant that person was elect. [26] Bullinger did then relate predestination and covenant. But he did so in such a way as to maintain human reponsibility and obligation. For him, the covenant was God's vehicle for dealing with humans. God's election only became binding in history as individuals maintained their conditions of the covenant. [27]

In England, the ethical aspects of Covenant thought were accented through the works of William Tyndale. Though exiled from his native land in 1524, never to return, Tyndale's theological works and his English translation of the Scriptures were important contributions to the English Reformation. His colleague John Frith (1503-1533) was instrumental in spreading Tyndale's books and ideas. Tyndale asserted that:

> the key to the Scriptures is to be found in that all of God's promises are conditional. God's promises constitute a covenant, or appointment, by which God promises certain blessings to men on the condition that they keep his laws. This covenant was first made with Adam after the fall. It is now entered into by persons at baptism. All strictly religious matters, public and private, all moral standards, public and private, and all sense of ethical and religious obligation are founded upon this sworn covenant of promise to obey God's law. [28]

While it is very difficult to establish firmly the sources of Tyndale's thought, whether from Bullinger, or Zwingli or neither, it is clear that he did teach a contractual covenant. [29]

For Tyndale, God's Covenant was of the nature of an agreement rather than a promise. He wrote that, " . . . God never made a promise, but upon an appointment or covenant, under which whosoever will not come can be no partaker of the promise." [30] In his 1534 Prologue to his Pentateuch translation he wrote: "For all the promises throughout the whole scripture do include a covenant: that is, God bindeth himself to fulfil that mercy unto thee only if thou wilt endeavour thyself to keep his laws . . . " [31] For Tyndale the contractual covenant includes all the promises of Scripture. Yet this was not a "salvation by works" since he maintained: "Faith justifieth thee; that is, bringeth remission of sins." "But," Tyndale continued, "If thou wilt not go back again, but continue in grace, and come to that salvation and glorious resurrection of Christ, thou must work and join works to thy faith." [32] Justification is by faith but continued salvation comes from fulfilling God's condition: doing God's law. [33] This conditional nature of the covenant came to dominate Tyndale's thought so fully that it functioned as a basic axiom of hermeneutical method for interpreting Scripture:

> The ryght waye, ye and onlye waye to vnderstonde the scripture vnto oure salvacion, is, that we ernestlye and above all thinge [sic], serche for the profession of oure baptyme [sic] or covenaunts made betwene God an vs. [34]

Thus in Tyndale as in Bullinger and Zwingli in varying mixtures is a theological view of covenant that stresses strongly the view of covenant as agreement with stipulations and conditions attached.

Promissory Covenant

The second stream flowing into early English Covenant thought was from John Calvin. In his works the Covenant assumed a different character than in Zwingli or the other Rhineland theologians. Here the stress is not so strong on the Covenant as God's agreement with humanity but rather that it is God's gracious promise to humanity. For Calvin the Covenant of grace ran through both the Old and New Testaments in that "the Lord always covenanted with his servants thus: "I will be your God, and you shall be my people (Lev 26:12)." [35] He dealt with this doctrine in the 1559 **Institutes** chiefly in the chapter on "The Similarity of the Old and New Testaments" (Book II, ch. X). The first six sections of this chapter are devoted to showing that the Old Testament Covenant is really the same as that of the New. The remainder of the chapter deals with arguments to show that Old Testament people of faith looked forward to the hope of eternal life as God's promises to be fulfilled (secs. 7-22).

A dominant note here is thus that the history of salvation is a continuous history--through Old and New Testaments. The Covenant of God in the Old Testament is a Covenant of Grace every bit as fully as God's Covenant in the New Testament in Jesus Christ. Calvin wrote: "Both can be explained in one word. The covenant made with all the patriarchs is so much like ours in substance and reality that the two are actually one and the same." [36] The Covenant set before the Jews in the Old Testament "was supported, not by their own merits, but solely by the mercy of the God who called them." It is Jesus Christ who is the sole Mediator between humanity and God, the reconciler, the promised seed of Abraham who was and always will be the one through whom even the Old Testament Jews "were joined to God and were to share in his promises." [37] As such, Jesus Christ is the "sole foundation" of the Covenant. [38]

The similarities in the Covenant do not obscure the differences however for Calvin (See II, ch. 11). For him, the covenant before the Incarnation: represented spiritual blessings by temporal ones (secs. 1-3); Old Testament truth was conveyed by images and ceremonies which typified Christ (4-6); the Old Testament is literal, the New, spiritual (7-8); there is bondage in the Old Testament, freedom in the New (9-10); and the Old Testament refers to one nation, the New to all nations (11-12). But in all of this, the Old Covenant anticipates the New, the Law anticipating the Gospel, and the "eternal," "never-perishing" Covenant is fulfilled when it is "finally ratified and confirmed in Jesus Christ." [39] The Covenants are different in form and administration because God has "accommodated diverse forms to different ages, as he knew would be expedient for each." He has "accommodated himself to men's capacity, which is varied and changeable." [40] But behind it all stands an inseparable unity.

The promissory nature of the Covenant as found in the Old Testament, for example in such places as Leviticus 26:12 or Psalm 33:12, and 144:15 means that God "preserves forever and keeps in his everlasting mercy those whom he has chosen as his people." [41] But this does not mean to deny to humanity the responsibility which such a Covenant entails. As Calvin wrote: "Indeed, in all covenants of his mercy the Lord requires of his servants in return uprightness and sanctity of life, lest his goodness be mocked or someone, puffed up with empty exultation on that account, bless his own soul, walking meanwhile in the wickedness of his own heart (Deut. 29:19)." [42] Or again, "In making the covenant, God stipulates for obedience on the part of his servant." [43] So ethical responsibility is not abrogated. But the great stress on God as the initiator of the Covenant returns when Calvin reminds that in the covenant with Abraham it is Almighty God who gave the Covenant and in giving it, it is as if God had said, "See how kindly I indulge thee: for I do not require integrity from thee simply on account of my authority, which I might justly do; but whereas I owe thee nothing, I condescend graciously to engage in a mutual covenant." [44] The Sacraments as "signs and seals" of God's Covenant did not become for Calvin "vows of obedience." Rather they were "mirrors of grace" or "God's promises as painted in a picture" and set before our sight. [45] They were for the believer as circumcision was for Abraham: "not for his justification but for the seal of that covenant by faith in which he had already been justified." [46]

Calvin's theology of the Covenant was transmitted to England in part through the influence of the translation of the Bible into English made in Geneva by scholars of Calvinian persuasion. The Geneva Bible, first published in 1560, became "the household Bible of the English-speaking nations; and it continued to be so for about three quarters of a century." [47]

Of chief interest here is that the term "covenant" is used in this translation "far more frequently in the text than in previous English Bibles." [48] Beyond this, however, one of the most important features of the translation was that it was accompanied by marginal notes which reflected and expounded Calvin's theology. The note on Jeremiah 31:31 for example proclaims the oneness of the Covenant:

> Thogh the couenant of redemptiō made to the fathers, & this which was giuen after, seme diuers, yet thei are all one, & grounded on Iesus Christ, saue that this is called newe because of the manifestation of Christ, and the abundant graces of the holie Gost giuen to his Church vnder the Gospel. [49]

But the difference between the Gospel and the Law or the Covenant and the Law is also noted as at Galatians 3:15:

> No more is the promes or couenant of God abrogate by ye Law, nor yet is the Law added to the pmes [promises] to take any thīg away that was superfluous, or to supplie any thīg that wanted. [50]

The Sacraments are the "signes" of the New Covenant (see on Luke 22:20).

III. THE SIGNIFICANCE OF PERKINS AND THE THEOLOGY OF THE COVENANT

From this background it is possible to see more clearly William Perkins' place in the development of the Covenant doctrine. It can be seen that in Perkins there is a fusing of the two preceding streams of Covenant thought. In him there are elements of both the Zwingli and Tyndale tradition as well as that of Calvin.

As shown above, Perkins taught both a Covenant of Works and a Covenant of Grace. While it is true that in Calvin "a covenant of works, or of nature, stand[ing] beside the covenant of grace is not anticipated." [51] Perkins always referred the Covenant of works to the Moral law of the Ten Commandments and not to a pre-fall Covenant as later Federalists did. [52] It is beyond the scope of this study to try to trace the full origins of the Covenant of Works/Grace idea. There are signs of it in Musculus and in Olevianus who "appears to have been the first to use the term 'covenant of works,' but linked it with Moses, not Adam." [53] Oecolampadius had the view of the caritatis lex being written

on human hearts at Creation, in a context which is highly contractual in nature. Yet the view that "from these beginnings the law-
covenant principle came quickly to be the organizing principle
of the entire Rhineland reformation movement despite whatever
other differences of opinion may have existed among the various
leaders" [54] has been seriously questioned. [55] What is true
too, though, is that "none of these writers give the doctrine of
covenant the precise formulation given it by Perkins." And yet,
"his account of the doctrine almost certainly owes a good deal
to these predecessors, most of whom he had read." [56] On the
other hand, Covenant of Works and Covenant of Grace appear
in a work by Gomarus in 1594 (Gomarus had been a student at
Cambridge when Perkins was there); in **Questiones et responsiones**
by Rollock in 1595; and in Polanus in 1598. [57] All of these
men knew Perkins' works. [58] So, it is perhaps safer not to think
of doctrinal change at this point as being done in clearly-defined
intellectual borrowings. Instead, seemingly, the Covenant idea
was one developed by various people, wherever the Scriptures
were read. Parallel developments do not necessarily imply direct
echoings.

The Zwingli and Tyndale stream emphasizing the "agreement" or "contractual" nature of the Covenant is certainly found
in Perkins as many of his statements indicate. Very clearly he
begins by defining the Covenant as God's "contract with man,
concerning the obtaining of life eternall, vpon a certen condition"
(I, 32; see above). In his **Exposition of the Symbole or Creed of
the Apostles** (1595) he puts it like this: "in the making of the
couenant there must be a mutual consent of the parties on both
sides, & beside the promise on Gods part, there must be also
a restipulation on mans part; otherwise the couenant is not made"
(I, 165).

But it is precisely here that the "promissory" stream
flowing from Calvin redirects Perkins' thought. For the "restipulation" that humanity makes to God is that man "bindes himselfe
by Gods grace to beleeue and to rest vpon the promise" (I, 164).
That is to say, in Perkins' thought, "God makes no couenant of
reconciliation without faith" (I, 164). That which God requires
of humans as their part of the Covenant--faith--God Himself
provides for humanity by His grace.

In line with Perkins' view of election, all are not included
in the Covenant of grace (see above p. 87), but "onely that little
part of mankinde, which in all ages hath bin the Church of God,
and hath by faith embraced the couenant: as Paul plainely auouch-
eth, Galat. 3.22" (I, 164). And this faith is the "gift of God,"
"which commeth none other way, but by the effectuall certificate
of the holy Ghost" (I, 79). Thus humans for Perkins in this Covenant
"do not so much offer, or promise any great matter to God, as

in a manner only receiue" (I, 70). Perkins can thus continue to follow Calvin in his views on the Sacraments, that they were ordained for "the better confirmation of our faith: for by [them], as by certaine pledges giuan, God of his great mercie, doth as it were, binde himselfe vnto us" (I, 72). A Sacrament is that "whereby Christ and his sauing graces, are by certaine externall rites, signified, exhibited, and sealed to a Christian man. Roman 4:11; Gen. 17.11" (I, 71).

Perkins thus cast his lot fully with the Calvinian emphasis on the priority of grace as the context in which the Covenant of God is given and in which human obedience and response is made. There could be no obedience or no "contract" entered into on humanity's part if God had not already in his grace chosen to make the offer of salvation available to humanity through His Covenant.

Perkins' thought on the Covenant, linked as it was to his views of Election and the Sacraments had other important consequences for his theology. It played a direct role in his understandings of Sanctification, the question of Christian assurance of salvation, and in the possible ways one might prepare one's self for "lively faith." [59]

As seen throughout this discussion, Perkins represents a fusing of the two streams of Covenant thought. While he speaks the language of ethical responsibility for humanity in responding to God's Covenant of Grace in faith and obedience, he recognizes also that God is the initiator and indeed the One who makes possible this response to His Covenant promises. In this latter respect, Perkins stands closer to Calvin's teachings though the Tyndale and Zwingli strain is not lost. [60] Further study would confirm that with William Ames and other later Calvinists in the English tradition an increasing divergence of these two streams became apparent. Following Ames such theologians as John Owen, Thomas Goodwin, John Bunyan and James Ussher stressed the Calvinist side. [61] The extremes of Antinomianism found in hyper-Calvinists such as Tobias Crisp was the result. The Zurich tradition found its adherents in writers like John Preston, Richard Baxter, John Ball, Anthony Burgess, and Samuel Rutherford. Thus William Perkins, the popular theologian of Elizabethan England, played a vital role in English Covenant thought in the Reformed tradition. He joined together two vital aspects of the Covenant, a marriage which others tore asunder.

NOTES

1. See his **The Lord Protector:** Religion and Politics in the Life of Oliver Cromwell (Grand Rapids: Eerdmans, 1974); "The Covenant in Church History," Austin Seminary Bulletin, XCVI (March, 1981) 38-50; and **The Atonement and the Sacraments** (Nashville: Abingdon, 1960).

2. **A Golden Chaine (Armilla Aurea,** 1590; English translation, 1591) was Perkins' major systematic theological work. Its heavy emphasis on predestination and election is well analyzed in Richard A. Muller, "Perkins' A Golden Chaine: Pre-destinarian System of Schematized Ordo Salutis?" Sixteenth Century Journal, IX, No. 1 (April, 1978) 68-81.

   In the present paper I have used the three volume collected works of Perkins published as **The Workes of that Famovs and Worthy Minister of Christ in the Vniuersitie of Cambridge, Mr. William Perkins,** 3 Vols. (Cambridge: John Legatt, 1616-1618). In most cases spellings and lettering have not been modernized. Volume and page numbers without explanation in this paper are from this edition.

3. See **Works,** I, 151ff. on Adam in Paradise. See Peter Toon, **The Emergence of Hyper-Calvinism in English Nonconformity 1689-1765** (London: The Olive Tree, 1967) 114ff. for a discussion of the development of the "covenant of works" in "Hyper-Calvinism."

4. Perkins does not conceive of the two Covenants as being ways of God's successive dealings with his people. For him they both run through history simultaneously.

5. Cf. III, 520: "We must for our parts make a couenant with him, vnto which is required a conset on either partie; first on Gods part, that he will be our God; . . . Secondly, on our part is required conset, of which ther be two degrees: first whe we make an outward professio of faith . . . Secondly, . . . an outward consent of the heart: whereby a man taketh God for his God."

6. This is developed in Calvin. See his 1559 **Institutes** II. vii. 12, 13. Cf. I. John Hesselink, "Christ, the Law and the Christian: An Unexplored Aspect of the Third Use of the Law in Calvin's Theology," **Reformatio Perennis:** Essays on Calvin and the Reformation in Honor of Ford Lewis Battles, ed. B. A. Gerrish (Pittsburgh: The Pickwick Press, 1981) 11-26.

7. See Paul, "The Covenant in Church History," 38ff. and the literature mentioned there, particularly the works of Perry Miller such as his "The Marrow of Puritan Divinity" in **Errand into the Wilderness** (New York: Harper, 1956) 48-98 and **The New England Mind The Seventeenth Century** (Boston: Beacon, 1970) ch. XIII and Appendix B.

8. See for example Robert G. Clouse, "Covenant Theology," **The New International Dictionary of the Christian Church,** ed. J. D. Douglass (Grand Rapids: Zondervan, 1974).

9. John D. Eusden, "Introduction," to William Ames, **The Marrow of Theology,** tr. John Dykstra Eusden (Boston: Pilgrim Press, 1968) 52. On Ames see the splendid work of Keith L. Sprunger, **The Learned Doctor William Ames** (Urbana: University of Illinois Press, 1972).

10. See Olevian, **Exposition of the Symbole** (London: 1581) 52 and the discussion in J. Wayne Baker, **Heinrich Bullinger and the Covenant:** The Other Reformed Tradition (Athens, Ohio: Ohio University Press, 1980) 200-204. On F. Junius see **Opera Selecta** (Amsterdam, 1882) 183ff. as cited in Ian Breward, ed. **The Work of William Perkins.** The Courtenay Library of Reformation Classics 3, Appleford, England: The Sutton Courtenay Press, 1970, p. 128. For a survey of the doctrine of the Covenant on the European continent see G. Schrenk, **Gottesreich und Bund im älteren Protestantismus** (Darmstadt: Wissenschaftliche Buchgesellschaft, 1967) as well as Baker.

11. Breward, **Work** 90.

12. Baker takes full account of the literature. See particularly however, Richard L. Greaves, "The Origins and Early Development of English Covenant Thought" The Historian, XXXI (1968) 21-35 and Kenneth Hagen, "From Testament to Covenant in the Early Sixteenth Century," Sixteenth Century Journal, III, 1 (1972) 1-24.

13. See Greaves, p. 32 for this summary. Others such as Hagen, Baker, William A. Clebsch, **England's Earliest Protestants 1520-1535** (New Haven: Yale, 1964), Leonard J. Trinterud, "The Origins of Puritanism," Church History, XX (1951) 35-57, and Jens G. Møller, "The Beginnings of Puritan Covenant Theology," Journal of Ecclesiastical History, XIV (1963) 46-67 all argue for a "dual covenant tradition" though they do not agree on the specific origins and developments of covenant theology.

14. See Hagen, 16-17.

15. See Hagen, 17-18.

16. See G. W. Bromiley, ed., **Zwingli and Bullinger.** Library of Christian Classics (Philadelphia: Westminster, 1953) XXIV, 148.

17. Bromiley, ed., 131.

18. Huldreich Zwingli, **Werke,** ed. Melchior Schuler and J. Schulthess (Zurich, 1828-38) V, 73 as cited in Greaves, p. 24. Cf. Bromiley, ed., p. 127 who criticizes Zwingli for a too strong emphasis on the covenant's bilateral character.

19. See Baker, p. 16 and his whole chapter I: "The Zurich Origins of the Covenant Idea." Baker cites Jack Warren Cottrell, "Covenant and Baptism in the Theology of Huldreich Zwingli," Diss. Princeton Theological Seminary 1971 as being the best analysis of Zwingli's ideas.

20. Zwingli, **Werke,** V, 71 as cited in Greaves, p. 24.

21. See Baker, p. 15.

22. See Heinrich Bullinger, **Summa Christenlicher Religion** (Zurich, 1556) 137ff. and 146. The Latin is: "Baptizari autem in nomen Domini, est inscribi & in foedus Dei recipi . . . " **Compendium Christianae Religionis** (Tiguri, 1559) fol. 118 verso as cited in Greaves, p. 24. Cf. Møller, p. 48.

23. Bullinger, **Sermonum decades quinque** (Tiguri, 1557) 324 as cited in Greaves, p. 24.

24. See Baker, 17.

25. **De testamento,** fol. 16 as translated in Baker 17.

26. See Baker 52 and his whole chapter II: "Predestination and Covenant in Bullinger's Thought."

27. Baker 53.

28. Trinterud 39.

29. See Baker 208. An important exposition of "Tyndale's Law-Covenant Theology" is found in Nathan P. Feldmeth, "The Development of Exegetical Method in England, 1496-1556," Diss. New College, University of Edinburgh, 1982, 179-196.

30. Tyndale, **The Testament of William Tracy Expounded,** Parker Society, Vol. 3, 276 cited in Feldmeth 188.

31. Tyndale, **Prologue Upon the Five Books of Moses,** Parker Society, Vol. 1, 403. Cited in Feldmeth 188. Tyndale's teachings about the law are important here. For him, "loving the law, and doing it, had become a necessary condition for continued salvation. As he stated it, ' . . . none of us can be received to grace but upon a condition to keep the law, neither yet continue any longer in grace than that purpose lasteth,' " Feldmeth 185 citing Tyndale's **Exposition, Matthew V-VII,** Parker Society, Vol. 2, p. 7.

32. Tyndale, **The Testament of William Tracy Expounded** 276 cited in Feldmeth 187-188.

33. Feldmeth shows in Tyndale's developing doctrine of law that he moved beyond Luther toward a love for the law so that "the new ingredient in Tyndale's doctrine is a love for the law which springs as a natural result from man's salvation. This love furnishes the power to fulfil the law," 183.

34. Tyndale, **The New Testament** (1534), reprint edition edited by N. H. Wallis (Cambridge: The University Press, 1938) 4, as cited in Feldmeth, 190. Feldmeth is perhaps the first to point out the interesting shift in Tyndale's terminology in his Genesis translation between 1530 and 1534 as evidence of the

coming dominance of the covenant motif in his thought. He notes that in thirteen passages in Genesis where the Hebrew b⁻rîth was translated by Tyndale in his 1530 edition as "bond" or "testament" (once, "made couenaunte"), in the 1534 edition, the term "couenant" is used in all instances instead. See Feldmeth, 189.

35. John Calvin, **Institutes of the Christian Religion,** ed. John T. McNeill, tr. Ford Lewis Battles, 2 Vols. Library of Christian Classics (Philadelphia: Westminster Press, 1960) II. x. 8. Cf. Anthony Hoekema, "The Covenant of Grace in Calvin's Teaching," Calvin Theological Journal, II (1967) 133-61 and Baker, Appendix B.

36. **Institutes** II. x. 2.

37. **Institutes** II. x. 2

38. **Institutes** II. x. 4.

39. See **Institutes** II. xi. 4.

40. **Institutes** II. xi. 13.

41. **Institutes** II. x. 8.

42. **Institutes** III. xvii. 5.

43. Calvin, **Commentary on Genesis** 17:1, Calvin Translation Society (Edinburgh, 1847) 443.

44. **Commentary on Genesis** 17:12, 445.

45. See **Institutes** IV. xiv. The phrases are from IV. xiv. 5, 6.

46. **Institutes** IV. xiv. 5. As Trinterud comments, for Calvin, "The sacraments are witnesses, attestations, or seals to the effect that God has long since fulfilled his covenant, his promise," 45.

47. See B. F. Westcott, **A General View of the History of the English Bible** (London, 1868) 125ff. and Lloyd E. Berry, "Introduction to the Facsimile Edition," **The Geneva Bible 1560** (Madison: University of Wisconsin Press, 1969) 1-28.

48. Møller, 57. On other English translations see Trinterud, 44.

49. **Geneva Bible** (1560), Old Testament, 320.

50. **Geneva Bible** (1560), New Testament, 88. It has been speculated that the note on Hebrews 9:15 which speaks of a "former Testament"--"made betwene God and Christ, who by his death shulde make us heires," could be one of the sources from which some seventeenth-century Calvinists and especially those with some Antinomian tendencies "formulated the theory that the covenant of grace was first made between the Father and the Son." See Greaves 29.

51. Note 1 to **Institutes** II. x (LCC edition).

52. On the later Federalists see Toon, <u>passim.</u> Perkins' disciple William Ames presents God and Christ in a contractual relationship from which then a juridical concept of the atonement is derived. See **Marrow** I. xx. 4ff. Calvin's relation to Covenant Theology is portrayed in Everett H. Emerson, "Calvin and Covenant Theology," <u>Church History</u> XXV (1956) 136-144 as well as in Baker, Appendix B. Cf. Joseph C. McLelland, "Covenant Theology: A Re-evaluation," <u>Canadian Journal of Theology,</u> III (1957) 182-188.

53. Ian Breward, "The Life and Theology of William Perkins," Diss. University of Manchester, 1963, 62-63. On Musculus of Augsburg, see his **Commonplaces of the Christian Religion**, tr. J. Man (London, 1562) 120b; 122, a, b; Cf. H. Heppe, **Geschichte des Pietismus und der Mystik in der Reformirten Kirche, Namentlich der Niederlands** (Leiden, 1879) 211.

54. Trinterud, 41.

55. By Breward, "Life and Theology," 61.

56. See for example Perkins' reference to Olevian's, **De substantia foederis gratuiti inter Deum et electos** (1585) at I, 234 etc.

57. See Schrenk, 64-65. Perkins' **Armilla Aurea** was published at Basel in 1594.

58. See Breward, "Life and Thought" 63.

59. See Breward **Work** 93ff. On Assurance see Gordon J. Keddie " 'Unfallible Certenty of the Pardon of Sinne and Life Everlasting,' The Doctrine of Assurance in the Theology of William Perkins (1558-1602)," <u>The Evangelical Quarterly,</u> XLVIII, No. 4 (October-December, 1976) 230-244. On Preparation see Norman Petit, **The Heart Prepared** (New Haven: Yale University Press, 1966), 61ff. Cf. the works by R. T. Kendall, **Calvin and English Calvinism to 1649** (Oxford: University Press, 1979) and "The Puritan Modification of Calvin's Theology," **John Calvin His Influence in the Western World,** ed. W. Stanford Reid (Grand Rapids: Zondervan, 1982) 199-214 who examines Perkins' doctrine of faith and finds it closer to Beza's views than Calvin's.

60. See Greaves, 21-22 for a critique of John von Rohr, "Covenant and Assurance in Early English Puritanism," <u>Church History,</u> XXXIV (June, 1965) 195-203 for his failure to consider the Zurich stream.

61. See Greaves, "John Bunyan and Covenant Thought in the Seventeenth Century," <u>Church History,</u> XXXVI (1967) 151-169 and his "English Covenant Thought," 32-33 as well as Baker, 166. The most elaborate Federal Theology was produced in 1648 by Johannes Cocceius (1603-1669), **Summa Doctrinae de Foedere et Testamento Dei.** Cocceius was a student of William Ames at Franeker. The Westminster Confession (1647) and Savoy Declaration (1658) show moderate forms of the Federal Theology.

TEN CHARACTERISTICS
OF ENGLISH METAPHYSICAL PREACHING

Horton Davies

Like 'wit', 'metaphysical' is a slippery, fugitive term that has meant different things at different times, especially to literary and homiletical critics. To Dr. Samuel Johnson the distinguishing characteristic of metaphysical poetry was the fact that "the most heterogeneous ideas were yoked together." [1] Dryden thought that Donne's poems were marked by wit, and considered him "the greatest Wit, though not the best Poet of our Nation." [2] He further considered that Donne's use of dialectics and far-fetched conceits inappropriate in his poems, for he "affects the Metaphysicks, not only in his Satires, but in his Amorous Verse, where Nature only should reign; and perplexes the Minds of the Fair Sex with nice Speculations of Philosophy, when he shou'd ingage their hearts, and entertain them with the softnesses of Love." [3]

What distressed the seventeenth and eighteenth century critics, delighted the twentieth century critics. Sir Herbert Grierson, for example, found the ingenious speculation and the intense emotion fused in the imagination, the captivating and distinctive quality of metaphysical poetry. [4] Earl Miner, while acknowledging the importance of the conceits in a combination of "the wit of fancy" and the "wit of judgment" (fanciful resemblances in dissimilar objects or ideas, or genuine analogical correlations), claimed that the essential of metaphysical wit was private, not communal. This is, of course, a characteristic wholly unsuitable for public discourse given with the intention of being understood, which is an essential constituent of a sermon.

The homiletical critics among the Puritans, by contrast, objected to the word-play in the quips, puns, and paronomasia, as trivializing the encounter between Divine revelation and human response mediated by the preacher. Gravity rather than levity should characterize the preacher. They also deplored the pedantic citation of the Church Fathers in the original Greek or Latin, and the historical narrations and "unnatural natural" history employed, not to mention the elaborate rhetorical ornamentation of style, since all drew attention to the preacher, not to the treasure (the Gospel) in the earthen vessel (the preacher).

1. Puritans and the Plain and not so Plain Style.

Samuel Clarke, the Puritan hagiographer, contrasts the plain style of the Reverend Richard Capel with the contemporary fussy, florid and recondite style of the metaphysical preachers:

> Whereas now adayes, whilest some of our great Divines seem to be too much taken up with quaint and Histori-call flourishes, there is a terrible decay of the power of God amongst us. An Exotick, or strange tongue in the publick Congregation (whatever men think of it) is set out as a sign of Gods displeasure I Cor. 14. 21, 22. It feeds such humours as should rather be purged out. It had no good effect in the Church of Corinth . . . The Gold upon the Pill may please the eye; but it profits not the Patient. The Paint upon the Glass may feed the fancy; but the room is the darker for it. The Sword of Gods Spirit can never wound so deep, as when it's plucked out of these gaudy Scabbards. [6]

The Puritans objected to the contrived nature of the style which militated against sincerity and conviction. Clarke also cited Sibbes, the famous preacher at Gray's Inn, as being "wont to say that great affection, and good affections seldom goe together." [7]

Another Puritan critic, Richard Baxter, who had been the leader of the Presbyterian ministers who had met with the Bishops at the Savoy Conference in 1662 to consider revision of the Book of Common Prayer to make it easier to include its critics, thought metaphysical wit wholly out of place in sermons, disliking its fantastic conceits and rhetorical jingling. He observed: "There's no Jesting in Heaven, nor in Hell." Sibbes and Baxter (who had read and admired Sibbes) emphasized the importance of the plain style, though both were happy to use similitudes for illustrative purposes. Sibbes felt that the metaphysical preachers were too often in the clouds, hiding their meanings by their obscurity of thought and diction. He contrasted the kenosis, or self-emptying of Christ, and the humble style which should witness to Him, with the high-flown language of the metaphysical preachers, in the following appeal to the brotherhood of Puritan ministers: "Christ came down from heaven and emptied himself of majesty in tender love to souls; shall we not come down from our high conceits to do any soul good?" [8]

Since the plain (and occasionally not so plain) [9] style of the Puritans from the time of Perkins onwards, was the direct opposite of the metaphysical style, it is worth considering what its practitioners saw as its characteristics and its advantages. Perkins in his famous **Art of Prophesying** claimed that the preacher's task was: (1) "to reade the Text distinctly out of the Canonicall Scriptures" [excluding the Apocrypha]; (2) "to give the sense and understanding of it being read, by the Scripture it selfe"; (3) "to collect a few and profitable points of doctrine out of the naturall sense" [avoiding allegorical and tropological senses]; and (4) "to apply (if he have the gifte) these doctrines rightly collected to the life and manners of men in a simple and plaine speech." [10] The Puritan sermon was clearly aimed at changing the mind of the congregation with a view to the improvement of its behavior; hence there was little interest in speculative philosophy or even divinity of that type. Of paramount Puritan concern was clarity in making everyone in the congregation understand that godliness seeks the will of God in order to obey it. Puritan theology, according to Perkins, was "the science of living blessedly for ever." [11]

Samuel Clarke summed up the characteristics of the Puritan plain style in his eulogy of Dr. Harris, its practitioner: "In those days godly Preachers stuffed not their Sermons with aiery notions, and curious speculations, but sought out profitable matter, which they delivered in sound words, and in plain method of Doctrine, Reason, and Use, accomodating themselves to every man's capacity." [12]

Thus the Puritan critics disliked the levity, obscurity, artificiality, pedantry, secularity, pride, and lack of application that characterized metaphysical preaching according to their view. In brief, they considered that a minister who was not in the pulpit--to use Milton's phrase--"ever under the great Taskmaster's eye", was overreaching himself. The servant of the Word otherwise became its master. The preacher's duty was to treat his text, not as a pretext, with respect, since it was God's oracle. After careful study of the Word of God in the original languages, and a pastoral knowledge of the states of the souls of his flock, he was to pray for the assistance of the Holy Spirit so to light up and apply the message that it would bring the transforming and sanctifying truth to the minds, hearts and consciences of the congregation before him.

If, however, we ask the metaphysical preachers themselves what they consider the essential components of metaphysical preaching to be, the answer would be a combination of wit and recondite learning. Richard Corbet, poet, practical joker, and possibly the wittiest member of the bench of bishops, included the following lines in his epitaph on John Donne:

> He that wood write an Epitaph for thee . . .
> He must have wit to spare, and to hurle down
> Enough to keep the gallants of the Town.
> He must have learning plenty . . .
> Divinity great store above the rest,
> Not of the latest Edition, but the best. [13]

Both terms, of course, need much fuller elaboration in order to include the subtle and complex apparatus of logic and rhetoric, which the prose writers as well as the poets of the late sixteenth and the first half of the seventeenth century employed so brilliantly.

Confining myself to the pulpit in its golden age in England, I have found the 'metaphysical' style of sermon distinguished from its major alternative 'Puritan plain' (not to mention the Ciceronian style of Bishop Hall and Bishop Taylor, nor that of the Cambridge Platonists) by ten characteristics.

2.   The Ten Differentia of Metaphysical Preaching.

The ten characteristics can be listed as follows: 1. Wit; 2. Patristic learning; 3. Classical learning: poetic, moral, and historical; 4. frequent citations from Greek and Latin originals, and occasional use of Hebrew etymology; 5. Biblical exegesis which not infrequently adds typological and allegorical senses to the primary literal or historical sense of Scripture; 6. plans with complex divisions and sub-divisions; 7. a Senecan, rather than a Ciceronian style, often interrogative, epigrammatic, and staccato; 8. a delight in paradoxes, tiddles, and emblems; 9. a liking for speculative doctrines in both philosophy and particularly theology; and 10. the relating of doctrinal and devotional preaching to the liturgy, and especially to the calendar of the Christian year.

It is, however, important to recognize that not all metaphysical preachers will adhere to this style throughout their lives or on all occasions, or exhibit all of the ten characteristics in their corpus of sermons. Bishop John King and Dr. Thomas Fuller begin by preaching series of sermons which continue to expound entire books of the Bible, but discard this approach later, and Fuller changes from Doctrine, Reason and Use, to sermons which for wit and erudition are indistinguishable from other metaphysical sermons when he is preaching before the King at Oxford or in Westminster Abbey after the Restoration. Similarly, John Gauden and Thomas Jackson, as they change allegiance from the Puritan to the Cavalier side, switch from moderately Puritan Plain to Metaphysical Ornamental--that is, to the correct party styles of preaching. Further, the degree to which a preacher uses wit and erudition will depend in part on the circumstances of place and time. A sermon at court, cathedral, university church or college chapel, or in a fashionable London parish, would obviously use more wit and erudition than one preached in a country chapel of ease. Similarly, whether the preacher was officiating on a Church festival such as Christmas, Easter and Whitsun, or on a fast-day or black-letter day, would determine the elaboration of learning and conceits and other ornaments in the style and diction of his sermon.

The first distinguishing mark is, of course, wit, which is analyzed in detail in the following chapter 5, in all its copiousness and variety. It consists in a great fondness for puns and paronomasia in English and ancient languages; in abstruse and often paradoxical expressions of thought; in memorable epigrams and striking imagery, deliberately intended to elicit curiosity or to shock, and drawn from unexpected quarters (science, hermeticism, rabbinics, voyages of discovery); in an admiration for antitheses; and in a combination of the lyrical and the satirical, itself the brilliant contrast between the adoration of God and the ironical flaying of human beings.

3. Patristic Citations and References.

The many citations from the Fathers served a double purpose. It enabled the preachers to gain the respect of both learned and illiterate for the lore expounded in the large folio volumes in the obscurity of Greek, Latin, and Hebrew. This was also the kind of knowledge imbibed at the Pierian springs of the two universities, whose graduates now filled the pulpits, whereas they were in short supply in the early days of Elizabeth's reign.

The second function citations from the Fathers fulfilled was more significant: it attempted to prove the identity of the Church of England with the undivided Church of the first five centuries. This served as an important controversial ploy in showing the Puritans of Presbyterian or Independent leanings that the liturgy and polity of the Church of England faith was the worship and government of the first Church. It provided an apologetical armory of arguments and examples for the defense of the claim that it was the Roman Church not the Anglican which was the innovator, and had departed from the central tradition in East and West. Thus the politicization of the Papacy, and the development of the doctrine of Purgatory and the means of commutation of its punishments, and the intercession of the saints and the veneration of their relics, could be claimed to be idolatrous deviations from orthodox faith and practice. An additional value of patristic quotations, though subordinate to the other two functions they fulfilled, was that such theologians as Ambrose, Augustine, Gregory the Great and Gregory of Nyssa, John Chrysostom, and Bernard of Clairvaux, as well as Tertullian (despite his Montanist heresy) and others, provided the preachers with tropes and figures which they were happy to borrow for exegesis and illustrations.

For example, Bishop Henry King wisely cites Calvin in opposing the Puritan dislike of Latin citations and patristic references, and in asserting that there is no necessary quarrel between eloquence and integrity and simplicity in religion. He is most critical of the denial of the value of learning in sermons and worship on the part of these men "that have such an unlearned conceit of Gods service that they think it a trespasse of high nature to staine their Discourses with a Latine sentence, or authority of Fathers quoted in their own Dialect, or that make it a nice case of Conscience to present God with a studied Prayer, or any other forme of speech than . . . what comes into their heads whilest they are speaking." [14] It will be intriguing to see how ready King himself is to use patristic citations in the very book from which he made the criticism of unlearned preaching. This is **An Exposition upon the Lords Prayer** (1611), a series of eleven sermons. In over 360 pages he has 160 citations from the Greek and Latin Fathers (58 from Augustine, 15 from Ambrose, 12 from Chrysostom, and 10 from Aquinas), 8 from Reformed divines, and 49 references to Roman Catholic commentators and apologists (15 from Hales, 13 from Biel, and 3 from Bellarmine). Classical authors are referred to 25 times (Seneca 6 times and Plutarch twice), and there are also references to Erasmus, Rabbi Jehuda, and the Qu'ran. Thus we have a grand total of 245 citations or references, amounting to an average of 22 per sermon. Moreover, this is not untypical of the metaphysical preachers.

It should not be assumed that each of the Jacobean or Caroline divines read the patristic theological treatises throughout. In fact, several kept commonplace books in which they noted such citations complied by or quoted by contemporary writers. In yet other cases, they simply borrowed them from contemporary printed sermons. The famous sermon of St. John Chrysostom on the Magi, used at Epiphanytide, was borrowed by both Andrewes and Donne, and their treatments of the same subject were borrowed by Bishop John Cosin. Hacket and Frank both borrowed as well from Andrewes. [15]

The real scholars, such as Andrewes, Adams and Hacket,

have a profound and detailed knowledge of the Fathers. This can be demonstrated in a single case by Andrewes. In his fifteenth Easter Day Sermon he indicates that Christ's rebuke to Mary Magdalene, Noli me tangere, is interpreted in three different ways by the Fathers Chrysostom, Gregory, and Augustine. The first, says Andrewes, suggests that Magdalene was too forward. The second declares that "her touch [was] no Easter-day touch; her tangere had a tang in it (as we say)." [16] The third, Gregory the Great, understands it as a way of saving time "so that Jesus might hasten the message, Vale et dic." [17]

It is significant that Andrewes usually summarizes briefly the content of the citations, rather than citing them fully, as most of the other metaphysical preachers do. It was typical of his modesty, and of Bishop Buckeridge's [18] too, who followed the example of Andrewes in this and other ways. Occasionally, however, Andrewes was given to citing snippets of Greek and whole passages of Augustine's Latin. [19]

Donne, too quotes copiously from the Fathers and does not in the least mind differing from their interpretations, especially when they differ among themselves. In his Easter Sermon of 1622, he chooses the difficult text from the First Epistle to the Corinthians 15:51, which reads, "We shall not sleep, but we shall all be changed." This, says Donne, is delivered by St. Paul as a mystery, but the commentators "have multiplied mystical clouds upon the words." Some Fathers, he continues, interpret this as meaning we shall not all sleep, and therefore we shall not all die (thus Chrysostom). The Vulgate reads this passage differently: Omnes resurgamus; we shall all rise again, but we shall not all be changed. St. Augustine concludes that both meanings are orthodoxly Catholic and acceptable. It is then only Chrysostom's reading that Donne denies, since it contradicts the Apostle's "it is appointed once to every man to die." [20] Donne, early in his preaching career insisted that it was important to go ad fontes, that is, to the Fathers in the original languages, and not to rely on chrestomathies or commonplace collections. He said: "We steale our Learning, if we forsake the Fountaines, and the Fathers and the Schooles [scholastics], and deal with the Rhapsoders, and Commonplaces, and Methodmongers." [21]

It is intriguing to note where Donne's own preferences among the Fathers lie. In an analysis of three of the ten volumes that comprise the Potter and Simpson edition of **The Sermons of John Donne** (Volumes III, VI, and IX), Donne has 226 citations from Augustine, 86 from Jerome, 58 of Chrysostom, 38 of Gregory the Great, and 37 each from Ambrose and Basil. [22]

Thomas Adams admires the Fathers, but he, on one occasion among several, dares to dissent from the interpretations of Ambrose, Augustine, and Jerome. They regard the struggle of Esau and Jacob in the womb of their mother to be the first-born as merely playful, but Adams believes it to be warlike. [23] Oddly enough, apparently none of the authorities stopped to consider whether any of them could possibly know the fact, being so far in time from the event and therefore utterly ignorant of it. But that was typical of patristic as well as of Jacobean and Caroline speculation.

In general, however, the Fathers are cited frequently and respectfully. Bishop William Barlow, for example, when invited by King James to preach at Hampton Court in the presence of the Melville brothers, stout Presbyterians, to try to convince them of the authority and superiority of the church government by bishops, cited 27 different authors in 76 references, and 18 of the authors were Fathers of the Church. [24]

The peculiar authority of the Fathers was thought to derive from their closeness in time to the days of the promulgation of the New Testament Scripture and its canonization by distinction from apocryphal writings. Fuller, who in his later days made a greater use of the Fathers, indicates the varied attractions some of the more popular Fathers supplied:

> Indeed we Modernes have a mighty advantage of the Ancients: Whatsoever was theirs by Industry may be ours, The Christian Philosophy of Justin Martyr; the constant Sanctity of Cyprian; the Catholick faith of Athanasius; the Orthodox Judgment of Nazianzen; the manifold learning of Jerome; the solid Comments [Commentaries] of Augustine; the excellent Morals of Gregory; the humble Devotions of Bernard: All contribute to the edification of us who live in this later age. [25]

4. The Use of Classical Literature and History.

The metaphysical preachers also delighted to stud their sermons with references to the pagan poets, philosophers, and historians of Greece and Rome. Their aim was four-fold. The poetical citations provided fancy in the midst of the ardours of argument, the philosophers inculcated moral lessons, the historical narrations supplied exempla, while the 'unnatural natural' history gave illustrations that elicited wonder. In all this the preachers were making use of the Renaissance rediscovery of the classical world.

So many of the metaphysical preachers were minor poets, or at the lowest estimate versifiers, that it is astonishing how relatively few of them cited poetry in their sermons, and then only rarely. Thomas Playfere quotes Homer's **Odyssey** in one sermon and Martial in another. [26] Adams cites Horace and Ovid in his sermons. [27] In one of them he paraphrases the Latin in colloquially witty fashion: "Many a Pope sings that common ballad of Hell: <u>ingenio</u> <u>peril</u> <u>qui</u> <u>miser</u> <u>ipse</u> <u>meo</u>: Wit whither went thou? woe is me; my wit hath wrought my misery." [28] These jingling translations, uniquely my own, were admirable aids to the memory. Bishop Henry King in his series of eleven sermons, **An Exposition of the Lords Prayer,** has two references to Homer, two to Horace, and one each to Virgil, Ovid, and Juvenal. [29] Among other preachers quoting Latin poetry, were Bishops Gauden [30] and Howson, [31] and the Reverend Thomas Goffe. [32]

The impact of classical poetry, whether epic, satire or ode, was not as great as might be expected considering that it was taught in almost every English grammar school. It was more clearly seen in the intriguing mixtures of classical mythology and Christian story, where the combination is often striking. Thomas Playfere, for one example, borrows from Ambrose the figure of Christ as "our heavenly Ulysses" to whose Cross the faithful must fasten themselves for safety. [33] He also draws a parallel between the retrospective look of Lot's wife, and of Orpheus looking back longingly at Eurydice in his Spittal Sermon of 1593. [34] In a third use of classical mythology, Playfere likens the Puritans, troubled as he thinks with trivia, to Atalanta, distracted by the golden apples. [35] Also, he can even find a parallel to Rahab's red thread which guided the Hebrew spies into Canaan with Ariadne's thread that led Theseus through Dedalus' labyrinth. [36]

John Wall draws an inexact parallel between Telemachus saved by a dolphin, and Christians carried through deep waters on the back of the Lamb of God, Christ. [37] The image of a lamb carrying a fully grown person on its back through dangerous waters is ludicrous. It was a legitimate complaint among farfetched analogies.

Occasionally, the correlations between Classical and Christian references are casual, but significant because it seemed natural to make such analogies. Andrewes slips into saying of the Anabaptist idea that all can be prophets, that to follow it would result in "a <u>Cyclopian Church</u>, [which] will grow upon us where all were <u>Speakers</u>, no body heard another." [38] Similarly, Josiah Shute, not a metaphysical preacher, speaks of the first sin of Adam and Eve as "the Trojan horse." [39] Henry King points out that the Lord's Prayer has seven parts, like Minerva's shield, or the targe of Ajax. [40]

Bishop Hacket can use a classical story to provide a Christian lesson, which thus leads us into the value of classical historical narrations in metaphysical preaching. His sermon was on the Temptation of Christ in the Wilderness, when Satan requested him to turn the stones into bread. The sermon begins with the following narration:

> A Roman Orator in the days of Tiberius the Emperour, Afer by name, had so often taken in hand the worst part of every Plea to defend it, that at last his credit was prejudicated, and it was enough to say, Afer pleads on this side, therefore the justice of the cause is on the other side.

The moral is that if Satan propounds anything, the opposite must be true. Also, Hacket points out that the Devil's proposal, though appearing good, actually contained two sins, gluttony and infidelity. [41]

The use of historical exempla was far more common than the use of classical poetry or drama for the purposes of illustration. They were chiefly used as ethical examples, and from the time of Aquinas at least to illustrate the four cardinal virtues common to paganism and Christianity. Exempla of the virtues would be drawn from such historians as Herodotus, Xenephon, Livy and Plutarch, and the wonder stories of beasts would be culled from such an unnatural naturalist as Pliny, not forgetting the fables of Aesop. The historical narrations continued to be employed throughout our period with unabated zeal, but the interest in 'unnatural natural' history weakened considerably. This diminishment may be attributed to two factors. The first is the advance of the scientific spirit, such as was expressed in the formation of Wadham College, Oxford of the experimenters who were later to form the Royal Society, during Commonwealth days when Dr. Wilkins was the Warden, and the membership included young mathematical and architectural genius, Christopher Wren. This sceptical spirit rightly challenged the credibility of these stories which seemed too good to be true. Further, this type of illustration had been used ever since the Middle Ages, and was simply worn out. [42]

Andrewes rarely used historical illustrations, but Donne, Adams, Playfere, and Hacket used them frequently. Also, it was not unusual for narrative examples to be taken from the history of other countries than Greece and Rome, and from post-classical times. Some examples must now be given.

Adams wishes to demonstrate how important it is to safeguard time. Hence he chooses Vespatian as a good exemplar: "The good Emperour Vespatian, if he had heard no causes, or done no charitable act, would complaine to his courtiers at night, Amici, diem perdidi: my friends, I have lost a day, I feare too many may say of the whole day of their lives, I have lost my day." [43] In another sermon Adams takes Julius Caesar's monition as his own, when he appeals for charity toward the needy: "Julius Caesar seeing women carry Dogges under their arms, asked if they had no children. God asketh you, that give your bread to dogges, if he hath no children for your charitie." [44]

Andrewes uses a historical narration in a Gowrie Day Sermon as a parallel to David sparing the life of his enemy King Saul, because it was inconceivable to kill the Lord's anointed ruler:

> It calls to my minde, what long since I read in Herodotus: that at the taking of Sardi, when one ranne at Croesus the King, to have slaine him, that a little boy borne dumbe, that had never spoken word in all his life, with the fright and horror of the sight, his tongue loosed, and he broke forth, and cried, O man, destroy not the King, and so saved his life. So writeth he, as of a wonder: and see if this were not like it. [45]

Both Playfere and Hacket retell the story of the first Christian Roman Emperor, Constantine, honoring one of his most loyal commanders. Hacket's is the briefer version, from an Easter sermon dealing with the women who ran to tell the disciples of the empty tomb:

> They that held him by the feet had had the occasion to honour those parts of the body which had been pierced with Nails for our sakes upon the Cross. And I doubt it not, but to shew themselves thankful for his death, they did offer to lay their modest lips upon his wounds. As when Paphnutius his right eye was pluck't out for being a constant Christian, the Emperour Constantine kissed the hollow pit from whence the eye was taken in reverence to his sufferings. [46]

Donne also used a military narration. This was of an unnamed general, who was threatened by the prediction that the arrows of his enemies would be so plentiful that they would block out the sun. He replied: "In umbra pugnabimus; All the better, says he, for then we shall fight in the shadow." Donne then makes the application: "Consider all the arrows of tribulation, even of tentation, to be directed by the hand of God, and never doubt to fight it out with God." [47] The aptness of the illustration is clear when the text is considered. It is from Psalm 38:22: "or thine arrows stick fast in me, and thy hand presseth me sore."

A comprehensive use of historical narration is exemplified by Cosin in a sermon of 1632 on the first commandment, in which he gave a minatory account of the horrific deaths of several ancient and modern atheists, including Macchiavelli, and which he drew from the works of Diogenes, Laertius, Sozomen, and Camden. [48]

5. Illustrations from 'Unnatural Natural' History.

The metaphysical preachers were particularly fond of using 'unnatural natural' history as well. Christ represented as the self-wounding pelican feeding her young with her own flesh and blood was a famous image of the Eucharist, to be seen to this day in the courtyard of Corpus Christi College, Oxford, and its copy outside the chapel of Princeton University, was a well-known medieval example. [49] So also was the phoenix reborn from its own ashes symbolizing the Resurrection of Christ after three days in the grave. Thomas Playfere uses an intriguing reference to a panther as an image of godliness: "A panther hath foure clawes and no more on each hind foote; but five clawes and no lesse on each fore foote: so the godly, though they bee weake to the worldward, yet they are strong to Godward." [50]

Bishop Barlow, wanting to vivify a situation in which every man would be master and all bishops, recalls Pliny's Amphisbaena, "a Serpent which hath a head at each end of her body, both striving which should be the maister-head, in the meantime toiles the body most miserably, & in the end rets and tears it self most lothsoly." [51] Brownrig is captivated by the salamander, a cold-blooded creature which supposedly cannot be warmed by the flames that surround it, and the application is made to persons who respond coldly to the flames of God's love. [52] Henry Smith uses the Unicorn, in typically brief form: "As the Unicorne dippeth his horn in the fountaine, and maketh the waters which were corrupt and noisome, cleare and wholesome upon the sodaine: so, whatsoever state Godlines comes into, it saith like the Apostles, Peace be to this house, peace bee to this heart, peace be to this man." [53] Smith also uses the old favorite, the Harpy. [54] Willan says it is reported that the birds of Norway fly more rapidly than the birds of all other lands, not because of any superior natural agility, "but by an instinct they know the dayes in that Climate to bee very short, not above three houres long, and therefore they make more haste unto their nests: Strange that birds should make such use of their observation, and we practically knowing the shortnesse of our lives, yet make no haste to our home, the house appointed for all living." [55] The theme of carpe diem is an old one, but the attempted rational explanation for the unfamiliar is new in 'unnatural history.' This may be because it appears in a sermon of 1630.

Donne has several exempla of this type. Snakes fascinate him, especially the kind that knows its skin is useful to humans suffering from the falling sickness, and so "out of Envy, they hide their skin when they cast it." [56] He is also intrigued by the Lithospermus, which he calls the greatest wonder of nature, which produces a very hard stone as its fruit. His application is strained, namely, "That temporal affliction should produce spiritual stoniness, and obduration, is unnaturall, yet ordinary." [57] And Hacket, as one might imagine, would have a far-fetched example, necessary to illustrate the fact that God's eye is on the evil even when they are unaware: "Wherefore one says of the Crocodile, that the Egyptians in that vain Idol did resemble a God, Quia ex omnibus aquaticis habet oculos obtectos ut cernat, ne cernatur; It hath both eyes so befilmed that perceives afar off, and is not perceived." [58] Another Egyptian tale is used by Henry King to illustrate the danger that comes for those who have itching ears for too much preaching: "A man may heare so much that he may ston the sense, and bee like the Catadupes, whom the continuall fall of Nile makes deafe. Cisternes that have more powred into them then they can hold, must needs run to wast; and men that affect to learne more then they have braine to comprehend, waste their Pastors labour, and their own patience." [59]

John White the controversialist is not the only one to perceive the value of an example drawn from unnatural history. He likens a bird which, when men are at a sacrifice, burns their houses, like the Jesuits do--a clear allusion to the Gunpowder Plot. [60] It is interesting that, in contrast, Andrewes, dislikes anti-Roman references in his sermons, rarely uses historical narrations, and even rejects using a natural historian like Pliny to learn the functions of the dove, since Scripture is sufficient. [61]

We have dealt at great length on the parallel use of the Fathers in Greek and Latin, with Classical learning in general, which the preachers learned in school and university, and which they used to enliven their discourses. The poetical references were chiefly included for delight, the moral maxims for instruction and to urge Christians to go further than the pagans who had not received the special revelation peculiar to Christianity. The historical narrations were intended to produce both variety of material and the four cardinal virtues of fortitude, temperance, prudence, and justice. The function of the fantastical accounts of strange creatures was to elicit wonder and to prepare the listeners for the transcendent gesta Dei, the wonderful works of God.

It was for the latter purpose that riddles were retold, and occasionally also the emblems with their mottoes. Riddles certainly held the attention. Thomas Playfere, one of the earliest metaphysical preachers, wished to illustrate a neuter, that is a Christian who goes backwards and forwards and makes no real progress in belief or behavior, and so he uses a quadruple riddle borrowed from Athenaeus' Deipnosophistai ('The Learned Banquet'):

> Panarches riddle was this, how a man and no man, can with a stone and no stone, kill a bird and no bird, sitting upon a tree and no tree? Athenaeus makes the answer, That an Eunuch, is the man, and a Pumeise is the stone, a Batte is the bird, and fennell is the tree. After the same sort a Newter is a very hard riddle. You cannot tell what to make of him. For going backward and forward, he is a Christian and no Christian. [61]

Hacket, who like Donne, always delights in the curious and arcane combines a riddle with a historical narration. Philip of Macedon was at a banquet when he propounded the question: What was the greatest thing in nature? Various answers were given including the servile one, Philip himself, and others such as Olympus, the ocean and the sun, all of which were wrong. Philip answered: "Sed cor quod res maximas despiceret; the greatest of all things was an heart that despises the greatest things which are in this world beneath." [62]

6. Quotations in Greek and Latin, and Etymology.

The fourth characteristic of metaphysical preaching need not occupy us long, since it was evident in the consideration of historical narrations which often included an epigram in the original classical languages, and will be seen again in some of the witty word-play of our following chapter. The interest in etymology was, of course, not only an echo of the schooling of the preachers, but a necessity for a learned Biblical expositor, who had to be familiar with the Hebrew of the Old Testament, the Greek of the Septuagint (of the translation of the Old Testament), the Latin of the Vulgate (for understanding of the Roman Catholic commentators of which the Jacobean and Caroline divines made good use. Further, the Greek was essential for exposition of the New Testament. Greek tags (and less frequently, citations), and frequently Latin tags and citations, and etymology were used without exception by all the metaphysical preachers from Andrewes and Adams to Gauden and Goffe, and from Hacket and Holyday to Willan and Wren.

Andrewes was the ablest scholar of the group in Biblical languages, but it is Barten Holyday, the archdeacon of Oxford, who uses them more often, and who positively revels in semantic history. He gives the usual translation of Proverbs 7:9, as "in the black and deep night," telling us that "it is in the original be ishon laylah as if we should say, in the apple of the eie of the night." His application is: "Yet out of the darkest sorrow, God will at last raise the most cheerful light." [63] Andrewes is less pedantic and more practical in his semantic illustration: "Sinceritie (that is) cleanesse of life: (a word thought to be taken from honie, which is then mel sincerum, when it is sine cerâ, unmingled, without wax, or any baggage." [64] It was typical of him also to illustrate hypocrisy, by deriving it from its Greek original and pointing out that a hypocrite is essentially a stage-player, an actor or pretender. [65]

7. Principles of Biblical Exegesis.

Another distinctive characteristic of metaphysical preaching was its type of biblical exposition. From the days of the early Church there had been two tendencies: the Alexandrian which favored allegorical, and the Antiochene which preferred literal or historical interpretation. Ambrose and Augustine combined both, and it was Cassian who schematized for the Western Church the four senses of Holy Writ. Each passage of Scripture could be interpreted in a literal or historical sense, or an allegorical sense, strictly so-called in which it was applied to Christ and the Church Militant, or in a tropological or moral sense in which it was to be understood of the soul and its virtues, or, in an anagogical or mystical sense, applying it eschatologically to the heavenly realities. Protestantism, especially in its Calvinist form, had virtually rejected all allegory, except where the sense was plainly metaphorical, as, for example, in the Johannine discourses, when Jesus says, "I am the door" [68] and "I am the vine: ye are the branches." [69] Medieval Catholics had used the four senses, especially the Schoolmen, and many of the sixteenth century Roman Catholics continued to do so. This approach had two advantages: it enabled apparent contradictions within the Scriptures easily to be resolved, and it allowed preachers to exercise considerable ingenuity in interpretation. It was the latter characteristic, which often led to digressions and even deviations from the primary historical meaning of Scripture that led Protestants to emphasize the literal sense and virtually to exclude the other senses. On the other hand, while Protestant commentators made significant contributions to Biblical studies in their zeal to understand the Bible in the original languages, they also sometimes fell into the very error they criticized the Roman Catholics for, namely, the peril of subjective interpretation, or making the Scripture a "wax nose" because of the peril of private interpretation, from which an emphasis on the interior illumination of the Holy Spirit did not always save them. The wilder sectaries of the Commonwealth period sometimes took the short step from the inner light to the outer darkness.

The distinctive contribution of the metaphysical preachers was that they were truly of the via media in choosing neither to use all four of the Roman way, nor the single sense of the Genevan or Puritan way. This we might expect of Donne, because he had been brought up as a Catholic, and because of the brilliant opportunities polysemous interpretation provided for his imaginative and rhetorical genius. But it also proved invaluable for Andrewes and his followers. It enabled them to use the Old Testament in their typological exegesis, so that they found anticipations of the New in the Old, as Origen and Augustine had done before them. They gave them the opportunity, especially in court sermons, to use the Psalms historically, referring to their authorship by a king, David, then to apply it to the circumstnces of another King (James or Charles), and, finally, to see in it a reference to the King of Kings, Christ.

Among a multitude of possible exemplars three must suffice for the present. Dr. John Cosin preached a sermon to the Protestant members of the exiled English Queen's household in Paris, whose chaplain he was, on the Octave of the Resurrection, April 16, 1651 on the text John 20:9 "For as yet they knew not the Scriptures, that he must rise from the dead." He provided a thorough typological exegesis of Abraham's willingness to sacrifice Isaac at God's command as a foretelling of Christ's Passion and Resurrection. He found no less than seven parallels between Isaac and Jesus. Both were the only beloved sons of their fathers, who were determined to put them to death. Both accepted their lot obediently. Both were bound up for sacrifice. The wood for that sacrifice was laid on their shoulders. Both were led to a mount, and Calvary and Mount Moriah are the same mountain. The ram that was caught in the thornbush and was offered up to save the life of Isaac is seen "as the figure and pledge of Him that came forth with the crown of thorns, and offered up himselfe to save ours". Finally, each was released for life again in three days. [69] Cosin followed this by adducing all the Old Testament passages from the Psalms and the Prophecies thought to point to the Resurrection.

Calvinist though he was, Thomas Adams could use an Old Testament text as a text for embroidering his fancies which were only partly determined by the Bible. He takes a text from Hebrews 6:7, "For the earth which drinketh in the raine that commeth oft upon it, and bringeth forth Herbes meete for them by whom it is dressed, receiveth blessings from God." The sermon is entitled, "A Contemplation of the Herbes." So far, so good. Then he starts allegorizing with a pun on "Herbes of our graces" and glosses "meete for the dresser" as "contentfull to God" and then refers to "the Garden of our hearts" and says God will require four virtues in them: Odour, Taste, Ornament, Medicinall Vertue." Then he allegorizes without limit, speaking successively of Hyssop (Humility), Bulapathumm (Patience), Balsamum (Faith), St. John's Wort (Charity), and several others, until he reaches Holy Thistle (Good Resolution). [70] Similarly, Adams has a sermon entitled, "Heaven-Gate: Or, The Passage to Paradise." The text Revelation 22:14, is allegorized with the Gate having the foundation of faith, the two sides are patience and innocence, and the roof is charity. [71]

John Donne can use an Old Testament text with a double typological reference, so that Babylon is its context at the time of Ezekiel, and allow it to point to Jerusalem in the time of Christ, and to England in the time of the Reformation, in each case showing how God's people were under the tyrany of the Church and the State being in collusion to oppress them. What makes it interesting is that Donne uses the correct exegetical terminology to introduce these different applications. He says of the text Ezekiel 34:19, "And as for my flock, they eate that which yee have troden with your feet, and they drinke that which yee have fould with your feet," that their deepest distress was "that their own Priests joyned with the State against them" translating this very aptly in a sermon before the court to " . . . the Church joyned with the Court to oppress them." On that very context he comments: "This is the literall sense of our text, and context, evident in the letter thereof." Then his next comment is: "And then the figurative and Mysticall sense is of the same oppressions and the same deliverance over againe in the times of Christ, and of the Christian Church." Then he declares a paragraph later that it concerns "the oppressions and deliverances of our Fathers, in the Reformation of Religion and the shaking off of the yoak of Rome, that Italian Babylon, as heavy as the Chaldaean." [72]

In similar fashion, Hacket can preach a Gowrie Conspiracy Sermon before the King. It starts with the text from Psalm 41:9, "Yea, mine own familiar friend, in whom I trusted, which did eat of my bread, hath lifted up his heel against me," which he thinks refers to Ahitophel's treachery against David, then he applies it to Judas' betrayal, and, finally, to the rebelliousness of the Earl of Gowrie and his brother. [73]

The distinction between metaphysical use of allegorical and typological exegesis, as contrasted with the Puritan almost exclusive adherence to the literal-historical sense, with very rare use of typology, is striking in our period.

8. Sermon Structure and Division.

Another striking difference between metaphysical preachers and Puritan preachers was the preference of the former for sermons with complex divisions in the plan, sometimes almost recovering scholasticism, compared with the simplicity of Puritan exegesis according to the text. There was also a further difference in structure. Some of the metaphysicals, like Andrewes and Cosin, structured their sermons so that the text was followed by a general introduction which might be contextual or refer to the special liturgical occasion for which the congregation had met, followed by a bidding prayer, succeeded by the division and the exposition. [74] All of them in the early days used the scholastical plan with complex divisions and sub-divisions, but these became increasingly simpler as time went on. The preferred Puritan structure of sermons, which, for example, Fuller used in his pre-Cavalier days and which was standardized in the Westminster Assembly of Divines, was that of doctrine, reason and use. [75]

Thomas Playfere's lengthy sermon, The Meane in Mourning (1595) is so ludicrously elaborate in its eight-fold division, that it would almost justify the Puritan determination to keep sermons simple so that they occasionally ran the risk of being simplistic. The division of the text which is brief enough (Luke 23:28; "Weep not for me, but for yourselves") proceeds as follows:

> In which sentence we may observe, so many wordes, so many parts, Eight wordes, eight parts. The first, Weepe not; the second, But weepe; the third, Weepe not, But weepe; the fourth, For mee; the fifth, For your selves; the sixth, For Mee, For your selves; the seventh, Weepe not for mee; the eighth, But weepe for your selves. [76]

The seventh and eighth divisions alone would be an adequate division of this two-fold, contrasting text.

A relatively simple example of scholastic division, with the major points made in Latin, is provided by Andrewes as the structure for his Christmas sermon before the King and court in 1611. The text is John 1:18 "And the WORD was made Flesh, and dwelt among us: (and we saw the Glorie thereof, as the Glorie of the Onely-begotten SONNE of the FATHER) full of Grace and Truth." The division of the text is given thus: "All reducible to these three words: Quod Verbum, Caro; Quid Verbum, Carni; Quid Caro, Verbo. That the Word became flesh; the Mysterie: What the _Word_ did for _flesh_; the _Benefit_: And, what flesh is to doe to the _Word_ againe; the _Duety_." [77]

It is perhaps most instructive to compare the changes from a Puritan to a Cavalier sermon structure in the life of one preacher, namely John Gauden, who had been given a silver tankard for his sermon before the House of Commons on November 29, 1640, and who changed allegiance when he found it impossible to take the Solemn League and Covenant. His Commons text is Zechariah 8:19 "Thus saith the Lord, The fast of the tenth moneth, shall be to the house of Iudah, joy and gladnesse, and cheerfull feasts; therefore love the Truth and Peace." The division is as follows: "In the words consider three things: First, the inference, _Therefore_; Secondly, the objects propounded, _Truth_ and _Peace_. Thirdly, the dutie required: _Love_." [78] Nothing could be simpler or more directly derived from the text, nor patterned more clearly on doctrine, reason, and use, with a strong concluding emphasis on the application to the affections, which was called "the patheticks." With this should be contrasted the future Bishop's sermon preached in 1659 to "the Lord Mayor, the Lord General, Aldermen, Common Council and Companies of the honorable City of London." He took his text from Jeremiah 8:11 "For they have healed the hurt of the Daughter of my people slightly, saying, Peace, peace, where there is no peace." It was an apt text for the day of thanksgiving appointed for the return of the secluded members of Parliament to the House. Now, a Cavalier parson, he not only shows off his knowledge of Latin, but expands his division doubly to a six-fold analysis, and the printed sermon balloons to 112 pages. Here is the clear but cluttered division:

> 1. _Persona laesa, icta, afflicta_, the _Patient_ or _afflicted_; whom the Prophet, yea God himself _deplores_ and owns; she is called the _daughter of my people_; 2. _Plaga_ or _laesio_; the _grief_ or _malady_, the _hurt_ or _lesure_. 3. _Ficta medela_, or _insana sanatio_, the pretended cure or verbal _healing_; they have _healed, with saying_, Peace, peace, slightly and superficially. 4. _Pseudos_ or _mendacium_; the fallacy and cheat, when there is no _peace_. 5. _Medicorum turba_; the _Physitians_ or _Empericks_; _They_, great Statists, grave Polititians, formal pretenders to do great feats, and miraculous cures in _Church_ and _State_, when really they are no other than _imperious_ Hypocrites, _magniloquent Mountebanks_, cruel and covetous, confident and careless _Boasters_ of their skill; but no way _Effecters_ of a real cure. 6. _Vera medendi Methodus_; the true way of _curing a diseased Nation_, a distressed Country, a sick and languishing Church, which is implied . . . [79]

While the division is clearly derived from the text, and the sermon is a declamation, the fifth section of the division ran away with the rest and this is precisely what the London congregation wished to hear at this critical juncture in their history with Monk in their presence, who was to engineer the Restoration of the monarchy.

9. The Senecan Style.

Another distinguishing feature of the metaphysical preaching mode was its preference for a Senecan pointed as compared with a Ciceronian periodic style.

It is Senecan in a double sense. First, its form is marked by directness, terseness, even occasional roughness, vividness, controversial nimbleness, and a love of epigram and antithesis. The Ciceronian style, in contrast, prefers the copiousness, smoothness, and braching style of the long paragraphs and periods. [80] It is also, in a way that became increasingly true of the later Puritan style, Senecan in content and emphasis. By this is meant that the Caroline divines do not only quote Seneca, but their emphasis is also strongly moral, which makes it approximate the third element in the Puritan schema of Doctrine, Reason, and Use, that is, the application. But the Puritans, of course, abominated the Ciceronian style generally, for copiousness and smoothness, to say nothing of the display of esoteric learning, was drawing attention to the eloquence of the speaker. The Puritan divines were ever mindful of the strictures of St. Paul against Apollos and his smoothly seductive style in the church at Corinth. [81]

The Ciceronian style was admirably exemplified by Richard Hooker and by Jeremy Taylor. Donne combines both, but he is dominantly Senecan, as is Andrewes and his followers. Donne's Ciceronianism in its superb balance is seen in the "Sermon of Valediction" preached to the benchers of Lincoln's Inn, when leaving for Germany in 1619. In this moving farewell and vivid anthropomorphic image "the ears of God" is the pearl in the shining oyster context of superlative prose:

> In my long absence, and far distance from hence,
> remember me, as I shall do you in the ears of that
> God, to whom the farthest East, and the farthest
> West are but as the right and left ear in one of
> us; we hear with both at once; and he hears in both
> at once; remember me, not my abilities; for when
> I consider my Apostleship that I was sent to you,
> I am in St. Pauls quorum, quorum ego sum minimus,
> the least of them that have been sent; and when

> I consider my informities, I am in his <u>quorum</u> in another
> commission, another way, <u>Quorum ego maximus</u>; the
> greatest of them; but remember my labours, and en-
> deavours, at least my desire to make sure your salva-
> tion. And I shall remember your religious cheerfulness
> in hearing the word, and your christianly respect
> towards all them that bring that word to you, and
> towards my self in particular far [a]bove my merit. [82]

With this may be compared Donne's Senecan style with
its colloquial idioms and interrogatories in an intriguing sermon
reconciling contradictory texts.

> He is speaking of God having the <u>judicium detestationis</u>,
> and hence he knows and therefore detests evil, and
> therefore flatter not thyself with a Tush, God sees
> it not, or, Tush, God cares not, Doth it disquiet him
> or trouble his rest in heaven that I breake his Sabbath
> here? Doth it wound his body, or draw his bloud there,
> that I swear by his body and bloud here? Doth it
> corrupt any of his virgins there, that I solicit the
> chastity of a woman here? Are his Martyrs withdrawn
> from their Alleagance, or retarded in their service
> to him there, because I dare not defend his cause,
> nor speak for him, nor fight for him heare? [83]

The jerkiness of the Senecan style, not an amble but
a series of stops and starts can be seen in the balanced antitheses
and terseness of the form and the practicality of the substance
in the following citation from Brownrig:

> Popery is a Religion for the Eye; Ours for the Ear . . .
> A Christian is described, <u>In auditu Auris,</u> At the Hearing
> of the Ear they shall obey. Hearing it is that breeds
> Faith. It is a comfort to have these Visions, Tastings,
> Feelings; but if all these fail us, or be denied us;
> yet if we can Hear, and Believe, it sufficeth. We
> must stick to this. In this sense, All <u>the Body must
> be an Ear.</u> <u>Miracula, muta sine voce;</u> but Seals to
> a Blank. [84]

The directness of the Senecan manner, with a vivid simile,
is shown in Bishop Morton's defence of the Book of Common Prayer
against the charge that it has passages taken from the Roman
Liturgy: Let us understand that truth is truth wherever it soundeth,
even as a Pearle is a Pearle of price, although it be taken out
of the head of a toade." [85]

How suitable a style it was for controversy can be seen
in an anti-Papal citation of Morton on the text of Romans 13:1,

"Let every soul be subject to the higher powers, &c." Morton
questions:

> Every soul subject? Not I, saith the Pope, and so all
> Popes of after-times, for we have power over all
> Powers, be they Emperours themselves, to kick off
> their Crowns with our feet; to depose their persons,
> and to dispose of their kingdoms. [86]

Thus the Senecan style succeeded in achieving vividness
and ingenuity by a variety of devices. These included rhyt mical
word play, alliteration, hyperbole, antithesis, and, of course, ra-
dox. Senecan brevity and epigrammatic concision, as well as abru *-
ness, was victorious over Ciceronian periodic expansiveness an
smoothness. [87]

10. Paradoxes, Riddles and Emblems.

Another distinguishing characteristic of metaphysical
preaching was a fondness for paradoxes, riddles and emblems.
They are, of course, interrelated. Each demands a teasing concentration on the meaning of what appears to be mysterious and thought-
provoking. They also represent a continuation of the medieval
delight in allegorization which also intrigued Renaissance minds
until the middle of the seventeenth century.

It belonged to the Platonic inheritance in which individual
objects were viewed as members of a class, rather than seen
in their individuality and particularity, or haeccitas (or thisness)
that the opposing Nominalists had stressed. Objects seemed to
be transparent pointing to the Divine pattern or idea in the mind
of the Creator God. Hence allegorical symbolization was built
on the conviction, equally flattering to the philosopher and the
mystic, that symbolic thinking penetrated the external nut to
reach the inner kernel of thought or union, and the harder the
nut was to crack the more valuable and esoteric was the mental
meat within. What Huizinga says of medieval understanding was
still true of much of the epistemology of those preparing sermons
in the Renaissance. He wrote:

> The Middle Ages never forgot that all things would
> be absurd if their meaning were exhausted in their
> function and their place in the phenomenal world,
> if by their essence they did not reach a world beyond
> this. About the figure of Divinity a majestic system
> of correlated figures crystallized which all have refer-
> ence to Him. The world unfolds itself like a vast

> whole of symbols, like a cathedral of ideas. It is the
> most richly rhythmical conception of the world, a
> polyphonous expression of eternal harmony. [88]

Such a conception lingered on in the Church after it had been given up by the world. Paradoxes are found throughout our period. Indeed, at the very time that contradictions or apparent contradictions in Scripture were acutely felt by the preachers, two such collections of paradoxes appeared. To use Rosalie L. Colie's fascinating title for her book, the contagion of paradoxitis had led to **Paradoxia Epidemica** . . . The two most popular paradoxers were Herbert Palmer and Ralph Venning.

Both flourished in the middle decades of the seventeenth century. Palmer was an honored member of the Westminster Assembly of divines and Master of Queen's College, Cambridge. He was the author of **Memorials of Godliness & Christianity** which appeared in 1644, and its second part, **The Character of a Christian in Paradoxes and seeming Contradictions** appeared in 1655 and was attributed to Lord Bacon, presumably because it seemed to be better at demonstrating Biblical contradictions than in resolving the difficulties it had disclosed. It was a compilation of 85 paradoxes. Many of them were more Scriptural inconsistencies than doctrinal paradoxes, though the latter were included.

Venning's **Orthodoxe Paradoxes, Theoreticall and Experimentall, or, a Believer clearing truth by seeming Contradictions** appeared in 1647 and five editions appeared in the first five years. It is better than Palmer both because it expounds a complete system of theology, and because it has clearer and more rational definitions. Palmer's first paradox read: "A Christian is one who believes things which his reason cannot comprehend." Venning's first read: "He [the Christian] believes that which reason cannot comprehend, yet there is reason enough why he should believe it." It is all the difference between the contra-rationalistic fideism of Tertullian who said, Credo quia impossibile est (I believe because it is impossible) and illuminating faith of St. Anselm, Credo ut intelligam (I believe in order to understand.) The strength and weakness of the over-paradoxical approach is revealed in the final paradox, number 127. This reads: "He is one who lives in another and for another; He seeks not himself when he aims most at his good: God is his all, and his all is God's; he aims at no end but the glory of God, of which there is no end." [89]

The strength is in the echo both of Christ's teaching that must lose the world to win one's soul and of the definition of man's true end in the Westminster **Shorter Catechism.** [90] Its weakness that it depends upon a verbal quibble on the two meanings of 'end'; namely, aim and terminus and thus sounds profounder than it is.

The doctrinal paradoxes, (as our chapter on metaphysical wit tries to make clear, in the many examples it offers) are integral to Christian doctrine and life. These include: The Holy Trinity, the Incarnation, the Atonement of the holy for the unholy and Love for the loveless, and the Resurrection as the death of death.

The value of the paradox to the preacher was that it helped him to elicit a sense of wonder in the listeners. George Puttenham called the genre itself "the Wondrer." [91] And in Andrewes and his followers the use of the paradox became orthodox.

While the paradox in the realm of thought from the days of Parmenides onwards aimed at forcing contemplation, the rhetorical paradox to quote Rosalie Colie has the "double aim of dazzling--that is, of arresting thought altogether in the possessive experience of wonder . . ." [92] Its other function is to encourage further question and possibly even contradiction on the part of the teased audience.

Two examples only will be given of a single paradox: that God immutably wills mutability. Dean Jackson's theme for his entire third sermon on Jeremiah 26:19 is to ask the question: In what sense is God said to repent? The answer he gives is: "God immutably willeth mutability." [93] Bishop Lake, however, shows himself to be a true scholastic in his illustrated explication of this paradox:

> True it is, that God is said to repent; but the Fathers joyntly agree that his repentance is mutation, not _affectus_, but _effectus_: hee changeth his creatures, unchangeable in himselfe. Even as a Chirurgeon who begins with one kind of plaister when that hath wrought his force, layeth another kind, doth not alter, but pursue his former resolution, which was, by those diverse plaisters to cure the sore: even so, whatsoever alteration befalls us, God did eternally decree it, and decree it as befalls. [94]

The metaphysical preachers also knew riddles, more frequently in Elizabethan than in Caroline days. It is interesting to observe two of them using the famous riddle of Samson recounted in the book of Judges. The riddle is: "Out of the eater came forth meat, and out of the strong came forth sweetness." The answer is almost equally obscure: "What is sweeter than honey? and what is stronger than a lion?" [95] The mystery clears when it is realized that Samson is referring to a honeycomb found in a lion's carcass. In an Easter sermon Bishop Brownrig following Augustine, applies the riddle as another proof of the transformation effected by the grace of God: " . . . the devouring Lyon shall bring hony in his mouth; the Church's cruel persecutours shall by the Gospel be made affectionate foster-fathers." [96] Thomas Fuller applies the riddle in an entirely different fashion: " . . . part of <u>Samsons</u> Riddel shall be fulfilled in your ears: <u>Out of the Devourer came meat</u>: <u>Gluttony</u>, that vice which consumeth and devoureth food, the discourse thereof by Gods assistance shall feed us at this time." [97]

Emblems became popular in the 1630's and later, when the emblem books of Quarles and Wither appeared in 1635. Quarles' work **Emblemes** [98] as also Wither's **A Collection of Emblems** were made up of symbolic pictures and explanatory words. The earliest English emblem book was Geoffrey Whitney's **A Choice of Emblemes and other Devises** (1586) and was published in Leyden.

Mario Praz has rightly stressed the link between the emblem and the conceit, maintaining that seventeenth century man needing the assurances of the senses wished "to externalize it, to transpose it into a hieroglyph, an emblem." [99] The aim of the device, associated with the emblem, was, like the paradox, to produce a sense of the marvellous, as its great exemplifier, Marino, had affirmed. [100] A further link between the brilliant analogy or witty conceit and the emblem is M. W. Croll's discovery that Lyly uses seventeen of Alciati's emblems as the basis of similes used in his **Euphues.** [101]

The great attraction of the emblem, as Rosemary Freeman has shown in her admirable **English Emblem Books,** is the wit, "the apparent lack of any relation between the two ideas [of the analogy] and the subsequent establishment of an intellectually convincing link between them that pleases . . ." [102] She claims that it is the same delight found in the Elizabethan drama and the modern English musical hall in puns, and in the <u>double-entendres</u> found in the cross-word puzzles of the Times of London, no matter how arbitrary the link appears to common sense or the feelings. Of direct interest to this study is the claim of Thomas Beachcroft that the emblem is simply a metaphysical conceit in miniature. [103]

The function of the majority of English sacred emblem books was to help Protestants to learn Christian doctrine through visual education and to enable them to meditate as Catholics had been taught to do. Louis L. Martz [104] has shown how Catholic meditation techniques assisted Donne, and certainly Crashaw, though it now seems unlikely that Donne ever had a Jesuit tutor because the work of Jesuits was so dangerous and they were so few in England, or that Herbert was unduly influenced by Catholic techniques. On the other hand the Ignatian technique of 'composition'--visualizing Biblical events, and the struggle for the <u>miles Christianus</u> to gain victory had a powerful effect on the religious imagination of Europe in art, architecture and meditation. As complement and partial correction of Martz, Barbara K. Lewal-

ski [105] has shown how important Protestant meditation techniques, aided by emblem books, were in their impact on the English
religious lyric. If such were influential on the English metaphysical
poets, they must have been at least as influential on the English
metaphysical preachers.

For Protestants emblems were derived from the natural
world (God's Picture Book since it was his creation), and the Scriptures (His living and transforming Word), and from other emblem
books, chiefly Catholic, which they borrowed and amended. Furthermore, history itself was seen by the eyes of faith as the saga
of the Gesta Dei per sanctos, themselves illuminated by the Holy
Spirit. Barbara Lewalski rightly sees that the major types of emblems are three: natural, historical, and moral, presumably including
the Scriptural as part of the historical. [106]

Space only allows us to illustrate the variety of homiletical
emblematic usage with concise examples taken from the late
Elizabethan and late Caroline periods. Playfere in his Spittal
sermon of 1593, using Philippians 3:14 as his text, illustrates
progress towards the high calling in Christ by referring to the
emperor's motto thus: "Hereupon Charles the 5. gave this Embleme,
Stand not stil, but go on further." [107] Henry Smith in a sermon
on the duties of marriage maintains that wives should stay at
home for homes are not prisons but paradises, continues: "Phidias
when he should paynt a woman, painted her sitting under a Snailes
shell, signifying, that she should go like a snaile which carrieth
his house upon his backe." [108]

Daniel Featley combines a natural symbol with a strong
moral meaning in a funeral sermon for a mercer named Benet.
This ends by saying that he will strew a few flowers on the hearse.
These are emblematic flowers. "The first flower is a Rose, the
embleme of charity. For a Rose is hot in nature, it spreadeth
it selfe abroad, and after it is full blowne scattereth both leaves
and seeds; so charity is hot in the affection; spreadeth it selfe
abroad by compassion, and scattereth seeds by almes-deeds." [109]
Similarly, the lily is the emblem of purity, and the violet of humility. Another late sermon in our period represents a fiery heart
as an emblem of a consecrated soul, a commonplace of its time.
This is from Bishop Hacket's sixth sermon on the Baptism of
Christ. He reports: "Truly did one say that the Emblem of a
pious was, Carbo ignitus divini amoris flammâ absorptus; a firy
coal wasting away all the gross and earthy parts of it with the
flame of divine love." [110]

John Donne, according to Joan Webber, obtained many
of his images from emblem books. [111] A common one that
he uses on at least three occasions is that of a balance drawn
from emblem books. Here is the use he makes of it in a Lincoln's
Inn Sermon:

> If you value God, weigh God, you cannot give him
> halfe his weight; for you can put nothing into the
> balance, to weigh him withall, but all this world;
> and there is no single sand in the sea, no single
> dust upon the earth, no single atome in the ayre,
> that is not likelyer to weigh down all the world,
> then all the world is to counterpose God; . . . [112]

11. Speculative doctrines and arcane knowledge.

A fuller consideration of this characteristic distinction of metaphysical preaching will be given in the chapter on "Learning Divine or Human." Only the briefest consideration will be given in this section to speculative thinking and a mention of the scope of arcane learning.

The metaphysical preachers, especially those like Donne [113] familiar with and fond of the medieval schoolmen, were far more inclined to speculation than the strict Calvinist divines. But even Donne, like any stoic Calvinist, warned against prying into the secret counsells of God [114] though he had often failed to take this advice. The rigid Calvinists contrasted the exclusiveness and profundity of Divine knowledge with the superficiality of merely human guesses. For them sola Scriptura was the authority for doctrine, whereas for the metaphysical preachers generally nature, reason and history, as well as the Scripture, were pointers to God.

Already we have mentioned the fondness of the metaphysical for knowledge ancillary to the Scripture: patristic and classical scholarship and parallels uniting their insights; historical narrations and natural history of the legendary type such as Pliny provided. They also enjoyed recounting Aesopian type fables with moral applications. Moreover, they read the many Biblical commentators, ancient, medieval and contemporary, in which the hermeneutical cruxes of the Bible were illuminated. They tried to reconcile them when possible or to select the most appropriate option when the interpreters differed. The learned Puritan divines were equally familiar with these sources in exegetical illumination and conveyed the insights in their sermons. They served the strong meat of the Gospel sauced with illustrations without bringing the recipes and cooking pots into the pulpit; or, to change the metaphor, they didn't drag their lexica, concordances, commonplaces and patristic folios into their sermons.

When thinking of mere speculation in sermons, one inevitably turns to Donne for his Faustian curiosity, now almost confined after his ordination to Scripture, patrology and the schoolmen. For example, he is fascinated in turn by the guesses from three sources on how to interpret "the messenger of Satan" in the Pauline letters. The possibilities include headache, gout, stomach-ache, heretics, and diabolical temptations. [115] On another occasion, he cites Origen to try to describe what is meant by the eternal generation of the Son of God, Christ. [116] On yet a third and typical occasion, using a suggestion of Justin Martyr's elaborated by Athenagoras, he wants to know what happens at the general Resurrection to a man's body which has been swallowed by a fish which, in its turn, is eaten by another man. [117]

There was considerable guessing about the nature of life after death and not only by Donne, whose morbid interest in death and vermiculation was equalled by a permanent fascination for "ouranology", as Hacket called the geography and architecture of heaven. Indeed Hacket says he rarely ventured into this area, because of its difficulty. "It is," he said, "one of the most difficult tasks in Divinity to understand the several quarterings and mansion-places of heaven. I confess I am not skilled in Ouranography." [118]

Yet Barten Holyday outreaches even Donne in his specula-tions on eternal life. He delivered a remarkable Easter sermon preached in St. Mary's Church, Oxford, in 1623, on the text "Now is Christ risen from the dead and become the first-fruits of them that believe" (I Cor 15:20). After a description of how he thinks the Resurrection was experienced by Christ, he insists that souls and bodies will be reunited although there will be no marriage of the sexes. He suggests that critics will consider it impossible to gather the bodies of those eaten by cannibals who descended from ancestors similarly nourished, "For by this wild reckoning there will bee such a Genalogie of debt, that the bodie of the Nephew must peradventure be paid to the great Grand-father." He concludes that God has decreed there will never be a human body consisting wholly of other human bodies. The eager soul will be renewed in an adorned body: "Mankind shall feel and expresse a youthfull spring: the walking-staffe and the wrinkle shall bee no more the helpe and distinction of age." He climaxes his description of renewal with accounts of the maturation and completion of child and dwarf and "when sleepe shall be commanded from the eylid, no more by care, but by immortalitie." [119]

The other set of theological questions which led to uncer-tainty and therefore to some speculation was common to both metaphysical preachers and strict Puritans: those of Calling, Election, Predestination and Assurance.

The Calvinist Fuller had a 'travelling' sermon preached again and again to help the serious Christian decide whether he was truly called and elected by God, a problem which John Downame addressed his Christian Warfare (1604). He offered ten "signes and infallible notes of our election." [120] Fuller's sermon on 2 Peter 1:10 "Give rather diligence to make your calling and election sure" provides a syllogistic answer to the problem:

> A Christian thus collecteth this Assurance of his Calling and Election by composing this practicall Syllogisme in his soule.
>
> The Major: He that truly repenteth himselfe of his sinnes, and relyeth with a true faith on God in Christ, is surely called, and by consequence Elected before all Eternity to be a vessel of honour.
>
> The Minor: But I truely repent myselfe of my sinnes, and rely with a true faith on God in Christ.
>
> Conclusion: Therefore I am truly Called and Elected, &. [121]

Donne's fondness for philosophical and theological subtleties, many of which had been propounded and answered by St. Thomas Aquinas, in the **Summa Theologica**, is well known. [122] His curiosity provides a natural bridge to arcane learning.

Thomas Goffe uses St. Paul's example as the authority for considering other than Biblical knowledge as of value to Christians. He claims that Paul was "able to cite their owne Poets among the then learned Athenians, and to apply a Satyricall Verse out of Epimenides, to reprehend the lying, gluttonous and bestiall manners of the Cretians." He continues: "His powefull language so ravish't the Lystrians, in the 14 of the **Acts**, that hee gain'd the repute of Mercury among them: and questionlesse, the sitting so long at the feet of Gamaliel, made him vas electionis . . . " [123] Hacket too, according to his biographer, Dr. Thomas Plume, followed Origen in that "he made use of all Heathen Learning to adorn the Doctrine of Christianity." [124]

Andrewes insisted, paradoxically, on the Biblical authority for using the Apocrypha, simply because the Epistle of Jude uses information from the Book of Enoch. [125] Andrewes [126] as well as Donne and King among others, were glad to use Rabbinic lore. John Chamberlin's **Increase and Multiply** [127] shows how Donne in his fascination with the Divine Names was intrigued by Cabalistic Studies derived from Notarikon in the **Essays in Divinity.** [128] Donne also alludes to the Cabalistic device of Gematriya in which not only words but syllables, letters and points reveal mysterious meanings to the instructed in as late as a sermon preached in 1626. [129]

Henry King gladly acknowledges in the conclusion of his series of sermons on the Lord's Prayer that Rabbi Jehudah

132

"thought the pronouncing of <u>Amen</u> so meritorious that hee who said <u>Amen</u> in this world, was worthy to say <u>Amen</u> in the next." [130] Other Rabbis thought it so effectual when devoutly uttered that it would accelerate the time of their redemption.

The inexhaustably curious Donne even refers to the **Qu'ran** to contradict its teaching:

> It was the poor way that <u>Mahomet</u> found out in his Alchoran, that in the next life all women should have eies of one bigness, and a stature of one size; he could finde no means to avoid contention but to make them all alike: But that is thy complexion, that is thy proportion which God hath given thee. [**131**]

Hacket also provides Muslim lore, about which he raises some doubts. He believes, however, that on completing their pilgrimage to Mecca, the zealots "presently draw hot burning steel before their eyes to put them out, that they may never see any other spectacle after they have been honoured to see that Monumant [tomb] of their Prophet . . ." [**132**]

Donne, from the wealth of his travelling experience and his visually acute imagination, can provide much recondite geographical and marine information. He uses images indicating his knowledge of the Northern Sea passage, [**133**] and even of how whales are caught. [**134**]

12. Liturgical--devotional Preaching.

The final distinguishing characteristic of metaphysical preaching is that Christian doctrine was related to the liturgical calendar. This stimulated Christian devotion.

There are striking differences between the calendar [**135**] of the Roman Catholic Church, the Church of England and the Puritan calendar of the Westminster Assembly days.

For both Catholics and Anglicans, the calendar had a retrospective look. It was a permanent christological reminder. Year after year, the calendar of these Churches renewed the remembrance of the mighty acts of the triune God in creation, Redemption and Sanctification. It centered on the climax of the Christian dispensation, the Incarnation. Preparation at Advent (with a brief prospective glance at the second Advent), The Nativity of Christ, (God-as-Man), the Epiphany (Wise Men bringing their triple tribute), Lent (the temptations of Christ) and climactic Holy Week, from the hollow triumph of Palm Sunday to the full triumph of Easter day--including the Passion--going through the Agony and Bloody Sweat of God on Good (bad) Friday--and the Resurrection. Then followed the Ascension at which the parabola of Christ's going "from God to God" [136] is completed, Pentecost, with the gift of the purifying, illuminating and inspiring Holy Spirit, and Trinity Sunday. Thus was completed the revelation of the Triune God, Father, Son and Holy Spirit.

The major calendric difference between the Church of Rome and the Church of England was that the former had many saints days celebrating the imitators of God in many lands and centuries, whereas the English Church celebrated exclusively the New Testament saints. This was amusingly reflected in a casual fashion by the observation: "One said to another that his face was like a popish almanck all holydayes because it was full of pimples." [137]

Continuing the same analogy, the Anglican's calendric complexion was clearer, while the Puritan's face was unspotted except for a blush. At the time of the Westminster Assembly, the Puritan calendar was prospective rather than retrospective. This sabbatarianism celebrated the Creation in which God rested on the seventh day, and looked forward to the Christian's future well-earned rest in eternity. It also meant that each Sunday (changed from the Jewish sabbath to the day commemorating Christ's Resurrection) the devout would maintain a firm family and personal discipline of prayer, attendance at worship and hearing the oracles of God preached, followed by the master of each household testing the servants and the children on their recollection of the expository sermon (with its emphasis on doctrine, reason and use). The Lord's Day would conclude with family prayer and private spiritual account taking. All this was appropriate for those who believed they were called to be saints in the New Testament sense of sanctification--a process, not an achievement. [138] The Puritan calendar was also contemporary in its insistence upon days of judgment and thanksgiving to acknowledge nationally, locally or privately the criticisms or comforts of God's providence, so strong a feature of Puritan diaries of this period. [139]

What were the contextual consequences for preaching? The Puritans could preach entire series of sermons from individual books of the Bible, or upon major Christian doctrines and their practical import whenever they chose, unhampered by liturgical cycle. They disliked the official Anglican calendar because of the immoderate merriment that took place at the Christmas season—ending only on the twelfth night after the Nativity--and on May day and night. They loathed the beery buffoonery, bawdiness and profanity that characterized such occasions. In particular, they

134

disliked the profanation of the Lord's Day which the royal Book of Sports, issued by James I in 1618 and renewed by Charles I in 1633, encouraged in their view. Royalist Anglicans considered them occasions of jollity and harmless fun, Puritans as occasions of triviality if not worse. [140]

The Puritan system of lectureships enabled the 'silver-tongued' Henry Smith and others like him, who scrupled the ceremonies of the Church of England, to supplement the leaner spiritual fare offered in many pulpits with the strongest meat of the Gospel, served up with the sauces of eloquence. [142] Similarly the Puritan chaplains of the court like Preston and Sibbes were not circumvented by ecclesiastical calendric conventions, because the lawyer's terms excluded the feast days.

On the other hand, the christological cycle of the Church of England provided the opportunity for the metaphysical preachers to ring the changes on the great festivals. So we have Andrewes, Brownrig, Donne and Hacket--to mention only the most outstanding metaphysical preachers--producing masterpieces of eloquence, doctrine and devotion at Christmas, Easter and Whitsunday (Pentecost), when their cathedral churches or the Court Chapel at Whitehall were filled with joyful listeners and communicants. The great introspective fast was, of course, the entire season of Lent when they had a searching task to perform.

There were, as we have seen, secular feast days also to commemorate. These included the accession days of the sovereigns, and days of thanksgiving for the deliverance of the King--the fifth of August, Gowrie Day, and the fifth of November when the King and Parliament were saved from the Gunpowder Plot. Ultimately, the Cavaliers during the Commonwealth as in the Restoration kept January 30th as a sacred day, that of the 'martyrdom' of Charles I in 1649.

Both Andrewes and Cosin almost always linked the liturgical lesson with the calendric context in their sermons. Most metaphysical preachers made much of the great christological occasions of Christmas and Easter. Cosin regularly followed a method which Andrewes occasionally used. [143] He began by connecting the sermon matter with the calendar year; he then introduced the bidding prayer, and then gave out the text. This indissolubly united the feast or fast, the appropriate devotion, and the apt text. Even in a marriage sermon, Cosin remains liturgically loyal by expanding a passage from the Gospel lection for the day, (the second Sunday after Epiphany). [144]

Donne's contribution to observing the Christian year, claims a modern Methodist minister, was massive. [145] As Dean of St. Paul's Cathedral, he was required each year to preach on

Christmas Day, Easter Day and on Whitsunday for almost ten years. He also preached extra sermons on Candlemas, Lent, Trinity Sunday and the commemoration of the conversion of St. Paul; nor should the Prebendary Sermons on the Psalms be forgotten which he was also required to preach. [146] Donne records his grave sense of responsibility in a letter to Mrs. Cockain towards the end of his life:

> I was under a necassity of preaching twelve or four-
> teen solemn sermons every year, to great auditories
> at Paul's, and to the judges and at Court . . . You
> know the ticklishness of London pulpits. [147]

Donne called the linking of the preacher's meditation on the text to the sacred occasion of the day "complication.' [148]

The contrast of the number of calendric sermons in their total output between the Calvinist ministers on the one hand, whose chief employment was as lecturers in either parish churches or chaplain in the Inns of Court, and on the other hand the parish priests who became prebendaries or deans, and in most cases (Donne is the exception), bishops, whether Calvinists or Arminians, is striking. It can be most succinctly indicated by providing a comparative table. (See page 136). Thomas Adams has been chosen to represent the first category; Andrewes, Brownrig, Cosin, Donne and Hacket, the second category.

Henry Smith had, it must be remembered, 'Decalogue God' as his mentor who was a strict sabbatarian [149] and, there-fore, objected to the Christian year but not to such topics as the Incarnation, the Atonement and the Resurrection. He had also doubts about some of the ceremonies of the Church of England which did not prevent him from being ordained but from being a parish incumbent who would have run foul of his bishop despite his influence with Cecil. Also his wealth saved him from the necessity of parochial charge.

Thomas Adams, as a lecturer for much of his life and as preacher at St. Gregory's near Paul's Wharf, London only had parochial responsibility for part of his life and was sequestered by Cromwell's Triers. Adams, however, did say, as a clear indication of his approval of the Church of England calendar, that Faith, Hope and Charity correspond to the three [150] festivals of the Christian Year. Oddly enough, though, he linked Faith (not Hope) with Easter, Hope with Whitsun (because of the transformation possible) and Charity with Christmas (although Augustine had taught that the Holy Spirit was the bond of Charity--vinculum caritatis--in the Holy Trinity.

All that requires comment on the part of the others

136

Table of the use of the Christological Calendar in Sermons

	Total of collected Sermons in print	Nativity or Epiphany	Lenten Passion	Easter	Ascension	Whitsun	Trinity (a) Transfiguration (b) All Saints (c) Candlemas (d) Conversion of St. Paul (e) Purification (f)	Total	%
Henry Smith			I			2		3	
Thomas Adams	63	4	1+2	1			1 (a)	9	14.3
Andrewes	96	17	14+3	18		15		67	69.8
Brownrig	65	7	1	7	1	4	7 (b)	27	41.5
Cosin (no Restoration sermons survive in print)	28	5	11	1	1	1		18	64.3
Donne	160	8	11	10		10	7 (a) 1 (c) 2 (d) 4 (e) 3 (f)	56	35.0
Hacket	100	15	27+5 (6 Baptism 21 Temptation)	9		5	7 (b)	70	70.0

is the great importance attached by Bishops Brownrig and Hacket to the Transfiguration, presumably because it links Old and New Testament and anticipates the glory that will be Christ's on the other side of his Passion and Death. It shows his sacred servant role in descending to the Valley of Humiliation from the Mount of Transfiguration.

Finally, we note that Andrewes, Cosin [151] and Hacket preach more calendric than other sermons, amounting to approximately two thirds of their total output: Their eloquence rose to its highest peak in these great festal occasions. A sense of their mid-century importance is conveyed by Davenant in the preface to his play, **Gondibert**. He writes:

> Divines . . . are the 'Tetrarchs of Time,' of which they command the fourth Division, for to no less the Sabboths and Daies of Saints amount, and during these daies of spiritual Triumph Pulpits are Thrones, and the People oblig'd to open their Eares . . .

*   *   *

In conclusion, the ten characteristics we have isolated did not distinguish all of the sermons of all of the metaphysical preachers all of the time. They were exemplified, however, by most of them, most of the time. In conjunction, they provide an index to the theological length and breadth in historical time and charity; the Biblical, patristic and classical learning; the controversial zest; the imaginative brilliance in wit and illustration; and the devotional spirit that marked the golden age of the English pulpit.

NOTES

1. Samuel Johnson, **The Lives of the Poets**, ed. G. B. Hill, 3 vols. (1903) I, 20.

2. Epistle Dedicatory to Eleanora, third paragraph.

3. Dryden, "Discourse concerning Satire," **The Poems of John Dryden**, ed. James Kinsley, 4 vols. (Oxford, 1958) II, 604.

4. H. J. C. Grierson, **Metaphysical Lyrics and Poems of the Seventeenth Century** (Oxford, 1922) xvi. Here Grierson speaks of "the peculiar blend of passion and thought, feeling and ratiocination, which is their greatest achievement."

5. **The Metaphysical Mode from Donne to Cowley** (Princeton, New Jersey, 1969) 47. Here Miner writes: "The chief literary radical of metaphysical poetry is, whatever the qualifications, its private mode."

6. Samuel Clarke, **A Collection of the Lives of Ten Eminent Divines . . .** (1662) 253-254.

7. Richard Baxter, **The Saints Everlasting Rest** (1650) 368. One may contrast this with Luther's assertion that if there were no laughter in heaven, he would not wish to go there.

8. Richard Sibbes, **The Bruised Reede and the Smoaking Flax** (1630) I, 53-54, quoted in J. K. Knott, Jr., **The Sword of the Spirit: Puritan Responses to the Bible** (Chicago, 1980) 185.

9. See Laurence Sasek, **The Literary Temper of the English Puritans** (Baton Rouge, Louisiana, 1967) for the range from naked to ornamental of pulpit styles.

10. William Perkins, **The Workes of that famous and worthie Minister of Christ, in the Universitie of Cambridge, M. W. Perkins . . .** (3 vols., 1613) II, 673. Perkins says the minister "may, yea and must privately use at his libertie the arts, Philosophy and variety of reading, whilest he is framing his sermon: but he ought in publike to conceal all these from the people, and not make the least ostentation. Artis etiam est celare artem: it is also a point of art to conceal art." He ruled out the use of Greek or Latin phrases because they distract the minds of the auditors, and the telling of stories and reciting of profane or ridiculous speeches. The most suitable style for a preacher, said Thomas Cartwright was "a speech both simple and perspicuous, fit both for the people's understanding, and to expresse the Maiestie of the Spirit." (**A Dilucidation or Exposition of the Apostle St. Paul to the Colossians,** ed. A. B. Grosart, 6.) Perkins, however, approved of illuminating (not obfuscating) metaphors and exempla as sermon illustrations.

11. Perkins, **A Golden Chaine** (1600) 1. Perkins, according to Fuller's **The Holy State,** 1681, 81, was said to have preached so that "his sermons were not so plain but that the piously learned did admire them, nor so learned but that the plain did understand them."

12. Clarke, **A Collection of the Lives of Ten Eminent Divines,** 285.

13. Izaak Walton, **The Life of John Donne** (1658) 145.

14. **An Exposition Upon the Lords Prayer. Delivered in certaine Sermons in the Cathedrall Church of S. Paul** (1628) 46.

15. See P. G. Stanwood, "Patristic and Contemporary Borrowing in the Caroline Divines" in The Renaissance Quarterly, Vol. XXIII, No. 4, Winter 1970, 421-449.

16. **XCVI Sermons** 547.

17. **XCVI Sermons** 551.

18. For example, in <u>A Sermon preached at Hampton Court 23 Sept.</u> <u>1608,</u> he has 38 brief patristic references.

19. As in the Spittal Sermon of 26 pages, with 21 patristic references, there are 11 references to Augustine (chiefly citations), 2 Greek citations from Chrysostom, and single references or brief citations from Jerome, Cyprian, and Gregory, and 2 to unnamed Fathers. The Sermon is among those bound in with the **XCVI Sermons** at the end.

20. **The Sermons of John Donne** (eds. Potter and Simpson) IV, 74–75.

21. **The Sermons of John Donne** I, 259.

22. The statistics will be found on X, 367. There is also the estimate that Donne has about 2200 Biblical citations and 700 citations or references to Augustine, far the most popular Father for Donne, who resembles him in his wild youth, and in his mastery of rhetoric and imagination.

23. **The Workes of Tho: Adams** (1629) 123.

24. One of the <u>Foure Sermons Preached before the Kings Maiestie</u> <u>at Hampton Court in September last.</u> <u>This Concerning the Antiquitie and Superioritie</u> <u>of Bishops.</u> <u>Sept. 21, 1606.</u> (1606). His sermon, <u>Christian Libertie</u> preached prior to his consecration, but printed in 1606, has 33 references in all, with Calvin having the lion's share, with 14 extensive citations from the **Institutes.**

25. **The Collected Sermons of Thomas Fuller, D.D.** (eds. J. E. Bailey and W. E. A. Axon, 2 vols., 1891) I, 311. It comes from <u>A Sermon of Reformation</u> <u>Preached at the Church of the Savoy, last Fast day, July 27, 1643</u> (1643).

26. Homer is cited in "Christs Wounds Our Health" (1598), and Martial in "God be with you" (1604), both court sermons.

27. Horace is cited in "The Sacrifice of Thankfulnesse" (1616) and Ovid in "Heaven and Earth Reconciled."

28. **The Workes of Tho: Adams**, 50.

29. The references to Homer will be found on 314 and 340, those to Horace on 157 and 229, and the references to Ovid and Virgil on 314 and to Juvenal on 114.

30. <u>Three Sermons Preached upon Severall Publike Oaccasions</u> (1642) 63, 77, and 130. There are several references to Homer in Gauden's <u>Kakourgoi</u> (1659).

31. Howson has two references to Juvenal in <u>A Sermon preached</u> <u>at Paules Crosse the 4 of December 1597</u> (1597) which was a criticism of simony,

and two further references to Juvenal in <u>A Sermon preached at St. Maries in Oxford the 17, Day of November, 1602</u> (second impression, 1603). Virgil, Juvenal and Horace, as well as Plautus and Pindar, are each cited once in <u>A Second Sermon preached at Paules Crosse the 21 of May, 1598</u> (1598). This particular sermon has a total of 94 references in 52 pages.

32. Goffe has a reference to Virgil in a Spittal sermon, "Deliverance from the Grave" (1627).

33. Thomas Playfere, **The Whole Sermons** (1623) 8. It is from "Hearts Delight" a Paul's Cross sermon of 1603.

34. **The Whole Sermons** 6. It is from "The Pathway to Perfection."

35. Also from "The Pathway to Perfection" in **The Whole Sermons** 177.

36. Yet again from "The Pathway to Perfection" in **The Whole Sermons** 185.

37. From **The Lion in the Lambe, Or, Strength in Weakness** (Oxford, 1628) 48-49. See also Wall's **Christ in Progresse** (Oxford, 1627) 34-35 for a parallel between Telemachus in Athens and Christ in Jerusalem.

38. **XCVI Sermons** 717. From a sermon preached at Holyrood Castle, Edinburgh, on Whitsunday, 1617 before King James.

39. <u>Sarah and Hagar: Or, Genesis the sixteenth Chapter opened</u> in **XIX Sermons** (1649) 180, and from a sermon originally delivered on January 19, 1641-2.

40. **An Exposition upon the Lords Prayer** 32-33.

41. **A Century of Sermons** 273.

42. See G. R. Owst, **Literature and Pulpit in Medieval England** (rev. ed., Oxford, 1961) 186-190. Pliny's **The Natural History** (in 37 books) was ably Englished by Philemon Holland in 1601.

43. **The Workes of Tho: Adams** 420. It is from the sermon, <u>The Spiritual Navigator Bound for the Holy Land.</u>

44. **The Workes of Tho: Adams** 869.

45. **XCVI Sermons** 793. From "A Sermon preached before the Kings Maiestie at Holdenbie, 5. Aug. 1608."

46. Hacket, **A Centenary of Sermons** (1675) 618. Playfere's <u>exemplum</u> comes from "Christs Wounds our Health" in **Nine Sermons** (1621) 111-112.

47. **The Sermons of John Donne** II, 69. For other examples see **Sermons** V, 233; VI, 85; and X, 161.

48. **The Works of John Cosin** Vol. I [Sermons], (Oxford, 1843) the conclusion to the Ninth Sermon.

49. See G. R. Owst, **Literature and Pulpit in Medieval England** 202.

50. **The Sermons** (1616) 162. From the 1593 sermon, "The Pathway to Perfection."

51. One of Foure Sermons Preached before the Kings Maiestie (1606) sig. C l.

52. **Sixty Five Sermons** (1674) 247.

53. **The Sermons of Maister Henrie Smith** (1593) 225-226.

54. Ibid., 593.

55. Eliahs's Wish: A Prayer for Death. A Sermon preached at the Funerall of the Right Honourable Viscount Sudbury, Lord Bayning (1630) 2.

56. **The Sermons of John Donne** X, 186.

57. Ibid., VII, 55. Other examples of Donne's can be found in IX, 299, and IV, 339.

58. **A Century of Sermons** 749.

59. A Sermon Preached at Paul's Crosse, the 25 of November, 1621 . . . (1621) 4.

60. **The Workes of that learned and reverend Divine, John White, Doctor in Divinitie** (1624) 13. From a Paul's Cross Sermon delivered 24 March, 1615.

61. **XCVI Sermons** 680. From a Whitsunday sermon preached before the King at Greenwich on 19 May, 1616.

62. **The Sermons** (1616) 175. From the Spittal Sermon "The Pathway to Perfection."

63. **Motives to a Good Life in Ten Sermons** (Oxford, 1657) 52. See 24 for another example. In the fourth sermon on "God's Husbandry" Holyday uses Greek etymology (pp. 97, 103), Latin (97), and Hebrew (103).

64. **XCVI Sermons** 455. From an Easter sermon before king and court, 1612. 1622. Other examples can be found on 36, 46, 77, 200, 404, 635 and 960-961.

142

65. **XCVI Sermons** 455. From a sermon on Ash Wednesday of 1622 preached before the king and court.

66. Cassian, **Collationes** XIV, 8.

67. John 10:5.

68. John 15:7b, 9.

69. **The Works of . . . John Cosin** Vol. I, (Oxford, 1843), **Sermons** 255.

70. **The Workes of Tho: Adams** 1036-1045.

71. Ibid., 656f. Among several allegorical sermons see "Loves Copie" 815; "Eirenopolis: The Citie of Peace," 995-1015, and "Mysticall Bedlam, Or, The World of Mad-Men" which includes a series of nineteen 'characters' from Epicure to Vain-glorious, 478-514.

72. **The Sermons of John Donne** X, 141-142.

73. **A Century of Sermons** 731-741. In similar fashion, the pattern of court preachers, Andrewes, preached the ninth of his Gunpowder sermons before King James and the court on November 5, 1617, from the Benedictus, applying the text first to salvation in Christ, which was evidently Simeon's confession of the messiahship of the infant Jesus but went on to apply it to the king and the nation's temporal salvation from the Gunpowder Plot. (**XCVI Sermons** 983-996.)

74. The Puritan structuring of sermons is analyzed by William Perkins in his influential The Arte of Prophesying contained in the complete **Works** II, 673. Perry Miller has attributed it exclusively to Ramist influence in his **The New England Mind: the seventeenth century** (New York, 1939) 338f. but there are some likenesses to the classical rhetoric of the modern modified kind also.

75. The Westminster **Directory** offers the following triple schema for preachers: "In raising doctrines from the text, his care ought to be, First, that the matter be the truth of God. Secondly, that it be a truth contained in, or grounded on, that text that the hearers may discern how God teacheth it from thence. Thirdly, that he chiefly insist upon those doctrines which are principally intended, and make most for the edification of the hearers." (**Reliquiae Liturgicae,** Bath, England, 1848, Vol. III: **Directory** 37).

Thomas Fuller's earlier style is described by his anonymous biographer thus: "But the main frame of his publique SERMONS, if no wholy, consisted (after some briefe and genuine resolution of the Context and Explication of the Termes, where need required), of Notes, and Observations with much variety and great dexterity drawn immediately from the Text, and naturally and without restraint, issuing or flowing either from the maine body, or from the several parts of it, with some useful Applications annexed thereunto . . . " (**The Life of that Reverend Divine, and Learned Historian Dr. Thomas Fuller,** 1661, 79-80).

76. Thomas Playfere, **The Whole Sermons** (1623) 3. Although the sermon was preached in 1595 it was only published in 1623 posthumously.

77. **XCVI Sermons** 45.

78. The Love of Truth and Peace. A Sermon Preached before the Honourable House of Commons Assembled in Parliament Novemb. 29, 1640, (1641) 5.

79. KAKOURGOI sive Medicastri: Slight Healers of Publick Hurte set forth in a Sermon Preached in St. Pauls Church, London . . . Febr. 28, 1659 (1660) 9-10.

80. See the descriptions of the styles of Cicero and of Seneca on 236 and 975 of **The Oxford Classical Dictionary** 2nd edn., ed. N. G. L. Hammond and H. H. Scullard (1970).

81. See I Cor 1:17: "For Christ sent me not to baptize, but to preach the gospel: not with wisdom of words, lest the Cross of Christ be made of no effect." See also I Cor 2:4.

82. **The Sermons of John Donne** II, 248.

83. Ibid., 315.

84. **Sixty Five Sermons** 83. From the fifth Transfiguration sermon.

85. The Presentment of a Schismaticke (1642) 15. Preached at St. Paul's Cathedral, on 19 June, 1642.

86. A Sermon Preached before the Kings Most Excellent Majestie, in the Cathedrall Church of Durham. (1639) 3. The sermon was preached on May 5, 1639 when King Charles was on his way to Scotland.

87. See for the pointed Senecan style of the Latin Silver Age, Michael Grant, **Greek and Latin Authors, 800 B.C. – A.D. 1000** (New York, 1980) 388.

88. J. Huizinga, **The waning of the Middle Ages** (New York, 1944) 203.

89. Ralph Venning, **Orthodoxe Paradoxes** (5th ed., 1650) 24.

90. The Westminster Assembly's **Shorter Catechism** goes: "What is the true end of man?" and answers: "To glorify God and to enjoy him for ever."

91. G. Puttenham, **The Arte of the English Poesie** (eds. Gladys D. Wilcock and Alice Walker, Cambridge, England, 1936) 225-226.

92. Rosalie L. Colie **Paradoxia Epidemica** (Princeton, N.J., 1956) 22.

93. **Three Sermons preached before the King upon Ier. 26:19** (Oxford, 1637).

94. **Ten Sermons upon Severall Occasions, Preached at Saint Pauls Crosse and elsewhere** (1640) 130-131.

95. Judges 14:14 and 14:18.

96. **Sixty Five Sermons** (1674) 281.

97. **The Collected Sermons of Thomas Fuller, D.D.** (eds. J. E. Bailey and W. E. A. Axon, 2 vols. 1891) I, 198.

98. Quarles, op. cit., Sig. A. 3, defines an emblem as "but a silent Parable" using a pointedly religious term.

99. **Studies in Seventeenth-Century Imagery** (2nd edn., revised and enlarged, Rome, 1964) 17.

100. **Studies in Seventeenth-Century Imagery** 55.

101. **Euphues** (ed. M. W. Croll and R. Clemens, 1916) passim.

102. Rosemary Freeman, **English Emblem Books** (1948) 3-4.

103. The article, referred to by Rosemary Freeman op. cit. is "Quarles and the Emblem Habit" in Dublin Review, vol. 188, Jan. 1931, 80-96.

104. Louis L. Martz's book is **The Poetry of Meditation; a study in English religious literature of the seventeenth century** (New Haven, 1954).

105. Barbara Kiefer Lewalski's book is **Protestant Poetics and the seventeenth century religious lyric** (Princeton, N.J., 1979).

106. Lewalski's **Protestant Poetics** 184f. This was the triple classification adopted by Georgette de Montenay's **Emblèmes ou Devises Chrestiennes** (1571), the first French Protestant book of sacred emblems, and of George Whitney's **A Choice of Emblemes and other Devises** (1586), the first English book of its kind.

107. Playfere, **The Whole Sermons** (1623) 155. Other emblems in Playfere are found on p. 161 " . . . a Crabfish and a Butterflie, with this Mot, Soft pace goes farre" - festina lente warning, 131, and "God be with you," royal sermon of 1604, 54.

108. **The Sermons of Maister Henrie Smith** (1593) 51.

109. Daniel Featley, **Clavis Mystica: A Key opening divers difficult and mysterious texts of Holy Scripture, handled in Seventy Sermons** (1636) 290. He rather improbably derives the humility of the violet etymologically 'ab humo' from the earth.

110. Hacket, **A Century of Sermons** (1675) 199.

111. Joan Webber, **Contrary Music. The Prose Style of John Donne** (Madison, Wisconsin, 1963), 81. The balances emblem image is explicit in III, 95; it is implicit in IX, 135 and IX, 137.

112. **The Sermons of John Donne** (eds. Potter and Simpson) III, 95.

113. Ibid., VIII, sermon 1; and VI, sermon 3.

114. Ibid., V, 298.

115. Ibid., V, 374.

116. Ibid., I, 293.

117. Ibid., III, 96-97.

118. **A Century of Sermons,** 1000.

119. **Three Sermons upon the Passion, Resurrection and Ascension of our Saviour, preached at Oxford** (1626) 55, 65-66.

120. The signs of the assurance of election will be found in Downame's **Christian Warfare** 235-247.

121. A Sermon of Assurance, Foureteene yeares ago Preached in Cambridge, since in other Places. Now by the importunity of Friends exposed to publike view. (1647). It was first preached in St. Benet's, Cambridge, later at St. Clement's, London, where Fuller was Lecturer. It was reprinted in **The Collected Sermons of Thomas Fuller, D.D.** (eds. J. E. Bailey and W. E. A. Axon, 2 vols., 1897) and the reference for the quotation is I, 475.

122. For example, how angels recognize one another, whether they were created before the world or after it, if they age or not, and what their hierarchical orders are. These are discussed in **The Sermons of John Donne** (eds. Potter and Simpson) VIII, Sermon I, 94f., and in VI Sermon 3, 331f. among other places.

123. Deliverance from the Grave (1617). This was a Spittal sermon preached on March 28, 1627.

124. Hacket, **A Century of Sermons,** biographical introduction, xiii.

125. **XCVI Sermons** 31. From a sermon preached at St. Giles, Cripplegate, London, in 1592 on the Second Commandment.

126. See also **XCVI Sermons** 31.

127. The full title is **Increase and Multiply. Arts-of-Discourse Procedure in the Preaching of Donne** (Chapel Hill, North Carolina, 1976) 106f.

128. Donne's **Essays in Divinity** (ed. E. M. Simpson. Oxford, 1952) 91.

129. **The Sermons of John Donne** IX, Sermon 2.

130. **An Exposition of the Lords Prayer** (1628) 361.

131. **The Sermons of John Donne** II, 243.

132. **A Century of Sermons** 93. This is from Hacket's tenth sermon on the Incarnation.

133. **The Sermons of John Donne** VI, 212.

134. Ibid., V, 199-200.

135. See H. Davies, **Worship and Theology in England** (5 Vols, Princeton University Press, 1961-1975) II, Chapter vi, 215-252, "Calendary Conflicts, Holy Days or Holidays." See also Howard Happ "Calendary Conflicts in Renaissance England," Ph.D. dissertation, Princeton University, 1974, for a more comprehensive study of the same topic.

136. John's Gospel 13:3: "Jesus knowing that the Father had given all things into his hands and that he was come from God, and went to God, took a towel and girded himself" to wash the feet of the disciples.

137. R. Chamberlain's collection of **Conceits, Clinches, Flashes and Whimsies newly studied** (1639) No. 38. The reference to this volume I owe to Paul Zall of California State University at Los Angeles.

138. See Edmund Morgan, **Visible Saints; the history of an idea.** (New York, 1963). See also Winton Udell Solberg, **Redeem the time: the Puritan Sabbath in early America** (Cambridge, Mass., 1977).

139. **Two Puritan Diaries, by Richard Rogers and Samuel Ward** (ed. with an introduction by M. M. Knappen, Chicago, 1933).

140. See Christopher Hill, **Society and Puritanism in pre-Revolutionary England** (2nd edn., New York, 1967) 160f., for proof that the establishment preferred the common man to disport himself at a tavern than to attend a Puritan religious lecture as shown by the case of the Somerset ales.

141. See Isabel M. Calder, ed. **The Activities of the Puritan faction of the Church of England, 1625-1633.** (1957), and John D. Eusden, **Puritans, lawyers and politics in early seventeenth century England,** (New Haven, 1958).

142. For Puritan Sermons, see William Haller, **The rise of Puritanism; or The Way to the New Jerusalem as set forth in pulpit and press, from . . . 1570-1643** (New York, 1938). For 'political' sermons see John F. Wilson, **Pulpit in Parliament** (Princeton, N.J., 1969). For exegesis, see J. S. Coolidge, **The Pauline Renaissance in England: Puritanism and the Bible** (Oxford, 1970).

143. Andrewes' sermons which follow this pattern of interruption of the sermon by a bidding prayer are Nos. 2 and 3. Heylyn and Basire also did so on rare occasions. See **The Works of the Right Reverend Father-in-God, John Cosin, Lord Bishop of Durham** (Vol. I **Sermons**, Oxford 1843), Introduction, vii.

144. **The Works of . . . John Cosin** 44.

145. **I Launch at Paradise** (1964) 173.

146. See Janel Mueller, **Prebend Sermons** (Cambridge, Mass., 1971).

147. Izaak Walton's **Life of Donne** (1658) 75.

148. **The Sermons of John Donne** IX, Sermon 5, lines 74-76, as noted by J. S. Chamberlin in **Increase and Multiply** 17.

149. Smith at least simplifies with sabbatarianism. See **The Sermons** (1593) 841:

> . . . he which will not allowe men to prophane the Saboth, but saith, that Cardes & dice, & stage plaies & Mai-games, & May poales, & May-fooles, and Morris-dauncers are vanitie, is a pratler, a disturber, an Arch-pustan, but the lawe which the Iewes had to kill Christ, the reason is, because men cannot be controlled of their pleasures.

150. **The Workes of Tho: Adams.**

151. We have only part of Cosin's sermons including those he delivered in Paris during the Commonwealth and Protectorate, coram Duce Iacobo. We can confidently guess this distinguished liturgiologist would have continued to preach liturgical sermons.

PORTRAIT OF A PEOPLE
Horace Bushnell's Hartford Congregation

Robert L. Edwards

My long-time friend and former parishioner Robert Paul observed in one of his first books that the work of the great nineteenth century theologian and preacher, Horace Bushnell of Hartford, Connecticut, had a fundamentally pastoral rather than metaphysical or academic origin. In his **The Atonement and the Sacraments** Paul devotes a number of pages to Bushnell's career, comparing it to that of his contemporary counterpart on the English scene, McLeod Campbell. Like Campbell, he writes, Bushnell came at his theological reflections "from the imperative claims of the pastoral ministry," and "was essentially an evangelist and a pastor." [1]

Biographers of Bushnell and general church historians, from Mary Bushnell Cheney in 1880 to Sydney E. Ahlstrom or Robert T. Handy in the 1970's, either have hinted at this point or made it quite explicitly--Bushnell used to say it about himself. Urged to accept the presidency of the College (now University) of California in 1856, he demurred and then declined, candidly explaining to the trustees, "I am a Christian pastor." [2]

For our day Paul has stated the insight as clearly as any and earlier than most, and his claim leads to a further historical question. If Bushnell was basically a pastor, who were the people whom he served? Bushnell himself we may well know, at least to some degree. But what of the other half of the partnership? What manner of Christian folk sat in the pews of the North Congregational Church, the only one Bushnell ever had, and heard his memorable sermons on "Every Man's Life a Plan of God," or "Unconscious Influence"? Who were some of the flesh-and-blood believers who bought his books and printed sermons in the bookstores, came to know him as man and friend, and benefited from his one-on-one pastoral care? Research into this side of the Bushnell

149

story can go only so far, given the sources available. [3] But it can go far enough to give us some engaging glimpses of local personalities, and help us see more plainly the primary context of his embattled yet uniquely influential ministry.

As a portrait frame, it may be well to review briefly the beginnings of the North Church and how it was that its people and Bushnell came together. After the less than harmonious founding of the Second, or South Congregational Church in colonial Hartford in 1670, there was a period of more than a century and a half when no new Congregational society was started in the community. The population being relatively stable, there was no urgent need of one. By the 1820's, however, growth began to set in, and the members of the First, or Center, Church were feeling crowded in their Main Street meetinghouse. It was decided in 1823 that there was room for a third Congregational fellowship, and just under a hundred Center Church people set out to establish it. They named it North Church, and, joined by a handful of others, they inaugurated worship in their new building in September of 1824.

Their first minister was a gifted but physically frail poet named Carlos Wilcox. When he left in 1826, the membership called Samuel Spring, Jr., son of a prominent New England family of ministers. Before he entered Andover Seminary, Spring had been a sea captain and was no stranger to facing human tensions. But after six years in Hartford, he found the theological differences among his people too frustrating, and, early in 1833, he left.

Thus it was that the church was again searching for a minister. In a way we cannot trace in detail, the Committee heard that young Bushnell was supplying various Connecticut pulpits, hoping for a call. He was one of Connecticut's own, born in Bantam (near Litchfield) in 1802, and a graduate of Yale in the unusually talented class of 1827. After dabbling in teaching, newspaper reporting, and law, he turned to the ministry and finished his studies at the Yale Divinity School in 1832. In the winter of 1833, he was falling in love, low on funds, and badly needed a steady job. The North Church invited him to preach for a trial period of six Sundays. He proved satisfactory, and in May was formally called and ordained. In neat fashion he became in 1833 the third pastor of the third Congregational society in one of the oldest cities in America. Here he remained for twenty-six years of active ministry, and for more than a decade and a half of a disease-ridden, but highly productive retirement.

Painting in the first brush strokes of a portrait of his North Church people, a word about numbers. By the time Bushnell arrived, the membership had more than doubled as compared with 1824 and stood at 264. By 1842, it had risen to 447, and when Bushnell left in mid-1859 the total was 490. Comparative church statistics before the Civil War are hard to come by. Probably with reasonable accuracy, however, the Hartford <u>Courant</u> for September 6, 1851, claimed the largest Congregational church in the state was in the North (now United) Church on the Green in New Haven, with a roll of 621. It reported further that the largest non-city Congregational fellowship in Connecticut was in Milford, which at that time numbered 540 souls. In this period, admission standards tended to be more exacting than they are today, so that Sunday attendance could frequently be larger than the core membership. But even without that bonus, Bushnell clearly had under his pastoral care a constituency, not of Henry Ward Beecher size (he never was, strictly speaking, a "popular" preacher), but one that as to numbers never lacked strength. Thomas Robbins, himself an experienced pastor, who came to Hartford in 1844 to be librarian of the then shaky Connecticut Historical Society, did not always think highly of Bushnell but fairly often sat as a visitor in the North Church pews. Entries in his famous **Diary** show that on one Sunday after his arrival in the city he found attendance at Bushnell's church, "great," and that on another occasion in the winter of 1852 he was part of "a large congregation," marked by "much religious interest." [4]

Not simply the numbers, but their origins, are worth noting. Socially, some of the old eighteenth-century Hartford names appear, such as Bunce, Goodwin, Olmsted, Pitkin, or Seymour, indicative of the many members who were of long-standing local background. Geographically, however, a surprising fraction came from beyond the Hartford area, reflecting a United States population beginning in a new way to be on the move from country to city, South to North, and from East to West and back. During Bushnell's tenure, about a quarter of his constituents were arrivals from afar--in 1836, as many as 29 percent, and, in 1859, 23 percent. They hailed from as far south as Alabama and Georgia, as far west as Kentucky and Illinois, and as far north as Maine and even Canada, from fifteen states in all, at a time (1859) when there were only thirty-three. This was gratifying, but a price was attached. If new members came from a distance, old ones as frequently went! After twenty years on the job, Bushnell remarked with more than a tinge of regret, "I have recommended members enough to the churches of New York and Brooklyn alone to make a respectable congregation. Others are sprinkled over the new world of the West." [5]

Numbers were ample, and from the start they included influential citizens. When Joel Hawes began his ministry at the Center Church in 1817 at a tender age, he felt he was looking down from his pulpit on a gathering of Roman senators, so distinguished and grave did many of his listeners appear. The impression left him anything but comfortable. [6] Bushnell faced a similar scene sixteen years later, and some of the "senators" who gazed critically at the untried minister in the North meetinghouse were the self-same Christian fathers who had caused Hawes such trepidation.

The deacons, for example, of whom there were at first only two: Senior in age and Hartford experience was Enfield native and former Center Church member, Seth Terry, a meticulous, no-nonsense attorney of orthodox Calvinist opinions, who lived to practice law in the city for sixty years. Once, when two talkative women were consulting him on a legal matter, he pointed his finger at them and exclaimed, "Women! Speak low! Slow! One at a time!" It was not too long before he was pointing a respectful, but admonishing, theological finger at his unorthodox new minister. In a careful letter to Bushnell in 1839, he confessed to being "exceedingly alarmed" by the modified views of total depravity and regeneration he had been hearing from his pastor, especially as they affected children. Just how Bushnell handled his disaffected parishioner we do not know, but, seven years later, Terry apparently could stand it no longer and transferred his letter to the South Church. There he promptly became a deacon again. While he remained in the North Church, however, he represented a type that helped make Bushnell's position delicate. [7]

Terry's junior colleague, Amos M. Collins, was also imposing, but had a markedly different temperament. Although by some kind of Christian accommodation they managed to get along for years, he and Terry agreed on almost nothing. Like Bushnell, Collins was a native of Litchfield, where his father had been one of Lyman Beecher's deacons. Unlike his new minister, however, Collins had received a minimum of schooling and while still young went directly into business in Massachusetts. He moved to Hartford in 1819, started from scratch, and by dint of drive and ability, became perhaps the leading wholesale dry goods merchant in the area. Twice in the 1840's, he was Mayor of Hartford, declining a third term, and he occupied a seat on almost every known charitable board in town. Theologically, he had been reared under Calvinist discipline, and he too may have had adjustments to make under the unusual lead of the young Bushnell. But there was a flexibility to his spiritual outlook, and his father's association with Beecher may well have tilted his views toward the slightly more liberal teachings of Yale's Nathaniel W. Taylor. As years went by, Collins supported his controversial minister in season and out. The two men and their families remained fast friends until Collin's death in 1858, and at the funeral Bushnell not only paid tribute to him as the most faithful Christian counsellor a pastor could hope to have, but claimed, "there is almost nothing here [in Hartford] that has not somehow felt his power." [8]

As the North Church grew, the number of deacons was

increased. Among those added was Normand Smith, Sr., another former Center Church personality, who sat under Bushnell's preaching from the first day. Thirty years older than Bushnell, he was a lifelong Hartford resident and in 1794 had opened a small saddlery shop "6 rods north of the State House at the sign of the Mounted Dragoon." With an expanding line of accessories, he developed a highly profitable, nationwide clientele, including markets in the antebellum South. So well did he build the business that nearly two centuries later, though on a smaller scale, it is still riding high. [9] An additional deacon close to Bushnell was Thomas Steele, a jeweler and watchmaker, and, yet another, Christopher Columbus Lyman, a self-effacing but eventually wealthy Hartford Fire Insurance Company official with musical tastes and a flair for composing hymn tunes. [10]

Mention of such key men is enough to indicate the mercantile cast of Bushnell's congregation. On any Sunday, it was peopled with manufacturers, bankers, commission merchants, insurance executives, and retailers, and with such figures Bushnell had frequent pastoral contact during the week. Charles Boswell was president of the Farmers' and Mechanics' Bank, and Oliver G. Terry headed the Aetna Bank. Silas Smith was engaged in the New England Shirt Manufactory, and Joseph Terry became the chief executive of the Hartford Bridge Company. Austin Dunham led a cotton commission house, and James C. Walkley was president of the Charter Oak Insurance Company.

Along with these captains of commerce was a sizeable company of shopkeepers and artisans. George Burnham dealt in artist materials, and DeWitt Pond in musical supplies. Zenas Rider sold ship timber. Drayton Hillyer was one of at least three grocers, and Lucius Hunt operated one of Bushnell's favorite bookstores. Arnold Holt sold shoes, and Alvan Hubbard, wood. Ira W. Ford was an auctioneer. Edward S. Cleveland was a joiner, Jason Howe, a machinist, and Simeon Stillman, a mason.

At these different levels, business representation was strong, but it was not typical of the whole membership. On any Sunday morning, professional men also entered the North Church doors in some numbers. Teachers were among them, and some of considerable importance. John P. Brace in the 1830's and 1840's was head of the Hartford Female Seminary, succeeding Catherine Beecher, to whom he was related by marriage. [11] Samuel Porter with his ever-friendly ear trumpet was a pioneer teacher at the American School for the Deaf. He was another of the remarkable offspring of Bushnell's long-time friend and backer, Noah Porter of Farmington. [12] As of 1859 there were seven lawyers, among them Thomas C. Perkins, husband of Mary Beecher. Asa Newton was one of two dentists, and Ebenezer K. Hunt, formerly a Presbyterian from Natchez, Mississippi, was one of at least two physicians.

154

Octavius Jordan, well-known English-born architect, was not himself
a communicant, but his wife was. A handful of ordained ministers
belonged, and a few ministerial wives and widows.

This last raises the matter of North Church women.
From the founding of the parish to the time of Bushnell's departure,
they were in a substantial majority, between 63 and 67 percent.
But as to official leadership, they were voteless and without
power, and few on the distaff side, with their bonnets and rustling
fashions, would have expected to have any. About the closest
they came to administrative position was to be matched with
a small number of men in making annual house-to-house rounds
to raise funds for mission enterprises. A few, but very few, had
identifiable breadwinning occupations, and even these were home-
centered. One pew-holder, Mary L. Steele, ran a boarding house.
Bushnell's unmarried sister-in-law, Elizabeth D. Apthorp, not
a church member, but a regular attendant during the 1850's,
managed in her own home an exclusive school for girls, including
at one time two Americans sent to her from Paris. [13] Most
women parishioners either were married and generally under the
sway of their husbands, or single and living at home with a limited
range of independence or opportunity.

This did not always mean, however, that they were without feelings and opinions. Sometimes these came out in restlessness
in worship. During Bushnell's early years in Hartford, he found
his people often "listless" during church services, which no doubt
meant, as in other churches, that women tapped their feet to
polka rhythms after entering church, while here and there men
read the newspaper if a prayer seemed too long! [14] More than
one North Church woman got up enough courage to vent her
views in a letter. In the summer of 1842 when millenarians were
proclaiming the end of the world was near, "Mrs. B." wrote Bushnell, urging him to re-examine the Bible and focus his ministry
more urgently on the Second Coming. He thanked her for her
friendly frankness, but as to studying the Scriptures more carefully
on this issue, he took her firmly to task. "Why, my dear woman,"
he reminded her, "I have done it with greater care . . . I am confident, than God ever vouchsafed to me in anything else, and I
am as certain as I can be that what you believe so earnestly
is all a delusion." [15]

For all their good works, the women of the church also
exerted social pressure, often of an aspiring, exclusive sort, encouraged by the growing material prosperity of their menfolk, and
the increasing comfort and culture that marked American society.
As men had a wary eye for the most advantageous business connections, women could be choosy about their social circles, even
within the fellowship of faith. Although no egalitarian, Bushnell
considered it a "vice" that some of his flock would have preferred

a more "select" gathering at the Lord's Table. [16] Yet even so sensitive a person as his own daughter, Frances Louisa, thought nothing of critically categorizing church guests at a party as the proper ones, the out-of-place simple souls, "and all the intermediates." She marvelled that her Christian hostess would dare bring together such "a queer combination." [17]

Women suggest the presence of children. Even if they did not, Bushnell himself would. Children were important to him, and his own children all but idolized him as a father. It was over children that his early theological disagreement with Deacon Terry arose, and over children that the first stage of his great controversy began in 1847 with the publication of **Discourses on Christian Nurture**--in its final form his most enduring book.

Names and numbers of children in the North Church family are not easy to dig out. But, whatever Sabbath School programming they had (nothing like what we know now), children were in the pews at adult worship week after week, brought by their parents whose authority in this was beyond challenge. So it was with little Charles H. "Charley" Clark. His family lived across Winthrop Street from the Bushnells, and the Doctor once saved small Charles from drowning. Clark remembered his church experience from about the age of four.

> Sundays I went regularly, because I was taken, to the Old North Church, where I counted the tassels on the pulpit cushion, thirty-nine of them there were-- the thirty-nine articles of the church as far as I knew any--studied the forms and the faces of the deacons, who presented some very interesting contrasts in American citizenship, wondered at the attire of certain old-school gentlemen among them who persisted in wearing swallow-tail coats, furtively calculated the different angles at which several mouths in the choir gave forth their sweetest notes, and went home, as no doubt children do today, with impressions of various things that were not all in the sermon. [18]

In time, Clark came to be the nationally known editor of the Hartford Courant, a director of the Associated Press, and a fellow of the Yale Corporation. He is a reminder that the children and young people of Bushnell's congregation grew to be men and women. Careers were not generally open to women as yet, but a number of the children and young men affected by his preaching and friendship came to be shapers of post-Civil War society in America. Among them were: Charles L. Brace, pioneer philanthropist and a founder of the Children's Aid Society in New York City; Aaron L. Chapin, for thirty-six years first president of Beloit College; Austin C. Dunham, cotton merchant and benefactor of the Sheffield Scientific School at Yale; Thomas K. Beecher, maverick preacher son of Lyman Beecher, who had a unique, forty-six-year ministry at the Park Congregational Church of Elmira, New York; Frederick L. Olmsted, landscape architect and, with his friend, Calvert Vaux, designer of New York's Central Park; and Henry C. Trumbull, influential leader in Christian education in the United States and widely abroad.

Any such roster must also mention young men Bushnell helped prepare for courage and sacrifice on the battlefields of the Civil War. One of them was artillery Lieutenant George Metcalf, a silversmith in civilian life. After two and a half years' service, he was killed in 1864 at Procter's Creek, Virginia. Another was Henry W. Camp, tall, attractive, somewhat introspective son of a teacher at the American Asylum for the Deaf and Dumb, and a Yale oarsman. He had an eventful career in the 10th Regiment, Connecticut Volunteer Infantry, at one point was captured in South Carolina, and eventually released. After being promoted to Major, he fell near Richmond in the autumn of 1864 during a brave charge that left half his ninety men sprawled in death. Bushnell had known Camp intimately since childhood and deeply lamented his loss. "He died," he wrote, "with his high bright future shut up in him." [19]

These were some of the Doctor's successes. His congregation, however, was far from problem-free. The common quota of human failings and struggles, pains and defeats was there, sometimes necessitating disciplinary measures long gone from our mainline churches. Bushnell was scarcely settled in his strenuous parish before he had to cope with the case of "Sister Dodge" (Mrs. Clarissa), an early member of the church and by 1834 a widow. That year the deacons accused her of keeping "a house of ill fame," despite repeated warnings that she was subjecting the North Church to "reproach and scandal." The rumors she admitted, but the truth of them she steadfastly denied. After more than a year of "tenderly and affectionately" pressing her to mend her ways and clean up her establishment, including a formal rebuke by Bushnell in the face of a church meeting, she failed to satisfy the membership, and one June day in 1836 found herself excommunicated. The church "catalogue" for 1839 shows that for unknown reasons Catherine Kelly and Sylvanus Jaggar, probably a spar-maker, recently had suffered the same fate. [20]

These more difficult souls were more than outnumbered by those devoted enough, but beset by all manner of "slings and arrows." Mental illness is no modern invention. References to "morbidity" and depression abound in accounts of nineteenth-century lives. A Case among Bushnell's people was Sophia A. Root. She had grown up in the North Church and professed her Christian faith in 1848. But she became too unstable and withdrawn to manage socially, and she needed frequent special support. When Bushnell was in California in 1856, Mrs. Bushnell undertook to do some pastoral calling in his place. One day she visited some of the more modest church members across the Connecticut River in the East Hartford meadow. "Here I found some widows," she reported to her teenage daughter Mary, "one living entirely alone in her home, no company but Christ . . . One, worse than widows, had been separated 49 [sic] years from a drunken husband, bearing still in her body the marks of his abuse; [and] one younger woman dying with consumption." [21]

A North Church communicant who meant much to Bushnell throughout his Hartford years was Thomas Winship. By trade a shoemaker, Winship grew prematurely hard of hearing and could catch almost nothing from a sermon. Nonetheless, he was faithfully in his pew, closely attentive with a "luminous, eager, listening expression" that Bushnell found encouraging as he preached. Winship had a daughter Mary who went from recurring illnesses to permanent invalidism, and hardly left her bed for nine years. With a commitment typical of his pastoral style, Bushnell made a point of calling on her Monday mornings when he was not away on travels or out-of-town on church business. One Monday when she was unable to stand she had herself placed in a chair, insisting she "knew he would come." And he did. [22]

Finer lines could be painted in, but such in broad brush were the people who made up the congregation that worshipped, governed and served from the Georgian-design North Church in pre-Civil War Hartford: the leaders and the led, the merchants, artisans, and professionals, the women and children, the strong and the weak, the fortunate and the inexplicably burdened. Individually and together they worked out their Christian lives in a dynamic city that tripled in population (from about 10,000 to 30,000) during the years of Bushnell's active ministry. [23]

As we look back on them, they prompt at least two observations. For one thing it is clear they were not an unusual assembly of the spiritually elite, somehow drawn out of the nineteenth century mainstream to appreciate and enable the rare kind of ministry Bushnell had to offer. They were the mainstream, in their variety and responses typical of an almost exploding, urbanized, middle class New England, economically optimistic and aggressive, politically involved but cautious, socially self-conscious climbers, who at their best were paternalistically kind to the disadvantaged--though often unashamedly racist--and religiously earnest. They were not noticeably different from the membership of the two older Congregational churches in the city, and must have been much like scores of metropolitan Congregational and Presbyterian fellowships elsewhere in this period.

The second observation is that just because they were
so nearly typical, the stage was set from the start for some sort
of exceptional interaction between them and Bushnell's original
brand of apostolate. He, too, of course, was in large measure
a post-Puritan New Englander, bone of its bone and son of its
most deeply intrenched traditions. Even when he was being assailed
as a heretic he saw himself as more truly conservative than his
critics. Yet it is also the case that from his seminary days he
had been different. Habitually he saw things from unconventional
perspectives, unwilling and likely unable to fit the regulation
mold. [24]

What came of this encounter is oft-told history, but
it may not be amiss to review it. The easier half to describe
is Bushnell's impact on his people. They themselves were not
unusual, but what he did with them was highly unusual. In 1833
he undertook to shepherd a flock that was largely orthodox in
its beliefs, whether leaning toward highly conservative Bennet
Tyler or moderately liberal Nathaniel W. Taylor. In 1859 he bequeathed to his successor a people open to, and generally accepting
of, a radical new understanding of Christian conversion and nurture;
a view of the Trinity that remained forthrightly trinitarian, but
was much more imaginatively believable; a recognition of many
aspects of the new science that still left the supernatural in
supreme place; and a knowledge of God that exalted his magnifi-
cence and his demands, but made his love and "tenderness" (a
favorite word with Bushnell) more ultimate than his terrifying
judgment.

All this was achieved against heavy odds in an era when
theological change came hard, and clergy and laity alike were
prone to fight with feeling over fine points of faith. So sharp
was the controversy Bushnell raised that his North Church congregation was all but isolated, their minister unwelcome in neighboring
pulpits, the Association of Ministers to which he belonged split
on his account, and the church's own ties with the North Consociation of Hartford County altogether broken. This is to make no
mention of the stigma that attached to any connection with Bushnell's ideas, a reproach that extended far beyond Congregational
circles. As late as 1864, when the peak of controversy had long
passed, the mother of the celebrated Episcopal preacher and
bishop Phillips Brooks cautioned him, indeed more than cautioned
him, against having anything to do with Bushnell. "I would rather
never have you preach Christ's blessed gospel," she wrote, "than
wickedly pervert it as Bushnell does." [25]

Yet, under this heavy pressure the North Church did
not buckle. Year after trying year, and especially from 1849
to 1854 when matters were at their worst, the merchant and
lawyer, the teacher and tailor, the jeweller and joiner loyally

stood by their unpopular minister. There was no exodus to other local churches, and such records as exist prove Bushnell's membership increased steadily. [26] Only three complaints from disgruntled parishioners would have been enough to start him toward the bar of formal ecclesiastical judgment. But those three votes were never found. The results of the turmoil radiated beyond Connecticut and even New England. The heart of Bushnell's accomplishment, however was right at home among his own people. The Hartford Central Association of Ministers played a valiant role. But without the pastoral foundation little else could have stood. [27]

When it comes to the reverse influence, that of Bushnell's people on him, the results are less easy to gauge. Given a relationship that is at all harmonious and fruitful, any Christian congregation probably does more for its minister than it knows, and likely more than a minister can be aware of. During his tenure in Hartford Bushnell grew greatly in faith and power. One can only surmise how much of this came from constant contact with his slice-of-life constituency, but a strong if quiet influence certainly was there.

There are signs of it in his writings. We have it in his own words that when he set about producing his manifesto on Christian nurture he was moved not simply by educational theory, but by the problems of puzzled parents in his pews. Many of them were baffled by "intractable" religious behavior in the younger generation, and Bushnell himself was troubled by adolescents he personally knew who had almost been lost to the church by well-intended but harsh Christian upbringing. [28] As he labored on **Nature and the Supernatural** he was trying to counter the Christian naturalism of his Boston friend Theodore Parker. But along with that he was seeking to put ground under the feet of his own people in Hartford, floundering as they were over miracles and natural law when geology and chemistry were almost daily announcing new things, and mechanical invention was harnessing the powers of an allegedly "fallen" nature to the dazzling improvement of material life. Bushnell did his major work on the atonement after he retired, but it is hard to doubt that as he wrote **Vicarious Sacrifice** and its sequel he had much in mind parishioners he once served, and still saw, who were baffled by extreme orthodox interpretations of the Cross.

In considering the effect of Bushnell's people on his ministry, the query sometimes surfaces as to whether the mercantile element in his church was so weighty that on social issues he virtually "sold out" to their conservative desires. The question is complex and needs fuller treatment than can be given here. It might be suggested, however, that everything we know of Horace Bushnell points to a figure too fearless and independent to do much selling out to anybody! Let it also be proposed that as to dealing with business pressures, surrender on Bushnell's part was not quite the central problem. He was well aware of Gospel warnings against being taken in by the riches of this world. Often he preached on that to his money-loving merchants. But victim of the myths of his age or not, he also, quite on his own, shared the optimism of the business community, and had it as an article of faith that commercial prosperity could be used as a vehicle for the Kingdom. When Hartford business hopes were in danger of being dashed, as they were more than once in his day, it was Bushnell who pumped new courage into fainting mercantile hearts, not they who were busy trying to twist his thinking their way. One has only to read his 1847 "Prosperity Our Duty," or his "Weekday Sermon to the Business Men of Hartford" ten years later, to catch something of his confidence in what commercial expansion could and should do to promote Christian values.

Inevitably an even more sensitive issue between him and his flock was slavery. Over the decades the North Church people had developed something of a network of connections with the slaveholding South. As we have seen, a number of members were engaged in profitable business there. Bushnell himself had travelled there and had personal friends in southern states. From time to time southern men came North to marry North Church women, and Bushnell officiated. There were those in his pews who came from southern churches, and more than once he gave letters to individuals and families who left Hartford to join congregations in such states as Georgia, South Carolina or Alabama. [29] Apart from any innate conservative leanings, these ties meant his parishioners were generally nervous about anything like abolitionism, and Bushnell well knew it.

Unquestionably influenced by this, he may not have been the passionate anti-slavery prophet we would wish to find, but neither was he always silent. It is only fair to recall that no uneasiness about congregational backlash deterred him from his controversial 1839 "Discourse on the Slavery Question," or from his gloves-off attack on Henry Clay--mainly on anti-slavery grounds--in a Whiggish North Church during the Presidential campaign of 1844. The latter pronouncement came within a hair of costing him his pulpit, and probably would have had he not determined not to let himself be "kicked out" (Bushnell's words), and talked back uncompromisingly but tactfully to his opponents. [30] After this he was less outspoken publicly for many years. But even then he was picking up personal acquaintances with a handful of Hartford blacks when few northern whites were willing to get that close. He began expressing high views of the coming significance of their race, some of them strikingly similar to paragraphs in Harriet Beecher Stowe's **Uncle Tom's Cabin**. By one of God's "grand inversions" of history, Bushnell predicted, powerless blacks would yet become "the topstone" of earth's most righteous peace and most inspired religion. "They are now the true Nazarenes and Galileans of the world," he said. "They are humble enough, and they know how to believe." [31] This was far from a full liberation message, but not many of his North Church members would have risked saying nearly that much.

As between Bushnell and his people adjustment took time. For some years he was not sure how long he wished to stay in Hartford, and with his new views, his young abrasiveness and his early tendency to over-confidence, there were those who wondered how long he should. But gradually respect developed, then acceptance, and finally deepening affection. In the spring of 1851, when theological attacks were beating on Bushnell unmercifully, he withdrew to the refuge of his own parish. From there he wrote his younger minister friend and protégé, Henry M. Goodwin in Illinois, that he was finding a new sense of "the usefulness of my ministry to my own flock." Then with evident relief and gratitude he added, "these know me and love me." [32] It was so, and the attachment by then was mutual.

The Yankee Christian members of the North Church congregation little knew what they were getting when Bushnell came to them, nor did he see clearly the way he would go. As it turned out, he led his people along paths that were neither smooth nor conventional, but as best they could they went with him, and discovered they had chosen better than they knew. In the happy idiom of Old World philosopher Miguel de Unamuno, he may have denied them peace, but he gave them a touch of glory. For loyalty and contribution on both sides, the relationship between them and their pastor-theologian is a bright page in New England church history.

NOTES

1. Robert S. Paul, **The Atonement and the Sacraments:** The Relation of the Atonement to the Sacraments of Baptism and the Lord's Supper (New York and Nashville: Abingdon, 1960) 150, 158.

2. Mary Bushnell Cheney, **Life and Letters of Horace Bushnell** (New York: Harper, 1880) 385.

3. I have relied heavily on triennial membership lists ("catalogues" as they were called) of the North Church for 1832, 1836, 1839, 1842, and 1859, Connecticut State Library, Hartford, and on annual volumes of Elihu Geer's **Hartford City Directories.** Geer became a member of Bushnell's church.

4. Increase N. Tarbox, ed., **Diary of Thomas Robbins, D.D., 1796–1854,** 2 vols. (Boston: Beacon Press, 1887) 2: 753, 1036. Entries were for October 6, 1844, and February 15, 1852.

5. Horace Bushnell, **A Commemorative Discourse . . .** May 22, 1853 (Hartford: Elihu Geer, 1853) 10.

6. Edward A. Lawrence, **The Life of Reverend Joel Hawes, D.D.** (Hartford: Hamersley, 1871) 55.

7. Stephen Terry, **Notes of Terry Families in the United States of America . . .** (Hartford: Case, Lockwood and Brainard, 1887) 38; James Trumbull, ed., **Memorial History of Hartford County, Connecticut, 1663–1884** (Boston, 1887) 1:127; Cheney, **Bushnell** 92–93; Records of the South Congregational Church, Hartford, Connecticut State Library.

8. Clarence L. Collens, **Collins Memorial**, 1959, 3–22; Trumbull, **Hartford County,** 1:669–70.

9. Hartford Courant, March 14, 1982.

10. Lyman Coleman, **Genealogy of the Lyman Family in Great Britain and America . . .** (Albany, New York: Munsell, 1872), 261, 288; **Encyclopaedia of Connecticut Biography** (New York: American Historical Society, 1917) 65–66; Hartford **Courant,** May 30, 1883, p. 2.

11. Mary Hewitt Mitchell, "John Pierce Brace," **Dictionary of American Biography** 2:541.

12. Precival Hall, "Samuel Porter," **Dictionary of American Biography,** 15:102–3.

13. Elizabeth D. Apthorp to Mary A. Bushnell, November 20, 1859. Bushnell papers in possession of Mr. and Mrs. Horace B. Learned, Avon, Connecticut.

14. Bushnell, **Twentieth Anniversary** 9; Barbara M. Cross, **Horace Bushnell: Minister to a Changing America** (Chicago: University of Chicago Press, 1958) 70.

15. Cheney, **Bushnell** 99–100.

16. Horace Bushnell, **Moral Uses of Dark Things** (New York: Scribner's, 1881) 226.

17. Frances L. Bushnell to Mary A Bushnell, November 13, 1859. Learned Papers.

18. Charles H. Clark, "Bushnell the Citizen," **Bushnell Centenary: Minutes of the General Association of Connecticut . . . Hartford, June 17, 18, 1902** (Hartford: Case, Lockwood and Brainard, 1902) 59.

19. **Record of Service of Connecticut Men in the Army and Navy of the United States During the War of the Rebellion . . .** (Hartford: Case, Lockwood and Brainard, 1889) 100, 398; Hartford Courant, October 21, 22, 1864; and Henry C. Trumbull, **The Knightly Soldier: A Biography of Major Henry Ward Camp** (Boston: Nichols and Noyes, and New York: Felt, 1865) 20, 310-318.

20. North Church Records, Connecticut State Library, Hartford, 1:61-77 passim; **1828 Hartford City Directory** (Ariel Ensign) 36, lists "Salvenus Jagar" as a "Pump, Block & Spar Maker."

21. Mary A. Bushnell to Mary Bushnell, November 4, 1856. Learned Papers.

22. Cheney, **Bushnell** 290.

23. **Connecticut Annual Register . . . for 1835,** and **1852** (Hartford: Huntington, and Brown and Gross) 65, 120.

24. Cheney, **Bushnell** 62.

25. Raymond W. Albright, **Focus on Infinity: A Life of Phillips Brooks** (New York: Macmillan, 1961) 106.

26. North Church Records, 1:180-99.

27. Edwin P. Parker, **The Hartford Central Association and the Bushnell Controversy** (Hartford: Case, Lockwood and Brainard, 1896) passim.

28. Horace Bushnell, **Views of Christian Nurture and of Subjects Adjacent Thereto** (1847). Facsimile reproduction with an Introduction by Phillip B. Eppard (Delmar, New York: Scholars' Facsimiles and Reprints, 1975) 6, 12-13. Bushnell here cites a case, "a fact and not a fancy."

29. North Church Records, passim. Prior to the Civil War Bushnell made journeys to North Carolina in 1845, and to Georgia and South Carolina in connection with his trip to Cuba in search of health in 1855.

30. Recollections of the Rev. Nathaniel H. Eggleston, **Supplements to the Connecticut Courant for the Year 1880 . . .** (Hartford: Hawley, Goodrich, 1880) 157.

31. Horace Bushnell, **Nature and the Supernatural, as Together Constituting One System of God** (London: Dickinson, 1887 edition) 341-44; and **Moral Uses** 315. Compare Harriet Beecher Stowe, **Uncle Tom's Cabin,** with an Afterword by John William Ward (New American Library, 1966) 197.

32. Cheney, **Bushnell** 248.

LEADING A HORSE TO WATER

Reflections on Church Union Conversations in Canada

John Webster Grant

In 1943 the general synod of the Church of England in Canada, wishing to mark its jubilee by taking some significant step forward, offered to meet "in conference and prayer with representatives of any Christian communion which shares its hopes and aspirations for a united Christendom." [1] The most significant result of this invitation was the initiation of conversations with the United Church of Canada, joined in 1969 by the Christian Church (Disciples of Christ) in Canada, that issued in 1972 in the publication of Plan of Union for consideration by the three churches. This promising train of events was aborted only three years later. On 4 February 1975 the House of Bishops of what had now become the Anglican Church of Canada, while affirming their "primary and deep commitment to the Unity of the Body of Christ," pronounced the plan "in its present form" unacceptable and held out little encouragement for "a successful outcome of a further revision process." [2] The Anglican general synod, meeting in the following June, reaffirmed its "commitment to the achievement of union" but cast similar doubt upon the existing negotiations. [3] Later that year, after hints that such a move would be welcome, the executive of the general council of the United Church offered the Anglicans a moratorium on union negotiations that was quickly accepted. [4] There the matter rests today. In conversation someone may occasionally wonder whether the project will eventually be revived, but the possibility of an imminent resumption of conversation is simply not discussed.

Although the sequence from Anglican initiative to Anglican withdrawal will be familiar to anyone who has followed the course of parallel movements elsewhere, Canada seemed an unusually favorable locale for the effort. Canadians have contributed relatively little to the formation of the ideal of union, but the necessity of coping with a formidable home missionary situation and the desire to shore up a fragile national identity have made them singularly receptive to it. [5] They set the pace in consolidation within denominational families, almost invariably bringing together particular Presbyterian and Methodist fragments in advance of corresponding unions elsewhere. By 1875 the Presbyterians and by 1884 the Methodists succeeded in bringing together the great majority of their members into nationally organized churches. Union of Presbyterians, Methodists and Congregationalists to form the United Church of Canada followed in 1925, a half-century before a comparable union in any other first-world country, although as in Australia a large Presbyterian minority stayed out.

Under the impulse of the Lambeth conferences Canadian Anglicans showed an early interest in union. In 1886 the synod of their eastern province appointed a committee to confer with other churches, and in 1889 a cordial meeting with Presbyterian and Methodist representatives took place. [6] It soon became clear, however, that the time was not ripe. The other denominations were not prepared to entertain seriously any suggestion that they should accept the "historic episcopate" and proceeded to union on their own terms. Before doing so, however, they raised again the possibility of Anglican participation, and their invitation was at least taken seriously. After the Lambeth conference of 1920 the Anglicans resumed the initiative, rather to the embarrassment of churches that were in the final stage of their own extremely delicate negotiations. Although these proposals seemed to lead nowhere, they encouraged an assumption that without Anglican participation the process of union in Canada would be incomplete. Shortly before the 1925 union the Disciples of Christ also made known their interest in the possibility of union.

After a long pause during which the United Church tested its new structures and all churches struggled to maintain services throughout the depression, the timing of the renewed Anglican initiative of 1943 seemed propitious. Plans for the Canadian and World Councils of Churches were well advanced, and a shortage of clergy due to wartime exigencies added a note of local urgency. The first fruit of conversations with the United Church was a proposal, put forward in September 1946, for the provision of a "mutually acceptable ministry" by the simple device of offering ministers of either church the opportunity of ordination by the other. [7] This procedure was based on the premise that the two ministries were "parallel to one another rather than identical", and was coupled with the assurance that "in neither case is any man denying the reality of the Ministry he has already received and exercised." [8] In practical terms it promised to meet the immediate need for joint ministries in burgeoning industrial communities. Despite these attractions the scheme soon died a natural death, striking most members of both churches as merely a transparent device for conveying episcopal ordination to United Church ministers. Conversations continued over the next decade, but with so little result that in 1958 the United Church general council asked the Anglicans whether they were seriously interested in continuing them. [9]

Mutual reassurance ushered in a period of more intense effort. A study entitled **Growth in Understanding** was issued, and a "League of Prayer for Christian Unity" launched. Newly appointed committees of ten from each church approached their task with an unaccustomed sense of urgency, although from the perspective of the present one is startled to note that only one of them was lay and none female. [10] By the early 1960's, as the Second Vatican Council revealed unexpected possibilities of openness in the Roman Catholic Church, the ecumenical tide was flowing and the "tens" were aware of mounting pressure to show results. Rising expectations seemed to solve none of their problems, however, and after each meeting the face of a colleague who was a member throughout its deliberations betrayed distinct disappointment. After a weekend session late in 1964, however, his countenance was noticeably brighter and he was speaking in terms of an unexpected "breakthrough" that could only be regarded as the work of the Holy Spirit. By 1 June 1965 the collaborating committees were able to issue a document entitled The Principles of Union between the Anglican Church of Canada and The United Church of Canada that was intended, in the words of its introduction, "to provide a sufficient basis for the two Churches to set about preparing concrete and detailed plans under the direction of the recommended commissions." [11]

The Principles of Union consist of two main sections. In "Principles of Faith and Order" the committees set forth the main elements of the faith as confessed by the two churches, and recommended acceptance of "the threefold ministry of Bishops, Presbyters, and Deacons in some constitutional form and with the same freedom of interpretation that is now permitted within the Anglican Church." [12] In "Principles of Organizational Union", besides acknowledging both ordained and lay ministries and providing for several levels of government, they made what was probably their key recommendation:

> The Acts of Union and Unification of Ministries shall be undertaken in the faith that God will act as he wills to establish this united Church and its ministry in Canada. It is our intention to enter into a new and unprecedented relationship with one another, under God the Author, Giver and Guide. We shall therefore place our ministries in his hands without question so that he may overcome what is inadequate and supply what is needed by us through the affirmations of faith and prayer and through the laying on of hands. [13]

Members of the committees tended in conversation to single out as decisive factors leading to this breakthrough the dawning recognition that their task was "to bring into being, not a merger of two existing ecclesiastical bodies, but rather a new embodiment of the One Church of God" [14] and their acceptance of the legitimacy of ambiguity on issues on which complete unanimity has never prevailed even within existing churches. A reading of their minutes suggests that agreement followed fairly quickly when, at the request of the House of Bishops and Executive Council of the Anglican Church, they turned their attention from learned papers on points of difference to the formulation of an actual proposal for union. They were also assisted by a Toronto Faith and Order study on the distinction between order and organization in the church, and the receipt late in 1964 of a plan intended for publication by the Anglican Diocese of Huron and the London Conference of the United Church may have prodded them to more intensive effort.

The immediate response to the Principles was overwhelmingly positive. The general synod of the Anglican Church, meeting that autumn, approved them almost unanimously after an extended debate. The general council of the United Church, which met only in the following year, also accepted them with virtually no dissent as a basis for further action. The churches proceeded to appoint a general commission along with special commissions on doctrine, liturgy, constitution, and law, as recommended by the Principles, and a special commission on "The Church and the World" was authorized at the first meeting of the general commission. Other churches were invited to send observer-consultants, to which were later added representatives of theological students and youth observers. Each church appointed an executive commissioner, and the two worked closely together. The first meeting of the general commission on 1 March 1967 marks the point at which the writer ceased to be a sympathetic observer of the process and became an active participant. For several years he chaired its executive committee, later presiding over the committee responsible for drafting a plan of union. From this point in the narrative the occasional use of the first person singular pronoun seems warranted, both to avoid artificiality and to prevent the concealment of an inevitable bias. [15]

From several points of view the work of the commissions was more successful than anyone could have dared to hope. For five years they labored together assiduously and, except on rare occasions, amicably. The general commission enjoyed such good rapport with its observer-consultants that it soon decided to invite other churches that had shown signs of significant interest to become full partners in the conversation. The decision of the Roman Catholic Church that it was unable to accept the invitation which came as no surprise, was overbalanced by the information that the bishops of Canada had taken it seriously enough to devote a full day to the formulation of their regrets. The Christian Church (Disciples of Christ) in Canada accepted the invitation in 1969 and took its place in the negotiations early in 1970. Despite the complications involved in dealing with the particular concerns of an additional partner, the general commission was able by November 1972 to agree unanimously on a document entitled simply Plan of Union for presentation to the churches.

Plan of Union was not born without struggle. Initially the task of the commissions had been expected to be fairly modest. The Principles contained solutions to the thorny problems that had hitherto made union unattainable. Now the doctrinal and constitutional commissions would put flesh on the bones, the liturgical commission would construct essential services of worship incorporating the agreed rationale of unification, and the legal commission would devise ways and means of carrying through the necessary formalities. If such was the expectation, it proved to be altogether unrealistic. The commissions were large--forty-five eventually on the general commission alone--and most of the members were new to the task. It was inevitable that every issue should be threshed again and that some should be threshed out practically de novo. The special commission on the church and the world, in particular, saw its mandate as bringing forward issues of mission and justice that had found no place in the Principles. There were always members on hand in the commissions to recall us to agreements embodied in the Principles, but they did not always heed their own advice.

Neither was it easy to establish the mutual trust that comes only with time and a sense of common commitment. In 1967 members of different denominations were not on the terms of easy familiarity that can usually be assumed today. At the first session of the general commission Anglican and United Church representatives could easily be distinguished as they sat in safely segregated rows, and the formality of posing for a group picture did little to break the ice. One could not even assume the enthusiasm of all members for the cause, for there had been a deliberate effort to ensure that the commissions would represent a broad spectrum of opinion. Carmino J. de Catanzaro, the most prominent member of an Anglican group opposing union known as the Council for the Faith, sat on the doctrinal commission throughout its deliberations. There he worked hard and constructively to improve a plan which he knew he could never conscientiously support. Some other members, better disposed toward union, were so forthright in the expression of their opinions as to alarm other commissioners every time they rose to speak.

Despite this heterogeneity of outlook, the commissions

were able to achieve consensus on a wide range of issues. In some surprising cases they seemed to reach agreement without effort, either because old controversies had faded or because the churches were moving independently to similar positions. Many armchair experts had predicted that the remarriage of divorced persons, which the United Church generally countenanced but the Anglican Church did not, would prove an insuperable stumbling-block to union. In 1967, however, the Anglican synod enacted a new canon that permitted remarriage in the case of irremediable marital breakdown, and the issue scarcely surfaced in the conversations. [16] The use of fermented wine or unfermented grape juice in communion caused no ripples either, although one correspondent informed us that the plan was splendid apart from the puzzling oversight of failing to rule out wine and bishops. Even the problem of deciding between assigned and composed prayers, which to many lay people seemed insuperable, had been overtaken by liturgical developments of the twentieth century; the liturgical commission was able to recommend a common shape into which either type of prayer might be inserted. Indeed, the commission took the liberty to use either approach so completely for granted that it was persuaded with difficulty to issue a statement on the subject. A thornier issue was the place that women were to have in the proposed church. At this time they were still not eligible for ordination in the Anglican Church, and the Council for the Faith was determined that they should not be. Through cowardice or foresight the commissions postponed consideration of the issue until the plan was almost ready. By this time the mind of the Anglican Church was changing, and the commissions were able with no more than one or two dissenting votes to approve the admission of women to all offices.

Perhaps the greatest surprise was the lack of disagreement about, or even interest in, arrangements for unifying the ministries of the existing churches. The liturgical commission, which was responsible for drafting the services of inauguration, seemed much more concerned to compose a worthy eucharistic service to contain them. The actual provisions for unification seemed to vary somewhat with each report to the general commission, and each report was accepted with little amendment or debate. The doctrinal commission more than once expressed concern about a lack of explicit indication of what the act of unification was intended to achieve, but neither the liturgical nor the general commission was greatly moved.

Some of the sharpest disagreements bore little relation to denominational lines. A proposal to make the basic local unit a pastoral zone consisting of several worshipping congregations as well as mission projects or "house churches" was referred back to the constitutional commission on its first presentation but later was generally accepted. A further suggestion that each pastoral zone should have a bishop as its chief pastor attracted a few avid supporters both Anglican and United, including the writer. It stood no chance of acceptance, but its rejection may have been a contributing factor to the defection of one of the most prominent Anglican supporters of the union. A proposal to restore the unity of baptism and confirmation, now widely accepted but then novel to many commissioners, was enthusiastically advocated by the theologians of the doctrinal commission but received with scepticism by the pastors and administrators who dominated the general commission. Determining the appropriate number of units of government proved the most chronically contentious issue of all. At least twice the general commission, fearful of an overly structured church, asked the constitutional commission to try to reduce the proposed four tiers of government to three, and each time the constitutional commission insisted that no other arrangement was practicable. Such disagreements, although sometimes deeply felt, at least helped to strengthen a sense of working as a single body rather than as representatives of negotiating denominations.

Some disagreements did follow denominational lines, and not all were resolved to everyone's satisfaction. A persistent bone of contention, rather unexpectedly, was the place of the laity in ordination. United and Disciple commissioners urged that only the laying on of hands by lay representatives would constitute adequate recognition, although at least in the case of the United Church this practice had only recently been introduced. To Anglicans, almost without exception, the proposal seemed a thinly disguised device for downplaying the role of the bishop in ordination. In order to deal with this and several other thorny issues, key members of several commissions were invited late in 1971 to a joint consultation on doctrine. Out of this meeting came several agreements in which each side gave a little in order to make possible a plan with which the other could be reasonably happy. They failed to impress those who did not attend the consultation, however, and by the next meeting of the general commission several of those who did attend had repented or forgotten their previous willingness to compromise.

These less than satisfactory episodes did little to dampen the general sense of satisfaction that greeted the completion of Plan of Union. The final session of the general commission, held in the Queen of Apostles Renewal Centre at Mississauga, Ontario, from 13 to 16 November 1972, stands out as one of the most memorable experiences of my life. It was my responsibility, as chairperson of the drafting committee, to stand before the commission for several days, from early morning until late evening, answering questions and receiving suggestions, and then to meet the committee each night to consider possible revisions. No one could have been more thrilled when at the conclusion, the entire commission, including several prominent members of the House of Bishops, rose to endorse the Plan of Union and to sing the customary doxology.

The Plan of Union, thus launched so jubilantly, was destined for speedy oblivion. The United Church and the Disciples stuck with it, officially at least, despite rumors of increasing dissatisfaction within their ranks. In 1975, however, the general synod of the Anglican Church responded to the bishops' disapproval not only by declaring the plan unacceptable but by pointedly withdrawing its commitment from all but the "Principles of Faith and Order" in the original Principles of Union. The work of the commissions had apparently been a tremendous success, but the union did not take place.

The abrupt termination of the conversations was bitterly disappointing to many, but warning signs had appeared at a much earlier stage. Even before the commissions began to meet, the enthusiasm so evident in 1965 had begun to dissipate. The almost unanimous vote for the Principles by the Anglican general synod that year may well have marked the high point of the entire enterprise. The lapse of a year before the next meeting of the United Church general council provided an opportunity for sober second thought and for the expression of the great variety of opinion that characterizes the United Church. Some commissioners freely expressed reservations about elements of the Principles, and in a successful effort to secure practical unanimity a special committee proposed to accept the Principles as "a working document . . . subject to such revision and addition as may become necessary during the negotiations" rather than "as a sufficient basis of agreement upon which to proceed." [17] The debate was well publicized, and it required several months to persuade Anglican leaders that the United Church was as seriously committed to the Principles as they were. That they were never fully persuaded is suggested by the general synod's reference to Plan of Union in 1975 as "one of the available study documents in our quest for unity." [18] Doubts about United Church intentions had the further effect of delaying the appointment of the commissions, and the assembling of a representative list occupied several additional months. There was to be no striking while the iron was hot.

Members of the commissions and other friends of union spoke to congregational and community groups as opportunity offered and thus had at least some inkling of the public mood. The atmosphere of such meetings was friendly, most of the questions predictable and not too difficult to answer. Noticeable almost from the outset, however, was a tendency to place the most threatening construction on every provision in the plan. United and Disciple members expected bishops in the proposed church to be tyrants, while Anglicans were sure that they would be figure-heads. One would also have supposed, from contrasting denominational reactions, that by the Sunday after union all the prayer books would have vanished from Anglican churches and reappeared in United pew racks. Neither did audiences seem prepared to accept reassurance, for questions one had thought satisfactorily answered had a way of coming up again repeatedly at the same meeting. One questioner, convinced that union would deprive the laity of the parity it enjoyed in the regional and national courts of the United Church, registered blank disbelief when assured that current Anglican practice already provided for lay majorities and that the plan would undoubtedly follow suit.

The questions raised by young people at public meetings, and even more conspicuously by youth observers in the commissions, were of a different and, at first, unexpected kind. They seemed much less interested in the provisions of the plan than in the credibility of the planners. How many of us were lay? female? What was our average age? An obvious answer, which never seemed to be given by those responsible, was that the commissions had been appointed by the existing churches and that the plan ensured that the judicatories of the united church would be more widely representative, although it is doubtful whether it would have satisfied many questioners. In fact great care had been taken to ensure that the commissions would be the most representative bodies of their kind that had ever been assembled, but expectations were changing with remarkable speed even during their short lifespan.

After a time it seemed that we could do nothing right. The inevitable period of silence when the commissions were being appointed and when they addressed preliminary tasks gave rise to a widespread belief that the whole project had quietly been shelved or else that the commissions were preparing a plan that would be forced on the churches without consultation. When the commissions responded by issuing a preliminary draft for general discussion at the earliest possible stage, the complaint became that we were rushing churches that were not ready; there was also a widespread assumption that this draft represented our final thinking and that our minds would be closed to further suggestions. Even a printer's accidental omission of the phrase "Where there is doubt, faith" from a well-known prayer of St. Francis was enough to convince one correspondent of the existence of a deliberate plot to make belief optional.

By the time that the Plan of Union made its public appearance, handsomely designed and bound within a striking azure cover, it was widely said that the general response was one of apathy. This was certainly not the whole truth, but to some extent it was a self-fulfilling diagnosis. A questionnaire sent out by the Anglican Church indicated that union could muster nothing close to three-quarters of each order that was proposed as a requirement for implementation and that less than half of the clergy were in favor. Although this sampling did not adhere to scientific procedures, it gave no comfort to unionists. Even within the membership of the United Church and the Christian Church (Disciples of Christ), where little active opposition manifested itself, there were rumors of widespread indifference. The prognosis of a prominent Anglican ecclesiastic that union had "a snowball's chance in hell" proved, in the event, to be correct.

Among factors leading to the rejection of the Plan of Union, some beyond the control of the planners were important and may have been decisive. The publication of the Principles coincided with a surge of optimism during the later stages of the Second Vatican Council, when traditional barriers among the churches were breaking down with astonishing rapidity and a new flexibility seemed to open up almost limitless possibilities. Even by the time the commissions began their work the public mood had changed perceptibly. Leaders of church and state, under suspicion of representing an invisible but sinister establishment, lost much of the prestige they had enjoyed in the 1950's, authority was admitted as legitimate only as "the people" participated directly in its exercise, and institutions as such were under a cloud. In this climate church union was widely dismissed as, at best, mere "tinkering with structures", and at worst as one more attempt by those in charge to consolidate their power. The new consciousness of the 1960's also introduced a vocabulary, based on direct perception and immediate experience, that made the reasoned logic of the Principles seem stodgy and archaic.

If the radicalism of the late 1960's put a damper on union by deflecting enthusiasm, it was not the radicals who in the end doomed it. Most of them were basically sympathetic to union, and some were genuinely disappointed when it fell through. Serious opposition in the later stages came mainly from people who sensed in union a threat of unwelcome innovation. Some of these were Anglo-catholics, some conservative evangelicals, some liberals of an older vintage. Their arguments were for the most part cast in traditional molds. A significant factor in disenchanting many Anglicans with the prospect of union with outright Protestants was the formation of the Anglican-Roman Catholic International Commission, which promised developments more in harmony with their natural inclinations. The suggestion has also been made that during the early 1970's the Anglican Church was called upon to deal with so many controversial issues, such as ARCIC, the ordination of women, and the rising demand for involvement in political causes, that it simply had no energy to spare for a proposal with such disturbing implications as church union.

It may be possible to discern a common element in radical and traditionalist disillusionment with union as an ideal. The ecumenical movement, with its attempt to embody in visible form the universal aspects of Christianity, has typically been based on what might be described in medieval terms as realist assumptions. During the 1960's there was a return to an attitude more reminiscent of nominalism, with emphasis shifting from global visions of reality to immediate experience and specific issues. Pluralism and diversity came to have greater appeal than unity, which seemed to carry the implication of homogenization. As office buildings, shopping plazas, and suburbs became increasingly indistinguishable, denominational peculiarities stood out as badges of identity to be cherished rather than deplored.

Whatever complications the Zeitgeist may have interposed, it seems unlikely that union would have taken place even if the most favorable conditions had continued. So long as union remains below the threshold of apparent attainability, the tendency is to bemoan its absence. The very existence of a basis on which it might actually be brought about compels a more serious facing of its implications. The reluctance that ensues cannot all be blamed on fickleness or loss of nerve. Differences among the denominations involved in these particular negotiations were serious enough to have kept them apart for many years and to have defeated previous attempts at union. The Principles of Union demonstrated that on the level of explicit theology there were no insuperable barriers to union. In some cases, however, differences in expression that seemed capable of resolution reflected deep-seated differences in mentality. Even in the Canadian setting there were times when debates recalled traditional confrontations between establishment and dissent. More fundamentally, Anglican commissioners tended to discuss the church in organic terms while those of the other denominations found contractual or instrumental descriptions more congenial. Such differences could not be resolved by problem-solving methods, for essentially they constituted not problems but different modes of conception. While closer acquaintance gave rise to new understandings, therefore, it also exposed unexpected threats to identities that had been largely taken for granted.

Merely to recognize that prospects for the immediate adoption of the Plan of Union were always slim and that they were especially so in a period when similar plans were running into heavy weather around the world, however, is to pass up an opportunity to learn possible lessons from the experience. Success in such enterprises is always relative, and one can at least ask whether a different approach might have resulted in an outcome more favorable than the outright rejection of the Plan of Union and the termination of conversations. Where along the line might opportunities have been more effectively seized and unnecessary obstacles removed?

The Plan of Union itself is the most obvious target of criticism. The Anglican Church eventually declared it unsatisfactory, and assuredly it contained both weaknesses and occasions of offense. Some agreements, such as that on the services of inauguration, were probably reached without sufficiently searching scrutiny. Other decisions, as on the role of the laity in ordination, represented the will of a bare majority rather than a consensus embracing all three denominations. The rhetoric of the plan, which was considerably affected by current pressures for the use of untraditional language and nomenclature, proved jarring to those who missed references to "dioceses", "presbyteries", or even "elders." Provisions for the episcopate proved especially troublesome to many Anglicans. A friend who was well disposed to union explained to me that for Anglicans the basic unit of church life is the diocese, which consists of clergy and laity grouped around a bishop who in Canada is elected by an unusually democratic process. Under the terms of the Plan of Union the bishop would be elected by a region, equivalent to the Anglican province, and assigned to a district or diocese for a limited period. Within the district he or she would share authority with a conference in a manner not precisely defined in the plan. Regardless of implications for church order, this friend urged, Anglicans would feel somewhat lost in such a system.

It seems scarcely likely, on the other hand, that any plan that might conceivably have been produced would have had a radically different reception. Any plan for uniting dissimilar churches is bound to call for the adoption of some unfamiliar procedures, and it should not be forgotten that the decision of the tens to try to transcend a mere combination of existing structures had been a major factor in making progress possible in the first place. Even the provision for attaching bishops to the regions, for that matter, is not unlike the present situation in the Anglican diocese of Toronto, where several bishops share responsibility for an area geographically larger than the corresponding region that was envisaged in the plan. After the reception of initial responses to the Plan of Union, the Committee on Union and Joint Mission addressed itself to the revision of some features that had caused difficulty, including the services of inauguration and the use of what had meanwhile come to be regarded as sexist language. These revisions were still unpublished in 1975 when the bishops issued their statement, and it is unlikely that they would have been welcomed at this stage. Any renewal of the impetus toward union in the future will certainly call for a new formulation, but the shape of the church that results is likely to resemble in many respects that forseen in the Plan of Union.

Some people blamed the collapse of the negotiations on a lack of effective promotion. While the commissions were busily engaged in their task, it was said, the mass of the people remained largely unaware of their activity. The executive was aware of this complaint and on one occasion called a conference of consultants from the media. To our amazement we were told that we had been receiving splendid publicity. The eggs provided in the budget for promotion were divided among three baskets: regular "church union reports" in the national denominational periodicals, occasional news releases, and the encouragement of joint study groups within the hundred-odd areas defined by United Church presbyteries. Each approach was at least partially effective. Canadian church papers, which have been remarkably successful in expanding their circulation, provided much broader coverage than could have been secured by the publication of a series of pamphlets, although the necessity of publishing commission reports in full gave rise to occasional complaints about their effectiveness as journalism. The news releases were largely ignored by metropolitan dailies, several of which were distinctly hostile, but regularly run in full by many local newspapers. Joint study groups were organized in a surprisingly large majority of potential areas, failing only in ignoring almost unanimously a portion of their mandate that urged them to sponsor study at the congregational level. This last was a serious setback, but it could scarcely be said that members of the three churches lacked opportunities to keep informed on the state of union.

If the message was delivered as vigorously as one could expect by commissioners who of necessity devoted the bulk of their time and effort to the facilitation of agreement within their own ranks, it obviously failed to convince the membership and especially the clergy of the churches. The most notable failures were in conveying a compelling rationale for union and in demonstrating to a sceptical membership that cherished elements of diversity would be protected. Communication faltered in large measure because many people heard simply what they expected to hear and discounted assurances to the contrary. The minutes of the commissions indicate constant concern that union should be an opportunity rather than a straightjacket, and the Plan of Union makes ample provision for regional initiative and local diversity. Nevertheless, hindsight suggests certain blind spots in our approach. Those most deeply engaged in the process tended to reflect the assumptions of a period of ecumenical formation when the desirability of union was assumed and only its attainability needed to be determined. And while our vision sought to embrace the concerns of our contemporary pluralistic society, it is doubtful that it had matured to the point where we were able to internalize them effectively. Many commissioners felt, with some justification, that their task was not to persuade the churches but to carry out on their behalf a specific assignment on which they had already placed their imprimatur. Nevertheless, one could wish that it had been possible for the commissions to spend more of their time in developing a theological imperative to union and less on resolving theological and other differences.

The uniting of churches, as traditionally conceived, consisted of the formulation of mutually acceptable terms followed by the merger of two or more existing churches into a newly constituted one. The process leading up to it was essentially diplomatic, culminating in a treaty setting forth the conditions of the new relationship. These steps are indeed essential but, as is universally recognized today, they do not constitute by any means the whole of the necessary process. Members must also be prepared, both psychologically and sociologically, to recognize the newly formed church as one to which they genuinely belong and to accept their new fellow-members as part of a single community of commitment. That success in these respects is seldom complete is suggested by the temporary erosion of membership that has followed most unions. A conspicuous lack of it was the most serious weakness of the Canadian effort.

Conventional wisdom had it that the enterprise was doomed from the start because it was "imposed from the top" instead of "springing spontaneously from the grassroots." Critics often called attention to the large number of congregational mergers that had preceded the formation of the United Church of Canada in 1925 and lamented the absence of a similar movement this time. The argument in this form is difficult to sustain. The organization of community churches in the early years of this century came about only after a good deal of official cultivation, and spontaneity was little in evidence until the publication of a basis of union in 1908 gave some assurance that there would be a united church to provide a denominational home for them. On the other hand, the number of co-operative efforts launched in the 1960's was more impressive than has generally been recognized. As for complaints of excessive encouragement from the top, those most deeply involved often regretted that there was not more. While some church leaders provided invaluable initiative and support, others were lukewarm or unwilling to divert energy from their own particular concerns. In any case, great ideas emerge not from indeterminate "grassroots" but from concerned and committed minds.

A lack of integration between the conversations and the ongoing programs of the churches, rather than excessive pressure from establishments, may well have been the most serious defect of the process. Members of the commissions had been appointed by the churches and regarded themselves as their agents.

Often, however, it seemed that the churches were saying to them, "Go ahead and produce a plan, and if we like it we may act on it." Meanwhile the committees responsible for the churches' long-range planning based their calculations on the assumption that union would not take place within the foreseeable future. At its fourth session in 1968 the general commission recommended that the churches anticipate organic union by taking such steps as the merging of mission boards, Christian education programs, and church papers. None of these suggestions was accepted, and the reasons offered in each case were cogent. The result, however, was that the Plan of Union had to be presented to churches that were little more accustomed to common action than they had been at the beginning of the process. [19]

Encouragement of co-operative activity, while necessary and helpful, is only one element in the program that needs to be devised in order to facilitate the process of union. By itself it can make further steps toward union seem less urgent and create additional structures that resist replacement. What seems to be needed is a series of stages of mutual commitment that are calculated to foster greater trust and thus lead to further commitment. Each stage requires a measure of agreement, and if it is not to become sterile each agreement needs to be followed by appropriate action. From the outset the general commission urged the churches to adopt a covenant that would pledge them to continue to the end along the path to organic union. The churches replied, too optimistically as events proved, that acceptance of the Principles had been such an undertaking. Probably such an all-embracing covenant would not have prevented the collapse that ultimately ensued, but some rhythm of agreement, commitment, and implementation might at least have brought about some tangible and irreversible steps toward closer relations rather than leaving the outcome to depend on the acceptability of a particular "new manifestation of the one church" to denominations that had had no opportunity to experience it.

Whatever the other defects of the Canadian process, none was more calamitous than the manner of its termination. To those who had invested much of the time over several years in the preparation of the Plan of Union, its curt dismissal seemed unfair and ungracious. In the relative calm of later reflection one can better understand and even appreciate the motives behind it. The continuation of negotiations that seem to be leading nowhere can be not only frustrating to individuals but debilitating to churches. Clearcut rejection may have seemed not only the most expeditious but even the most merciful way out of this situation. Experience since that time, however, has demonstrated that cutting the thread may not only stop the shuttle but cause the existing fabric to unravel. Personal relations among members of the former partner churches continue to be cordial. At the official level, co-operation may even be closer than before. Despite a stated intention to abide by the Lund principle, however, local ventures in co-operation are in difficulty and suggestions for further steps in unity are under a virtual taboo. Union conversations in a number of countries have survived periods of suspended animation and been resumed successfully later. A categorical refusal can set back the process for many years.

NOTES

1. Journal of Proceedings of the 15th Session of the General Synod of the Church of England in Canada, 1943, 333.

2. Journal of Proceedings of the 27th General Synod of the Anglican Church of Canada (in continuity with the last, despite the change of name), 1975, 82.

3. Ibid., M-37-9.

4. **The United Church of Canada Year Book** 1976, 5f.

5. I have told the earlier part of the story at greater length in **The Canadian Experience of Church Union** (London: Lutterworth, 1967).

6. T. R. Millman, "The Conference on Christian Unity, Toronto, 1889", Canadian Journal of Theology 3:3 (July 1959), 165-74.

7. The text is reproduced in G. K. A. Bell, ed., **Documents on Christian Unity:** third series, 1930-48 (London: Oxford University Press, 1948).

8. At the time the United Church of Canada ordained women, while the Church of England in Canada did not. The document contains no suggestion that the difference might constitute an obstacle to the plan.

9. Record of Proceedings of the Eighteenth General Council of the United Church of Canada, 1958, 53, 221.

10. The minutes of the tens are in the United Church archives at Victoria University, Toronto, "Interchurch, Anglican-Christian Church (Disciples of Christ)-United Church Union" papers, box 5, file 49.

11. Principles, 7.

12. Ibid., 11.

13. Ibid., 12f.

14. <u>Ibid.</u>, 12.

15. The minutes of the various commissions are included in the "Inter-church . . . Union" papers. The minutes of the General Commission are in box 9, while box 17, file 98, contains successive drafts of the <u>Plan of Union.</u> Most of what follows is based on personal reminiscence, checked against these documents.

16. <u>Journal of Proceedings of the 23rd Session of the General Synod of the Anglican Church of Canada,</u> 1967, 27, 346f.

17. <u>Record of Proceedings of the 22nd General Council of the United Church of Canada,</u> 1956, 54, 52.

18. <u>Journal of Proceedings of the 27th General Synod of the Anglican Church of Canada,</u> 1975, M-38f.

19. The United Church has suggested co-operation in world mission and church extension when it approved the <u>Principles of Union</u> (<u>Proceedings,</u> 1966, 578).

IMPULSES TOWARD CHRISTIAN UNITY IN
NINETEENTH CENTURY AMERICA

Paul A. Crow, Jr.

After the Revolutionary War (1783) the American churches found themselves confronted by two fundamental tasks. The first was the need to ignite a vital faith throughout the new nation. The post-war period was bleak for the churches marked by a low morale and a lack of zeal among Christians. On the eve of the nineteenth century the Congregational ministers in once-pious Massachusetts lamented "the present decay of Christian morals and piety, and the awful prevalence of speculative and practical infidelity." [1] The second task was to evangelize and minister to the swarms of people who were migrating westward beyond the Allegheny mountains and were "building a new society in the great unoccupied stretches of the continent." [2] The Massachusetts and Connecticut Missionary Societies sent missionaries, such as Samuel J. Mills, on exploratory tours through the West and the South to "preach the gospel to the destitute, explore the country, examine the moral and religious state of the people, and promote the establishment of Bible societies wherever they went." [3] Mills found countless communities without churches or ministers, and estimated that in 1815 there were 76,000 families between the Alleghenies and the Mississippi who were without Christ and the Bible. A major program of evangelism and Bible distribution would have to be launched or the people of the Western frontier would become as ignorant of God's Word as those in the heart of Africa. Especially, said Mills, the West could not be won by divided churches. [4] The religious situation of the American frontier was both a threat and call to the mission of the Church.

At the turn of the nineteenth century the American churches were terribly and conspicuously divided. The young nation had inherited most of the divided traditions of Europe, all made worse by the geographical, cultural, and language isolation of the new land. And if that was not enough, the religious climate of America permitted, even encouraged, a pattern of division. Revivalism had quickened the tempers and caused conflict and schism. The gifts of religious liberty and voluntary church membership were used to create churches of all shapes and persuasions, and to release a divisively competitive spirit among them. The established churches of the old country and the free churches of the new nation were molded into a new type of ecclesial community, called the "denomination." Even in evangelism the result was a free-for-all. As John Howard Yoder quips: "There were no ethics in the battle for the souls of the pioneers. Baptists were obliging enough to immerse any stray Methodists they could find; mounted Methodist circuit-riders were glad to rope and brand Calvinistic sheep with the marks of Arminius and Wesley . . . In this complete freedom to be different, Americans pulled sectarianism to the end of its rope." [5]

The sectarianism of this era can be illustrated in the biographies of that triumvirate of Disciples saints--Thomas Campbell, Alexander Campbell, and Barton W. Stone. Thomas and Alexander's early ministerial credentials identified them with the divisions of 18th century Scotland and Ireland. They were Old Light, Antiburgher, Seceder Presbyterian ministers. (Imagine trying to make sense out of these labels to the unchurched people of Western Pennsylvania, Kentucky, or Ohio!) The Seceder, or Associate, Presbyterians had separated from the established national Church of Scotland in 1733 in protest against the law of patronage which gave the power to elect ministers not to the congregations but to wealthy land owners or patrons. This meant that persons were chosen who often belonged to another church or claimed no religious convictions. The large Secession Church in Ireland also believed the National Church had watered down true Calvinist theology. In 1747 the Secession Church divided into two groups-- Burghers and Antiburghers--over whether these local magistrates [burghers] should be required to take a Holy Oath to uphold "the religion presently professed in this realm" [Scotland]. Then both the Burghers and Antiburghers each divided into Old Lights and New Lights, a contention based on whether subscription to the Confession of Faith was required of those ordained to the ministry. An American version of this Old Light-New Light controversy-- which Barton Stone battled--developed around those who supported and those who opposed the revival ideas of the Great Awakening. The complexity of this chart of schisms is not the only issue. What was divisive of religion and politics in Scotland had no relevance to Christians in Ireland. These divisions were even more incomprehensible to the American scene.

The problem faced by the churches of the frontier was how to evangelize and teach the Christian faith in a society marked by secularism and through churches tempted by sectarianism.

But this was not only a matter of new geographical territory. As Sydney E. Ahlstrom accurately points out, "The 'frontier' in America is not a region but a process," a process which began with the arrival of the Mayflower and continues until today. [6] In the midst of this expansive and divisive nineteenth

In the midst of this expansive and divisive nineteenth century there is a sequence of bold and courageous efforts toward Christian unity. Since some Disciples tend to think their forefathers and mothers were lone voices in the wilderness, it is important to hear this interesting collection of ecumenical witnesses. Ironically some of the same forces which created hostility and schism also were instruments of Christian unity for those who grasped the vision of the one People of God. Revivalism, with its emphasis on the value of religious experience, tended to overcome those doctrinal differences which had been obstacles to fellowship. The separation of church and state, which gave no church a status of privilege, made real the view that all churches are equal in the sight of God. This encouraged among all at least a mutual toleration which in some instances was later followed by mutual recognition and cooperation. Religious liberty opened the door for voluntary cooperation and unity. The Lockean idea of the Church as a voluntary society formed by contract encouraged cooperation among Christians around certain issues and goals. Equally important in this century, however, was the theological struggle among key persons for whom the Biblical faith and the missionary movement called for a church united in order that the world may believe. In brief, the crisis of the nineteenth century American churches had to do with the nature of the Church. To this often unknown panorama of witnesses to unity and union we shall now turn our attention.

According to the typology of Princeton historian Lefferts A. Loetscher, three approaches to Christian unity marked nineteenth century American Christianity: (1) cooperation by individuals in non-denominational bodies; (2) federative action by denominational bodies; and (3) organic union, usually "on the basis of the minimal tenets of the initiating group." [7]

I

The first of these types of Christian unity--cooperation by individuals in non-denominational bodies--was expressed in a proliferation of voluntary societies which brought Christians from many denominations to witness together on common concerns. These societies grew out of the revivalism of the Second Great Awakening and constituted an ecumenical phalanx against the isolated divisive denominational loyalties which were so characteristic of the young American churches. Together these cooperative societies made such an impact that they are called the "Evangelical Empire" (Loetscher) or the "Evangelical United Front" (Foster).

One group was created for the purpose of evangelism and religious education. Among them was the American Board of Commissioners for Foreign Missions (1810), the first American missionary society initiated by Congregational, Presbyterian, and Reformed Christians; the American Home Missionary Society (1826), an agency for uniting the efforts of several denominations in a comprehensive plan for evangelizing the nation; the American Education Society (1815), inaugurated to aid in the education of ministers; the American Bible Society (1816), whose purpose was to supply the Holy Scriptures, "without note or comment," to every "destitute" person in the United States; the American Sunday School Union (1824), drawing its membership from many denominations resolved to publish lessons and organize "a Sunday School in every destitute place where it is applicable"; the American Tract Society (1825), which published millions of gospel leaflets, devotional guides, and hymnals; the American branches of the Young Men's (1852) and Young Women's Christian Association (1866) whose evangelical mission was to unite those women and men--separately in those days--"who regard Jesus Christ as their God and Saviour according to the Holy Scriptures, and desire to be his disciples." A second group of nondenominational societies were pledged to social reform. Such agencies as the American Society for the Promotion of Temperance (1826), the American Peace Society (1828), and the American Antislavery Society (1833), sought to establish a Christian American nation, trying to incarnate the ideals of pietism and the Puritan theocracies of Puritan New England. It is not accidental that "American" was in the title of those voluntary societies for Christian witness and service. In one sense, they represented a naive national self-confidence, the doctrine of Manifest Destiny with the millenial hope of a Christian America winning the world for Jesus Christ. In another sense, these nationalistic titles represented a broader vision of Christian responsibility which challenged the local and regional loyalties. The prospect of authentic ecumenism in the 19th century "faced the problem of transcending not only denominations but also geographical localism . . . It was necessary therefore to assert the national character in order to maintain hegemony over those local interests." [8] The inevitable temptation, however, is to identify Christian with American culture and national interest; sectarianism is merely replaced with nationalism.

Another ecumenical dimension of those societies was the prominent leadership given by lay persons. "The nineteenth century in America," observes C. Howard Hopkins, "was the age of the lay worker in religion quite as much as it was the day of the common man on the democratic stage." [9] This involvement of lay people facilitated an easier cooperation and gave many laity ecumenical experiences from which they would never again rest with a divided church.

Since all this was bursting across the American horizon at the same time the Christians and the Disciples of Christ were being born, it is worth noting that in 1845--nearly 30 years after its origins--Alexander Campbell cautiously favored the American and Foreign Bible Society and later became a vice-president of the American Bible Society when it broke away from its inter-national parent body. [10] He and other Disciples positively pro-moted the American Sunday School Union, the American Protestant Association, and other "ecumenical councils" (Campbell's term). After his temporary--and immature--suspicion of missionary soci-eties he became the first president of the American Christian Missionary Society, which sought to evangelize the world in partner-ship with the societies of other traditions.

The pinnacle of this approach to Christian unity--coopera-tion of individuals from different churches--was reached in 1846 when in London some 800 Christian leaders from Europe and America formed the World's Evangelical Alliance. The Alliance was shaped by "the basis of great evangelical principles" with the purpose "simply to bring individual Christians into closer fellowship and cooperation on the basis of the spiritual union which already exists in the vital relation of Christ to the members of His body in all ages and all countries." These principles were nine, including "the Divine Inspiration, Authority, and Sufficiency of the Holy Scriptures," the right of private judgment in interpret-ing the Scriptures, the Trinity, the Incarnation and the work of atonement of Jesus Christ, and other conservative doctrinal points. [11] Many had hoped that the Evangelical Alliance would be a federation of churches but instead it became an alliance of individual Christians. Nevertheless it had truly remarkable achieve-ments in setting up an annual week of prayer for Christian unity, in holding international conferences which stimulated the experience of unity among different nations and churches, in advocating world-wide missions, and in defending religious liberty for minorities in countries where an established church discriminated against them. Americans participated in the Evanglical Alliance from the beginning in 1846, but an American branch was unable to be organized until 1867, two years after the Civil War; the Alliance would not admit members who owned slaves. Once in action, however, the American Evangelical Alliance was a powerful ecu-menical presence and attracted major leaders such as layman William E. Dodge, church historian Phillip Schaff, and social activist Josiah Strong (1847-1916).

With a slight change of events in 1846 the Disciples of Christ would have been influential in constituting the World's

Evangelical Alliance. As Eva Jean Wrather, the eminent scholar on Alexander Campbell, points out, several Disciples congregations offered to pay Mr. Alexander's expenses to the London inaugural assembly, but pressing matters at Bethany kept him away from that major ecumenical meeting. [12] None among us doubts that if Mr. Campbell had attended he would have played a formative role! Apart from this missed opportunity it is not surprising that no Disciples were among the eighty Americans who attended the London Assembly. As W. E. Garrison observes, Disciples

> were then a relatively young and unknown people who would naturally not be invited; they were a middle-western people, to whom a trans-Atlantic voyage was an even more unaccustomed and formidable adventure than it was at that time to the residents on the Eastern seaboard (but Campbell did visit Great Britain the following year); and the related British Churches of Christ had not yet begun to emerge from the isolation involved in their exclusive devotion to the reproduction of what they conceived to be the pattern of the primitive Church, one feature of which was strict adherence to close communion. [13]

After the meeting Campbell wrote a five-article series in The Millenial Harbinger [14] heralding the Alliance and comparing it with his father's "doctrinal scheme of union," and calling both "indications of a spirit at work in the conscience and affections of Christian men." [15] He commended the architects of the Alliance for making Christian union and cooperation their central idea. In particular they had agreed to plead "the cause of visible and real union of Christians, and to devise ways and means of accomplishing that great desideratum." His profuse celebration of the Alliance is hardly rivaled by his comments about any other ecumenical venture during his lifetime.

> We thank God for the Evangelical Alliance, and we take courage from it . . . I am happy to add that no convention that has met since the Protestant Reformation has had so strong a hold upon my affections and esteem . . . I wish the Alliance God's speed in every effort to gather the dispersed of Israel into one . . . We can very cordially sympathize with the Evangelical Alliance, and anticipate for them a brighter and a better dispensation; and for my part, I will, to the utmost of my power, cooperate with them just as far and as long as they please to permit me. [16]

Circumstances of overseas travel precluded his participation in the World's Evangelical Alliance. His death came in 1866, one year before the American branch was formed.

5

We can facilely critique the Evangelical Empire. Collaboration on common causes did little to lead the churches toward visible, organic union. But in a sense their non-ecclesiastical cooperation was all the ecumenical traffic would bear at the time. In fact, any ecumenical relations in this century seem like a miracle. In the mid-nineteenth century a young minister commented on the hostility among the churches: "'Sectarian jealousies were fierce; ministers of the different churches were hardly on speaking terms; an exchange of pulpits was a thing never heard of.'"[17]

By 1840 the energies of the Evangelical Empire were waning under an avalanche of a reborn, powerful denominationalism. The benevolence budget of America began to take on a denominational cast. The ecumenical status of a number of the cooperative societies was reduced to one denomination; both the American Board of Commissioners for Foreign Missions and the American Home Missionary Society became Congregational agencies. In the same decade the Calvinism which had been the source of theological consensus for the voluntary societies experienced schism and splintering. Congregationalists mounted their pulpits against Unitarians, Presbyterians divided into Old School (Old Light) and New School (New Light) parties.

Yet these missionary and benevolent societies made a courageous ecumenical witness which at the least set a trajectory toward the Federal Council of Churches in 1908, and in 1950 the National Council of Churches of Christ in the U.S.A. Dr. Loetscher's assessment is worth noting: "In spite of defects and superficialities, the Evangelical Empire was the most vigorous and effective Christian unity movement in the United States during the first half of the nineteenth century. It was aware of some of the deepest spiritual and moral needs of the country . . . It bequeathed to the later years of the century a precedent of unitive Christianity." [18]

II

The second movement of Christian unity in America in the nineteenth century was federative action by the denominational bodies. In this approach the focus becomes not individuals but the churches in official ties of cooperation. The quality of this "federative action" is defined by the preservation of each church's separate identity, authority, and decision-making. This approach was given articulate expression by two American-German theologians--a Lutheran, Samuel Simon Schmucker (1799-1873) and a German Reformed, Phillip Schaff (1819-1893).

Born in Hagerstown, Maryland, Samuel Schmucker studied theology at Princeton, that bastion of Calvinism. His roommate was Robert Baird who has been described as "the first American scholar to trace American religious history not in patriotic denominational terms but in terms of the contributions of all the churches." [19] While many Lutherans at the time were isolationists, Schmucker gave himself toward making Lutheranism indigenous to the American scene and boldly ecumenical in its perspective. His ecumenism came from his pietism. As a young pastor and professor at Gettysburg Theological Seminary he vigorously participated in many of the voluntary movements for evangelism and social reform already mentioned as the Evangelical Empire.

Schmucker gained national attention in 1838 when he issued his Fraternal Appeal to the American Churches, with a Plan for Catholic Union, on Apostolic Principles. [20] In this proposal he was a pioneer in the federation of the churches, a concept which captured many American Christians of the time. Schmucker's plan envisioned the formation of an "alliance", a loose federation through which Protestant churches would cooperate and have intercommunion without affecting the authority, polity or discipline of the denominations. An advisory council would visibly show forth their common loyalty to Christ, and be an agent of understanding and closer relations. A distinctive part of his Fraternal Appeal is his emphasis upon a doctrinal agreement, expressed in an "Apostolic Protestant Confession," which would be a twelve-point summary of "all those doctrines which the great body of all Christians agree upon." He also emphasized the joint relations of local congregations in cooperation and annual joint communion services.

In 1870 Schmucker reissued his proposal for federal unity in a modified form under the title, The True Unity of Christ's Church; Being a Renewed Appeal to the Friends of the Redeemer, on Primitive Christian Union, and the History of its Corruption. [21] He called upon the churches to abandon their party names and think of themselves as branches of a united church, to practice intercommunion, to mutually recognize each other's ministries. In this edition he sought to encompass the plans for the World's Evangelical Alliance. Indeed, years before, Schmucker was one of the key Americans who planned the Alliance's 1846 meeting in London and effectively helped to make it a more ecumenical body. One enthusiastic Irish leader at the London meeting called him "the father of the Alliance." [22] Schmucker's plan was never accepted. In fact he was rejected by his own Lutheran church which was skeptical about any ecumenism outside Lutherans. But his vision enabled later concepts of federation and federal union.

Again we discover Alexander Campbell's alertness to

the ecumenical movement as in 1839 he wrote about Schmucker's Fraternal Appeal in a complimentary manner, then made his own proposal for an international congress which would work for Christian Union. [23]

Another voice was Phillip Schaff, a Swiss Reformed historian and theologian who came to the U.S.A. in 1844 to teach at Mercersburg, the German Reformed Seminary nestled in Pennsylvania's Allegheny mountains. In 1870 Schaff became professor of Church History at Union Theological Seminary in New York, and distinguished himself by publishing multitudinous works, e.g., **Creeds of Christendom** and the **History of the Christian Church,** and the **Schaff-Herzog Encyclopedia of Religious Knowledge.** Schaff's historical and theological works were scholarly testimonies of the unity of the Church. His teaching and writing of church history from an irenic perspective made an immense ecumenical impact--though it did not always please those with parochial or defensive minds. He also became a formative leader in the Evangelical Alliance. In 1893, two months before his death, at a meeting of the Alliance in Chicago, gathered concurrently with the World's Parliament of Religions, he gave a classic address on "The Reunion of Christendom" which was a dramatic appeal for federal union. "Federal union," he said "is a voluntary assocation of different churches in their official capacity, each retaining its freedom and independence in the management of its internal affairs, but all recognizing one another as sisters with equal rights, and cooperating in general enterprises, such as the spread of the Gospel at home and abroad, the defense of the faith against infidelity, the elevation of the poor and neglected classes of society, works of philanthropy and charity, and moral reform." [24]

III

The third type of unity articulated in the nineteenth century American ecumenism was organic or church union. In union two or more churches assume a common identity; they express a common ecclesial life. Yet most of the nineteenth century proposals carried the veiled assumption that the ecclesiology of the proposing church would become the basis and shape of the eventual united church. Here the Lutherans, the German Reformed, the Episcopalians, and the Disciples of Christ are the most noteworthy.

Within the German Reformed Church came Phillip Schaff and his teaching colleague John Williamson Nevin (1803-1886), who became principal voices in a movement of the 1840's called the Mercersburg Movement. Mercersburg theology taught a high doctrine of the Church and the sacraments. They emphasized the corporate, organic nature of the Church, historical continuity from the early Church through the Reformation to the present day, and the centrality of the Eucharist. The nineteenth century Mercersburg theology had a distinctive perspective on the unity of the Church. The unity of the Church is a reality. It is given by God's act in Jesus Christ, and is not an achievement of human efforts. It is to be celebrated and made visible by the use of ecumenical symbols, namely the sacraments of Baptism and the Lord's Supper and by those confessions of faith which belong to the whole Christian Tradition.

Nevin's concept of the Church and its unity was in pronounced contrast to the prevailing evangelistic theology--individualistic and non-historical--which reigned among German Reformed and Lutheran churches in Pennsylvania. For this reason Nevin seemed to be to many of his contemporaries "a crabbed critique of ecumenical endeavors." [25] His work sometimes frustrated the efforts toward union between the Reformed and Lutherans in that part of the U.S. But Nevin's vision of the future one Church of Christ required a theological basis for unity. "He knew and demonstrated that there are no administrative short-cuts to Church unity, that the prerequisites are repentance, religious renewal, and faith in the Church as the locus of Christ's continuing presence." [26] In a startling way the Mercersburg theologians anticipated the church union agenda as it came a century later.

Another example came in the first quarter of the nineteenth century when leaders of the Lutheran and the German Reformed churches began to push for cooperation and church union. In part they were inspired by the mandate to mission of the American frontier; in part they were inspired by the Prussion Union of 1817 (now the Evangelical Church of the Union). Their common language, common cultural background, and their common pietistic heritage led Lutherans and German Reformed in Pennsylvania to experiment with "union churches" at the local level. "Union" churches in this instance were interim relations, which essentially were places where Lutherans and German Reformed congregations owned the same church buildings but worshipped on alternate Sundays. At this stage the relationship was primarily cooperation with the goal of organic union. Several hundred of those local unions were born until about 1900 when the rigid denominationalism of both synods ended this church union experiment. [27]

Another celebrated union development was the Plan of Union of 1801 which united Presbyterians and Congregationalists in their evangelism to those who immigrated from New England to Central and Western New York and Ohio. This venture was one of the earliest ecumenical ventures of national proportion in the United States. In reality the Plan effected a regional union, but its significance cannot be down-played. The demands of an expanding mission field convinced these two strong churches that they needed each other. As a later report declared:

> The wants of the mission field already opened to Christian effort in New York and Ohio demanded the united efforts of Presbyterians and Congregationalists . . . It was of the highest importance that there should be no denominational conflict or collision. The claims of missionary evangelization were felt by all parties to be paramount to all denominational interests. [28]

The Plan of Union grew naturally out of long years of cooperation between Presbyterians and Congregationalists during the colonial period and out of close similarities in their polities. Congregationalism in Connecticut with its "consociations" approximated Presbyterianism in the Middle Colonies by giving decisive power to church councils. The consociation was a Congregational association of ministers and lay representatives entrusted with substantially the same authority as a presbytery. These two factors made union seem appropriate in the midst of an otherwise sectarian climate. [29]

In the Plan, approved by the Presbyterian General Assembly and Congregational General Association of Connecticut in 1801, each church agreed to recognize each other's ministry and polity and to establish a procedure for common mission in "the new settlements" along the frontier. The Plan had four articles. (1) It "strictly enjoined" all missionaries and ministers to "promote . . . a spirit of accomodation" between Presbyterians and Congregationalists. (2) It provided for a Congregational church to call a Presbyterian minister and still "conduct their discipline according to Congregational principles"; any difficulties between the minister and the congregation would be referred to the presbytery. (3) A Presbyterian church could call a Congregational minister and still manage its affairs according to Presbyterian polity; disagreements would be submitted to the Minister's Association. (4) Finally, in new communities the Plan made provision for union congregations between Presbyterians and Congregationalists "uniting in one church and settling a minister." A revision was made in 1808 in what was called the Accommodation Plan which allowed Congregational congregations and ministers to become members of the presbyteries while retaining their Congregational commitments. These "accomodated" churches were good-naturedly called "Presbygational" or Congreterial." In this plan these two churches were intimately bound together for over fifty years, particularly at the association and presbytery levels, as they moved across the frontier of New York, Ohio, Indiana, Illinois, Michigan, and Wisconsin.

Later a heightened denominational consciousness led the two churches to set their union aside. Termination was voted in 1837 by the Presbyterians and in 1852 by the Congregationalists. The statistics reveal that during the fifty-one years a large percentage of the Congregational churches became Presbyterian in name. But to an earlier generation that development was not judged as a loss. The ill-fated outcome was not so much, say some historians, the product of a denominational rivalry between the two churches as it was the divisive power of the conditions of the frontier. As Robert H. Nichols concludes, "However one-sided the ecclesiastical advantage of the operation of the Plan proved to be, it was the missionary need and nature which determined the course of events." [30] The Plan of Union of 1801 was a victim of what has been called "revived denominationalism, demanding conformity to denominational standards of polity and doctrine." [31] Yet the issues were far deeper. Douglas Horton, the beloved ecumenist and one of the architects of the United Church of Christ, maintains the Plan of 1801 failed because it was "an attempt to unite the fully-formed Presbyterianism with a half-formed Congregationalism. The latter was in process of losing its seventeenth century structure, and had not yet acquired its present one. The congregationalism of early New England was not a type of church polity merely; it was a philosophy of civilization in that it involved both the Church and the State." [32] There was a rivalry not merely between two denominations but between two doctrines of the Church. Further, while it was never acknowledged at the time the issue of slavery was a hidden element in the failure of the Plan of Union of 1801. It failed because "it tried to yoke those who tolerated slavery with those who did not." [33] The Congregationalists and Presbyterians walked away from union because "the spirit that created the Plan was replaced by one less Christian." Such a commentary covers more than a nineteenth century plan!

The Episcopalians also occupy a special place in the 19th century search for church union. In 1841 a pastor from Hartford, Connecticut, Thomas Hubbard Vail (1812-1889) published his apologia for a united church which conveyed a particular perspective and approach. "Instead of endeavoring to strike out an entirely new system of ecclesiastical unity," Vail argued, "the proper and only feasible course is to select, for the purpose of uniting within it, some system already established, and which realizes most nearly the idea of a Comprehensive Church, and if it be not in every respect perfect, to improve it, if it will allow improvement into perfection." [34] Such a church capable of being the haven for union did, he believed, exist and it was his own Protestant Episcopal Church. He therefore invited all denominations to "cast in your lot with us." Vail assumed that Christian unity required an outward, visible church union. He said, "We do not think that any progress can be made toward Church Union except upon the basis of a United Church."

In 1853 William Augustus Muhlenberg (1796-1877) made a proposal for organic union called the Muhlenberg Memorial. The essence of his proposal was to expand the Episcopal Church into a wider ecumenical fellowship by a recognition of ordained ministries of other churches and by creating a church system "broader and more comprehensive" than the Episcopal Church. Muhlenberg did not offer any practical indications of how this comprehensive, united church could be achieved. [35]

The most serious Episcopal proposal for a united church was made by William Reed Huntington (1838-1909), the rector of an Episcopal parish in Worcester, Massachusetts. In 1870 Dr. Huntington preached a sermon to his congregation and published "an essay towards unity" entitled, The Church-Idea, which received wide public interest. Christians "have become possessed with an unwonted longing for unity," he said, "and yet they are aware that they do not grapple successfully with the practical problem. Somehow they are grown persuaded that union is God's work, and separation [the] devil's work." [36] Proclaiming the desired union as the Church of the Reconciliation, Huntington offered a quadrilateral, a four-point platform, as the basis for all union attempts. These four points of agreement were (1) the Holy Scriptures as the Word of God, (2) the primitive creeds (Apostles and Nicene) as the Rule of Faith, (3) the two sacraments ordained by Christ himself, and (4) the episcopate as "the keystone of governmental unity." [37]

Huntington's plan captured the imagination of the Protestant Episcopal Church and later the entire Anglican communion. The quadrilateral was accepted in substance and rewritten in language in 1886 by the Episcopal General Convention in Chicago. At the Lambeth Conference in 1888 the bishops of the whole Anglican communion adopted the quadrilateral, in a slightly modified form, as the beginning point for all future Anglican unity conversations. Henceforth it was known as the Chicago-Lambeth Quadrilateral.

This dramatic proposal was sent to a number of American churches, and as would be expected few of the contemporary responses were favorable. The Quadrilateral was sent in 1887 by the Protestant Episcopal Church to the General Christian Missionary Convention of the Disciples of Christ at its annual meeting in Indianapolis. The convention president, Charles Louis Loos, appointed a Committee on Christian Unity to draft a response. The blue-ribbon committee involved Isaac Erret, D. R.

Dungan, A. R. Benton,. J. H. Garrison, B. J. Radford, and J. W. McGarvey, and C. L. Loos, president of Kentucky University. The report typically disclaimed any authority to speak for Disciples, but made four observations. (1) It celebrated the Episcopalian's commitment to Christian unity, an historic commitment shared by the Disciples of Christ. (2) It concurred that the Scriptures of the Old and New Testaments are the only rule of faith, but questioned that a diocesan episcopacy could be justified on scriptural evidence. Hence, it should be declared non-essential. (3) It expressed pleasure at the freedom proposed in the methods of practical work in the Church. (4) It commended the "gentle and loving spirit" of the resolution of the House of Bishops which disavows any selfish aims. [38] The Episcopal declaration rightly understood that union does not seek to absorb other communions or to promote the interests of only one denomination. In 1888, when the Lambeth Conference approved the Quadrilateral, J. H. Garrison, editor of The Christian-Evangelist, took a more negative stance, declaring, "We question both the desirability and feasibility of the Episcopalian idea of Christian union as we understand." [39] In 1891 a Disciples minister, George Plattenburg assessed the Quadrilateral in a book of essays edited by J. H. Garrison and put forth his "fatal objection," viz., nowhere in apostolic teaching is the being, or even the well-being, of the Church guaranteed by any form of church government; only faith in Christ can be required as the basis for church union. "It is wholly inconsistent with the nature of Christianity to condition unity upon a mere ministerial function. The basis lacks catholicity." [40] The Episcopalians and the Anglicans did not waver in the face of these critiques, and the Quadrilateral became one of the primary documents in the 20th century's Faith and Order Movement where ironically Anglicans and Disciples played such important roles. Later, the rector of Grace Church in New York, Huntington proposed to the Episcopal General Convention an amendment to their constitution to allow a bishop to take under his spiritual oversight any congregation of any tradition which accepted the Quadrilateral; it was voted down.

In 1897 Huntington revised his proposal in his book **A National Church**, changing his assumption that Anglican tenets are the basis of a united church in America. He rejected the idea of the Episcopal Church or any other church being the via media. Rather he longed for the Episcopal Church to commit itself to organic union on the basis of the equal contribution of all the churches. [41] This new position on organic union was clearly put in an address entitled The Four Theories of Church Unity (1909). Each church has an essential contribution toward organic union. A united church is formed by "constitutionalism," a union in which the rights of all parties would be conserved and the different polities would be mingled. "It means unity by contribution, not by subtraction." [42]

It now remains for us to sketch the place of the Christians and the Disciples of Christ on our landscape of nineteenth century efforts toward unity and union. They pre-date many of the ventures we have described, and rival them all in terms of their antipathy for disunity and their passion for visible unity among all Christians. As we have noted, in each of the three approaches to Christian unity we have discussed, the Disciples had a happy awareness and usually a critical comment. But their primal vision and their preoccupation was with the search for a united church through organic union. Indeed in early nineteenth century American Christianity their voice uniquely raised the plea of union. Their approach was also distinctly American, shaped by the Western frontier, that mission field of the century, but with echoes of their British origins. The first voices we hear are those of Barton Warren Stone, Thomas Campbell and Alexander Campbell.

Barton Warren Stone (1772-1844) ranks as one of the earliest proponents of Christian union in America. Born in Port Tobacco, Maryland, his family moved to Pittsylvania County, Virginia, near the North Carolina border. Stone was formed by the American culture and the religious experience of the American frontier. His passion for religious freedom, his skepticism of ecclesiastical structures, his preference for the Bible alone over speculative theology and creeds were frontier American teachings. With his abhorrence of division Barton Stone became one of the chief actors in the Cane Ridge Revival (1801), a major ecumenical event which took place in Bourbon County, Kentucky. It was planned as a "sacramental meeting" for Presbyterians, but Methodist and Baptist ministers and lay people also came to preach and hear the Word of God and to celebrate the Lord's Supper. As Stone later reflected, at Cane Ridge "all appeared cordially united-- of one mind and one soul . . . We all engaged in singing the same songs of praise--all united in prayer--all preached the same things-- free salvation urged upon by faith and repentance." [43] This ecumenical revival convinced Stone that he wanted to be not the defender of "partyism" but a servant of the one Church of Jesus Christ. From that moment on his conviction about the embracing love of God thrust upon him the mantle of leadership in the movement for Christian unity.

Alienation soon developed between Barton Stone and the rigid Calvinism of the Kentucky Presbyterians. As a result he and four other ministers withdrew (or were expelled) in 1803 from the Synod of Kentucky, and immediately constituted their own Springfield Presbytery. But this was only a momentary way station on their pilgrimage. Having pledged themselves "to take the Bible alone as the only standard of faith, practice and discipline" and claimed only the name "Christian as legitimate", Stone later wrote, "It was frequently cast up to us that we were as much a party as others, having assumed a party name, the Springfield Presbytery." So they met at Cane Ridge, June 28, 1804, and agreed "to cast off our assumed name, and power, and to sink into the general body of Christians, taking no other name than Christian." [44] This dramatic proposal was announced in a document which if not written by Stone--and evidence supports the authorship of Richard McNemar--does articulate Stone's understanding of the Church and its unity.

The Last Will and Testament of the Springfield Presbytery which Walter C. Gibbs, professor of church history at Lexington Theological Seminary, called "the first plea for the union of all Christians promulgated in America," [45] was not a particular design for Christian unity. Those five signers primarily intended to defy the dominant disunity which marked their times and to offer the dismantling of their church structure as a beginning. The first item of the document lists their primary ecumenical principle: "We will, that this body die, be dissolved, and sink into union with the Body of Christ at large; for there is one Body, and one Spirit, even as we are called in one hope of our calling." [46] Stone and others in his Christian movement were talking about a costly unity which came through the surrender of separate denominational identities. "The Witnesses Address", a statement appended to The Last Will and Testament also made clear their ecumenical intentions:

> Let all Christians join us, in crying to God day and night, to remove the obstacles which stand in the way of his work, and give him no rest until he make Jerusalem a praise in the earth. We heartily unite with our Christian brothers of every name, in thanksgiving to God for the display of his goodness in the glorious work he is carrying on in our Western country, which we hope will terminate in the universal spread of the gospel, and the unity of the church. [47]

Stone often spoke of four kinds of union: book union, head union, water union, and fire union. Book union was based upon an authoritative creed, confession of faith or church discipline. Head union was based upon a common opinion, and Stone warned that this approach was characteristic of many who denounced creeds and made the Bible their creed. He warned that to make interpretations of the Bible a system of salvation is equally wrong. Water union was based upon baptism by the immersion of believers; if made the primary criterion of faith, said Stone, immersion baptism can become sectarian. These three concepts of union Stone rejected in favor of the fourth: the union of fire or the Spirit. This is the perfect union achieved not by the agreement of human opinion but faith in the "Lord Jesus Christ, the Saviour of sinners, and by cheerful obedience to all his known commands."

[48] The road to union is the road toward the Lordship of Christ.

Barton Stone interacted with the ecumenical agenda of his day in two specific ways. In 1841--preceeding Schmucker, Schaff, and others--he was one of the first Christian leaders in America to propose a national conference on Christian unity at which the various denominations could "consult upon some general points respecting the union of Christians." Beyond the idea, Stone offered no specific items about this conference except that it should be held in a central place in America and the conference should be promoted by all religious journals. [49] In a second progressive move Stone made clear his opposition to the anti-Catholic movement in the 1840's. The growing strength of the Roman Catholic Church in the United States had brought anxiety and veiled anger. Anti-papal organizations were formed; the Native American Party was begun in 1837 with the purpose to oppose liberal immigration laws which permitted the steady flow of Roman Catholics to America. Among some Protestants church union was even proposed as the development of a power base vis-à-vis the new Catholic power. Barton Stone was dismayed with such views. This sort of strategy would neither succeed nor express true Christian unity.

> Practical Christianity can only save Protestantism from popery and skepticism, and also from external ruin. If all parties among the Protestants would agree to reform their lives, to be holy, humble, and obedient to all God's commandments--if they would agree to cease from their unhallowed debates and striving against each other, and to unite as one to promote Godliness and brotherly love in the earth--if they agree to meet together at the throne of grace in fervent, solemn and faithful prayer, then the spread of popery would cease, and skepticism be confounded and silent, if not converted to the Lord. [50]

As we learn from Barton Stone, unity comes through ecumenical persons who live and help others live in God's atmosphere of love and trust. Here we gain insight into the irenic spirit which Stone felt alone would bring about Christian unity. More than anything else unity comes through humility, meekness, gentleness, long suffering, and "daily searching to find the will of God." [51]

Luther A. Weigle, the former dean of Yale Divinity School, once described Stone as "a 'grass roots' practitioner of Christian Unity rather than a debater about it." [52] Stone was not a theologian, and when he made theological statements he often became immersed in controversy. His individualism and his simplistic restorationism did not encourage him to develop a full ecclesiology or a design for a united church. Stone's contribution was his ecumenical charisma, his unadulterated passion for the unity of God's people, and his personal witness that visible unity is the essential calling of the Church. His memorable words launched an ecumenical movement: "Let the unity of Christians be our polar star. To this let our eyes be continually turned, and to this let our united efforts be directed--that the world may believe, and be saved." [53]

Thomas Campbell (1763-1854), a scholarly and irenic preacher, left Ireland at a difficult time. Not only were Presbyterians rent asunder. Both Presbyterians in the north and Roman Catholics in the south were agitating against the government in Dublin, which was dominated by the Anglo-Irish aristocracy-- which used Ireland as a playground--and the Anglican Church of Ireland. Already Presbyterians and Roman Catholics were vying for control in Ireland. (These tensions were shades of the sad spectacle of division which strangles Ireland today.) Thomas Campbell left the schisms of Ulster-Scot Presbyterianism and migrated to Western Pennsylvania, only to find that a divided church frustrated Christian witness in this new land. Indeed, the denominational rivalries and schisms became more intense in the United States than in Ireland or Scotland. Upon his arrival at Philadelphia, Thomas Campbell identified with the Associate (Seceder) synod of North America, and was promptly assigned as an itinerant pastor to the Presbytery of Chartiers in southwestern Pennsylvania. He soon developed a conflict with the presbytery over his rejection of creeds as the basis of union and communion and his ecumenical gesture of offering the Lord's Supper to non-Seceder Presbyterians and even to other Christians. If Christ died for all persons, he affirmed, then all who believe in him are welcome at the Table. Treated like a heretic for this ecumenical practice, Thomas Campbell felt he could only walk away from this excessive and exclusive Calvinism. This he did in 1808. The following year (1809) he gathered some thirty women and men and formed the Christian Association of Washington (Pennsylvania). The Association was understood to be not a church but a temporary society of "voluntary advocates for Church reformation." So began the Disciples' pilgrimage toward a doctrine of the Church which would fit their vision of Christian unity.

To articulate more fully the motives and mission of this Christian Association, Thomas Campbell wrote a thirteen-point document called the Declaration and Address. Judged by ecumenical scholars as "one of the great milestones on the path to Christian unity in America," [54] it clearly projects a vision which was dramatically to challenge the sectarian spirit on the American frontier. "Sick and tired of the bitter jarrings and janglings of a party spirit," he set forth thirteen propositions, appealing to the Christian world to discover its integrity in the "primitive unity, purity, and prosperity" of the New Testament Church. In that simple community is found a constitution for the worship, discipline, and government of the Church. "It is the grand design and native tendency of our holy religion to reconcile and unite men (and women) to God, and to each other, in truth and love, to the glory of God, and their own present and eternal good." [55]

Four of the propositions declare the mandate for Christian unity. The first one stands among the most famous statements in ecumenical literature:

> 1. The Church of Christ upon earth is essentially, intentionally, and constitutionally one; consisting of all those in every place that profess their faith in Christ and obedience to him in all things according to the Scriptures, and that manifest the same by their tempers and conduct . . .

Thomas Campbell's three aspects of unity are worth some exegesis. To be "essentially" one carries the note that unity is not extraneous or a luxury but belongs to the very essence of the Church. A divided church is a contradiction. The only true Church is a united Church. To be "intentionally" one conveys that unity is not accidental or casual. It does not come from cordiality or the mutual choice of others. It is given by God, and is part of the divine design for the Church. To be "constitutionally" one conveys structural unity. The church's unity is in its faith and order, signs of its visible community. This visible unity is the only adequate expression of what it means to be one in Christ.

> 2. Although the Church of Christ upon earth must necessarily exist in particular and distinct societies, locally separate one from another, yet their ought to be no schisms, no uncharitable divisions among them. They ought to receive each other as Christ Jesus hath also received them, to the glory of God.
>
> 9. All that are enabled through grace to make such a profession (of faith in Jesus Christ), and to manifest the reality of it in their tempers and conduct, should consider each other as precious saints of God, should love each other as brethren, children of the same family and Father, temples of the same Spirit, members of the same body . . .
>
> 10. Division among Christians is a horrid evil, fraught with many evils. It is antichristian, as it destroys the visible unity of the body of Christ . . .
> [56]

The other nine propositions deal with practical implications which will lead to the achievement of union. Nothing can be an article of faith or a test of communion except that which is expressly taught by Christ and his apostles. The primary assumptions of the <u>Declaration and Address</u> are that Christians are separated by non-essentials, matters of private opinion; they are in reality at one "in the great doctrines of faith and holiness" as well as "the positive ordinances (sacraments) of Gospel initiation."

Among the ecumenists we have surveyed in nineteenth century America none was more catholic in his ecclesiology or more irenic in his strategy for unity than Thomas Campbell. His eclipse as a leader after his son took the reins may well have contributed to the atmosphere of contention and legalism which tempted later generations of Disciples.

Thomas' son, Alexander Campbell (1788-1866), arrived on the American scene from Scotland when the <u>Declaration and Address</u> was in galley proofs. Alexander, who had been grappling with the schisms of the Church in the Old World, immediately became the leading spirit of the Reformation for unity in the nineteenth century. The contrasting roles of Thomas and Alexander Campbell in early American ecumenism was later colorfully described by J. H. Garrison. To Thomas Campbell was given the vision of a united church. "To him it was given to see the evils of division; to hear God's call, in the condition and events of the times and in his Word, for the unity of the church; and to perceive and announce the great fundamental principles by which this unity might be realized." [57] To Alexander Campbell was given the leadership in applying these ecumenical principles to the work of religious reformation.

Alexander Campbell had the same disdain for Christian divisions and the same enthusiastic advocacy for union as did Barton Stone and Thomas Campbell (Stone died ten years before Thomas Campbell). The great fundamental principles which he fully articulated in his books, **Christianity Restored** (1835) and later in his **Christian System** (1836), centered upon unity as the missionary principle for the conversion of the world. Nothing is more essential for the conversion of the world than the union of all Christians, and "nothing is essential to the union of Christians but the Apostles 'teaching and testimony.' " "Neither truth nor union alone," wrote Mr. Campbell, "is sufficient to subdue the unbelieving nations, but truth and union are omnipotent." The union of all Christians is the fundamental purpose of the Church. The restoration of primitive Christianity is the method, Campbell believed, by which this unity can be achieved.

Unity and restoration were the distinctive genius of those early Disciples, but they became a demonic paradox for later Disciples. Due to a contradiction in Campbell's own thought and to the hermeneutical views of later Disciples, the restoration of the New Testament faith was sadly made a legalistic biblicism. The result was that the vision of union was eclipsed. This tension between restorationism and visible unity led to the two schisms among the followers of Stone and the Campbells--the first separating the Disciples and the non-instrumental churches of Christ, the second dividing the Disciples and the Independent Christian Churches.

In conclusion, the nineteenth century produced a panorama of amazing perspectives on Christian unity. (i) It was not an era which supported Christian unity. All these witnesses were achieved when the signs of the times were against them. Their society accentuated division, approved individualistic understandings of the Church, and blessed the diversity in the divided denominations. These attitudes allowed people to accept a vivid competition and denominational self-justification as a natural grace rather than a horrid evil. (ii) The nineteenth century gave birth to some of the most heroic ecumenists in Christian history (rivaling the 17th century with such ecumenical luminaries as Dury, Baxter, Calixtus, Zinzendorf, Leibniz, et al). The leaders we have studied advocated cooperation and union even when it meant risking their careers. Their passion was a spiritual gift not a calculated strategy for success. (iii) From this period we have inherited some of the most articulate books and tracts as well as far-reaching proposals on Christian unity--all which anticipated the fervor of the twentieth century ecumenical movement. They were the architects of Christian unity in America. Their irenic spirit and their practical efforts prepared the foundations for later laborers who would move the churches closer toward union. Their pilgrimage was a tenacious and glorious witness to the one people of God.

NOTES

1. Panoplist and Missionary Magazine, Vol. I (1808-1809) 402; quoted in Lefferts A. Loetscher, "The Problem of Christian Unity in Early Nineteenth-Century America," Church History, Vol. XXXII, No. 1 (March, 1963) 3.

2. William Warren Sweet, Religion in the Development of American Culture, 1765-1840 (New York: Charles Scribner's Sons, 1952) 97.

3. J. B. McMaster, A History of the People of the United States Vol. IV, 551.

4. Samuel J. Mills and Daniel Smith, Report of a Missionary Tour

204

Through That Part of the United States Which Lies West of the Allegany [sic] Mountains (Andover, Massachusetts, 1815) 47.

5. John Howard Yoder, "Christian Unity in Nineteenth-Century America," in **A History of the Ecumenical Movement, 1517-1948** (**HEM**). Ed. Ruth Rouse and Stephen Charles Neill (Philadelphia: Westminster Press, 1954) 232.

6. Sydney E. Ahlstrom, **A Religious History of the American People** (New Haven and London: Yale University Press, 1972) 452.

7. Loetscher, op. cit., 6.

8. Ibid., 12.

9. C. Howard Hopkins, **History of the YMCA in America** (New York: Association Press, 1951) 12.

10. See Millenial Harbinger, 1842; and M.H., 1852, 211.

11. See Ruth Rouse, "Voluntary Movements and the Changing Ecumenical Climate," in **HEM** 318-324.

12. Eva Jean Wrather, "Alexander Campbell on the 'Union of Christians,' " The Christian Evangelist, Vol. XCI, No. 21 (May 27, 1953).

13. W. E. Garrison, **Christian Unity and Disciples of Christ** (St. Louis: The Bethany Press, 1955) 111.

14. "Evangelical Alliance," (five parts), Millenial Harbinger, 1846-1847.

15. Millenial Harbinger, January, 1847, 33.

16. Ibid.

17. Washington Gladden, **Recollections** (Boston: Houghton Mifflin, 1909) 34.

18. Loetscher, op. cit., 15.

19. Yoder, op. cit., 244.

20. Samuel Simon Schmucker, **Fraternal Appeal to the American Churches, with a Plan for Catholic Union, on Apostolic Principles** (New York, 1838). See Seminar Edition (Philadelphia: Fortress Press, 1965).

21. Schmucker, **The True Unity of Christ's Church; Being a Renewed Appeal to the Friends of the Redeemer, on Primitive Christian Union, and the History of Its Corruption** (New York, 1870).

22. E. B. Sanford, **The Origin and History of the Federal Council of**

the Churches of Christ in America (Hartford: S. S. Scranton Co., 1916) 90-92.

23. Millenial Harbinger 1839, 211f.

24. Phillip Schaff, **The Reunion of Christendom** (New York: Evangelical Alliance, 1893).

25. James H. Nichols, "John Williamson Nevin: Evangelical Catholicism," in **Sons of the Prophets; Leaders in Protestantism from Princeton Seminary.** Ed. Hugh T. Kerr (Princeton: Princeton University Press, 1963) 78.

26. Ibid.

27. See Yoder, op. cit., 242-243.

28. Quoted in Charles L. Zorbaugh, "The Plan of Union in Ohio," Church History, Vol. VI, No. 2 (June, 1937) 147-148.

29. Robert Hastings Nichols, "The Plan of Union in New York," Church History, Vol. V, No. 1 (March, 1936) 35.

30. Zorbaugh, op. cit., 162.

31. Nichols, op. cit., 50.

32. Douglas Horton, "The Plan of Union of 1801 in the United States," The Reformed and Presbyterian World, Vol. XXVI, No. 6 (June, 1961) 249.

33. Ibid.

34. Yoder, op. cit., 248.

35. See William W. Manross, **A History of the American Episcopal Church** (New York: Morehouse-Gorham Co., 1954) 285-289.

36. William Reed Huntington, **The Church-Idea; An Essay Towards Unity,** 5th ed. (Boston: Houghton Mifflin Co., 1928) 2.

37. Huntington adapted the word "quadrilateral" from the military lore of his day. In 1870 there was much public attention with the famous "quadrilateral of Lombardy," the four great fortresses which played such a critical role in Napoleon III's campaign in Sardinia. His quadrilateral was for Huntington the four fortresses in the campaign for church union. See John Wallace Suter, **Life and Letters of William Reed Huntington, A Champion of Unity** (New York and London: The Century Company, 1925).

38. This report is published in full in B. B. Tyler, **A History of the Disciples** [American Church History Series] (New York: Christian Literature Co., 1894) 82-94.

39. Ibid.

40. George Plattenburg, "The Unity of the Church--How Broken, and the Creed--Basis on Which It Must Be Restored," in The Old Faith Restored, ed. J. H. Garrison. (St. Louis: Christian Publishing Co., 1891) 335.

41. See John F. Woolverton, William Reed Huntington and Christian Unity: The Historical and Theological Background of the Chicago-Lambeth Quadrilateral. (Unpublished Ph.D. dissertation, Columbia University/Union Theological Seminary, New York, 1963).

42. William Reed Huntington, The Four Visible Theories of Church Unity (New York: John H. Smith, 1909) 11.

43. John Rogers, The Biography of Elder Barton Warren Stone, written by himself with Additions and Reflections 6th ed. (Cincinnati: American Christian Publication Society, 1853) 37-38.

44. Declaration and Address and Last Will and Testament of the Springfield Presbytery (St. Louis: The Bethany Press, 1960).

45. Walter C. Gibbs, "Cane Ridge and Barton W. Stone," The College of the Bible Quarterly, Vol. XXIV, No. 4 (October, 1947) 5.

46. Last Will and Testament 17.

47. Ibid., 22.

48. Christian Messenger, Vol. VII (1833) 315 (C.M.).

49. C.M., Vol. XI (1836) 247.

50. C.M., Vol. XIV (1844) 4ff.

51. C.M., Vol. II (1828) 37ff.

52. William G. West, Barton Warren Stone; Early American Advocate of Christian Unity (Nashville: The Disciples of Christ Historical Society, 1954) xvi.

53. "An Address to the Churches of Christ," C.M., Vol. VI (1832) 266.

54. Yoder, op. cit., 237.

55. Declaration and Address op. cit., 27.

56. Ibid.

57. J. H. Garrison, The Story of a Century (St. Louis: Christian Publishing Co., 1909) 55.

THE AUSTRALIAN LIFE STYLE--SPIRITUALITY "DOWN UNDER"

Geoffrey Barnes

The Portugese explorer, Pedro Ferdandez de Quiros, resolved that terra australis incognita should be known as the land of the Holy Spirit. [1] Seventeenth century Spanish officialdom was less enthusiastic about missionary endeavor in the unknown Southland and de Quiros died a disappointed man. Dutch navigators came next to the Southland in search of wealth but, "finding no good to be done there", left it to Captain James Cook, the English explorer, to claim for Britain what was then New Holland and to name the Eastern half of it New South Wales. [2] Six years later in 1776 the American colonies won their independence and the ensuing years clearly indicated that British convicts could no longer be transported across the Atlantic to the new world. Captain Cook's fellow explorer and distinguished botanist, Sir Joseph Banks, proposed that the British government should found a new colony at Botany Bay in New South Wales. It was American independence that finally forced the circumstances which made the first white settlement in Australia a convict colony. Dreams of spiritual conquest and merchant utopias in the land "down under" gave place to the realities of colonization by convicts.

Taking the Puritans of old and new England as his field Robert Paul has argued that the aim of the church historian is to discover how far they succeeded or failed in translating what they believed into a credible way of life. [3] The interaction of the circumstances in which they found themselves with their adherence to Reformation theology led the Puritans to establish a style of spirituality which continues to invite respect as an authentic response to the Gospel. Given the different circumstances of the respective settlements the contrast between the northern and southern hemispheres is so striking as to pose the question whether, in their formative years, the Australian colonies could give rise to any believable pattern of spirituality at all. [4] No sense of participating in a great Christian experiment, nor responsibility to fulfill an errand in the wilderness, activated the first arrivals of the European world in Australia. They came as prisoners and prison keepers, not as pilgrims and puritans. [5] The mood of many historians has been to discover not the roots of an Australian spirituality but a pervasive secularity. Captain Cook, it has been noted, held religion in such low esteem that he would never tolerate a parson aboard his ship. [6]

It was the children of the enlightenment rather than the Catholic enthusiasts or the Dutch calvinists who eventually planted the institutions of civilization on Australia's shores. [7] Persuaded not by religious dogmas but the necessity to find a practical solution to a social problem, the British government despatched an Anglican chaplain, Richard Johnson, with the first fleet of convict settlers in 1788. The authorities believed that the Church, as by law established, should play its part in founding the new colony and maintaining order. Johnson was followed by Samuel Marsden in 1794. The task of the chaplains was unenviable. Both were of the evangelical or low church party within the Church of England. [8]

As evangelicals the chaplains felt the call to secure the eternal salvation of the reprobate souls that provided the bulk of the new colony's population. As officials they were expected to act as moral policemen. But a prison mends no morals even with a chaplain. [9] They needed the respect their official position gave them to get a hearing and yet the combination of evangelical piety with the inevitable harsh authoritarianism of penal life was not calculated to win many converts from those long since antipathetic to the niceties of ecclesiastical office and the comforts of religion. Apparently in defiance of Governor Hunter's order compelling attendance at church by all denominations the convicts burnt down the first church which Johnson had by dint of long perseverance built five years before. [10] Impatience with imposed authority in church, and in the state, has left its mark on Australian spirituality. Within and without the churches an uncritical equation of religion with traditional morality lingers on.

A definitive religious history of Australia has not yet been written but a new tradition is emerging in Australia which has to do with a search for national identity. [11] Writers have taken up the task with fresh enthusiasm in order to assess the extent to which religion is being translated into a believable way of life. [12] The first chaplain's ministry could be considered a failure; yet a failure not entirely of his own making, and it is a too simple reading of the history to conclude that secularism triumphed and that the role of religion was minimal. [13] The churches and their leaders adapted as best they could. More importantly Marsden survived over many years preaching and planting Christian institutions. His most recent biographer calls him "a great survivor." [14] Indeed spirituality in the land once called the land of the Holy Spirit was indeed a matter of human survival. The penal discipline and the harsh alien bush inevitably tested human endurance as well as the inherited patterns of human identity. Irish convicts were permitted no priest of their persuasion, though in 1840 there were three times as many Irish in New South Wales as in the British Isles. [15] Such piety as survived among them was born of the need to maintain their religious and racial identity over against the predominantly English institutions of the colony.

The reasons why institutionalized religion eventually survived and flourished towards the end of the nineteenth century were not very different from those which applied back in Britain. Sheep and wheat and gold played their part in developing a middle class not unlike that at home. The "hell" of the penal colony became "a workingman's paradise." It seemed to be in the interests of those now enjoying the comforts of the middle class to defend the institutions of Christianity. [16] Once established however the churches found the convict origins of Australia an embarrassment. G. A. Wood, first professor of history at Sydney University, claimed that the "first fleeters" were the victims of a system that transported people for very trivial offences. Catholic historians sought to remove the stains from Irish beginnings by declaring that the convicts were the innocent victims of social circumstances and political expediency. [17] In fact the majority of early settlers in Australia, whatever their nominal church allegiance, were hardened criminals, not the victims of "hideously unjust penal system." [18] Romanticized versions of the early settlers have failed the test of time, adding no luster to the beginnings of denominationalism. The shape of Australian spirituality was determined early on by the human capacity for survival not by the triumph of injured innocence and righteous indignation. Tracing one's ancestry to convict beginnings has now become a popular hobby providing an interesting commentary on the changing canons of respectability and suggesting a new focus of spirituality, in the human struggle for existence and identity rather than in the traditional institutions of religion.

Recent research has also indicated that several elements of survival spirituality are not as characteristically Australian as once was thought. Colloquially Australians still address one another as "mate." "G'day, 'ow yer goin', mate?" is a common greeting. The mateship philosophy has been explored by Russell Ward in **The Australian Legend.** [19] The typical Australian is commonly regarded as

> . . . a practical man, rough and ready in his manners, and quick to decry affectation . . . He is a great improvisor . . . willing to 'have a go' at anything, but . . . content with a task done in a way which

is 'near enough'. Though capable of great exertion in an emergency, he normally feels no impulse to work hard . . . He swears hard and consistently, gambles heavily and often, and drinks deeply on occasion . . . He is usually taciturn . . . stoical . . . and sceptical about the value of religion, and of intellectual and cultural pursuits generally. He believes that Jack is not only as good as his master, but . . . probably a good deal better, and so he is a great 'knocker' of eminent people, unless, as in the case of his sporting heroes, they are distinguished by physical prowess. He is a fiercely independent person who hates officiousness and authority--especially when . . . embodied in military officers and policemen. Yet he is very hospitable and, above all, <u>will stick to his mates through thick and thin</u> . . . He tends to be a rolling stone, highly suspect if he should chance to gather much moss. [20]

The legend has reality because it is not only rooted in the nation's real past, but because it continues to influence how Australians behave. Thus the harsh conditions of the convict era have made human solidarity a necessity for the sense of personal worth. In the nineteenth century the legend accorded well with the experience of agricultural and pastoral workers scattered across the vast lands behind the coastal settlements. To those in the cities the conquest of the bush seemed to promise the realization of a distinctive Australian way of life. It was celebrated and popularized in the ballads and stories of Henry Lawson.

> The hottest drought that ever blazed
>   could never parch the hearts of men;
> And they were men in spite of all,
>   and they were straight, and they were true. [21]

It was as if, 'the bush people knew as well as the author of the Book of Ecclesiastes, or of Psalm 39, what life was all about.' [22] A. B. ('Banjo') Paterson epitomized the men who knew and loved the bushland in **The Man from Snowy River and Other Verses**--the men who knew the bushman's creed about kindness in another's trouble and courage in their own. [23] The question is whether the mateship philosophy was the product of the convict experience of Australia or whether it was already in existence among the criminal classes of England and Ireland. [24] Clearly mateship has been influential in Australian life. The question of originality arises however because the twentieth century is becoming aware that the recitation of the bushman's creed by Lawson and Paterson was an escapist spirituality, indeed a failure to come to terms with the realities of the city. Life in the cities demands a different ethos from that of the bushman legend. [25]

The mateship legend is chauvinistic. It was the qualities of manliness and independence which the Australian writers of the late nineteenth century celebrated. Women played little or no part in the social image of "the coming man" that activated the ambitions of the British Empire at the time. And "the typical Australian" was readily assimilated to the coming man philosophy. [26] The exception was one bush girl whose anguished cry was expressed in her novel **My Brilliant Career** published in 1901. Stella Miles Franklin was making her plea against the male domination of Australian society. The comparative ease of her country way of life was threatened by the immoderate habits of her father; but she had better dreams of womanhood in her changing social circumstances than to perpetuate the tradition of the submission of women to men. She would make her own decisions. [27]

The classical mateship legend might have died sooner had it not been for the first world war. Threats to Britain were seen to be threats to Australia and the Australian way of life and inevitably the apron strings of mother England were tightened. In 1915 Australian volunteers were first called into service at Gallipoli in the Dardanelles. In the face of fierce Turkish defences they dug their trenches and in the midst of unbelievable slaughter they needed all the qualities of manliness, independence and mateship of which their image makers had lately sung to maintain their sanity. Gallipoli was a military disaster; but for the Australian and New Zealand Army Corps, the Anzacs, it was the triumph of "the diggers", the fulfillment of the ethos of "the coming man." [28] They had given sacrificial proof of that comradeship and fighting spirit nurtured beneath the suns of the Southern Cross. Australians, the official war historian declared, "were made to fight, be it drought, fire or unbroken horses. More loyal to his mates than submissive to authority he was as fine a fighting man as exists." [29] When the rhetoric of war is removed it is clear that something of the mores of the convict days had come to fruition redeeming the taint of Australia's beginnings. Mates had become heroes. Latterly the Australian film industry has joined the new opinion makers in a critique of the Anzac legend. Though not dispensing with the mateship symbol altogether, **Breaker Morant**, the story of an Australian soldier's trial by British officers in South Africa, and **Gallipoli,** which presents a young athlete from the wide open spaces in Western Australia racing across the field of battle only to be sacrificed to the ineptitudes and cruelty of war, question militarism as the cradle of nationhood and authentic human self-understanding. For some significant groups within society Australia's national celebration of Anzac Day has a hollow ring. It no longer sets forth a vision designed to inspire patriotism; it celebrates past glories without establishing their relevance for the future. [30]

Following the first world war, the onset of the great

depression and a second world war, there was little creative reflection on the Australian character and the old symbols had to suffice. [31] There remained nevertheless a hint of dissatisfaction. Floods of new migrants from Europe made Australians, if not self-righteous, a little uncomfortable as they sensed levels of self-understanding related to cultural and artistic traditions the exploration of which their march to the workingman's paradise had prevented. [32] Faced with the sophisticated world of international affairs allegiance to "Uncle Sam" seemed more sensible than to look to Britain. The Vietnam veterans, however, served not to glorify the diggers of Anzac but to remind Australians that once more they had been party to policies doomed to failure and destined to fight against overwhelming odds. The image of "the little aussie battler" emerged drawing upon the old symbols--the often unrewarding engagement with the bush and the failure of the average Australian to project the confident image of the person determined to make every post a winning post. Since the 1960's Australians have sensed that they need to find a life-line to deeper levels of cultural and spiritual identity. They have been able to hear again what D. H. Lawrence once said about them:

> They're awfully nice but they've got no inside to them.
> They're hollow . . . They're marvellous and manly
> and independent and all that, outside.
> But inside they are not.
> When they are quite alone, they don't exist . . . [33]

The recognition that Australia's received and ritualized traditions are in need of re-assessment and re-interpretation has led religious historians in particular to insist that there is nevertheless a future for the study of Australia's past. [34] During the last twenty years a group of Sydney historians has published The Journal of Religious History in order to attack the view that religious history is merely an appendage to the more important discussions of politics and economics. Keith Hancock's pioneering history of Australia mentions religion only once and that in brackets! [35] Sociology these days instructs the work of historians and so religion finds its place as one of the basic "structures" in any total national history. In American history the structures of religion are clearly evident, for example, in puritanism, revivalism, catholicism and, their impact upon and relationship to society are discernible. Australia began in the age of the Enlightenment and religion as a structure of society does not figure nearly so clearly in its national development. Comparisons with America may be instructive but not determinative, for Australia may well have to find its own way towards a religious or spiritual understanding of its identity. [36] "Down under" depends, of course, on how the globe of the world is viewed. In Mercator's projection of the terrestrial globe Australia's position down under is correct. Figuratively speaking it has perhaps a pejorative, certainly a non-triumphalist connotation and, viewed from the latter half of the twentieth century, the Australian experience as a whole accords well with that. It is the seemingly negative response to spiritual values and the apparently secular life-style which delineate the Australian character.

Strangely the churches have been slow to recognize the latent spirituality in a non-triumphalist, non-authoritarian approach to life. When the churches battled through the nineteenth century to achieve towards its end a measure of success, it was with British middle class notions of respectability and institutionalized Christianity that they aimed to make and maintain Australia as a civilized nation. [37] The dream of Australia for Christ was not realized. [38] Unlike America revivalist preachers were not greatly successful. [39] The churches themselves have reluctantly become part of the Australian experience never quite able to get on top of the situation. No new religion has come to birth in Australia; the British versions were adapted to the new conditions. Even the Great Disruption of Scotland in 1843 was reproduced in Australia where patronage, the causative factor in Scotland, was entirely unknown! [40] In the nineteenth century Australia was a "derived society" and the churches were no exception to the rule. That they survived is a tribute to the strength of the traditions they inherited and the leadership of the clergy in adapting to the new environment. Not until towards the end of the century had a significant lay leadership emerged. [41] And not until 1901 were the first moves made in the direction of an Australian church.

It was the New South Wales Presbyterians who first proposed a union of the Protestant evangelical churches despite their own sorry history 'by schisms rent asunder." The vision of "one grand church" was no doubt inspired by the federation of the Australian colonies into the commonwealth of Australia in the same year. Delayed by wars and economic depression the vision failed to catch the imagination of the Australian people until the 1950's when the process began which culminated in 1977 with the inauguration of the Uniting Church in Australia. Claiming to be the first truly Australian church it brought together the Methodists, the Congregationalists and a majority of the Presbyterians. [42] That a significant number of Presbyterians has chosen to maintain their separate identity is a testimony to the strength of the Scottish tradition and the failure as yet for a mature Australian spirituality to emerge. During the negotiations for union a proposal to have bishops in the new church, the validity of their order transmitted by means of a concordat with the Church of South India, was rejected. The proposal ran counter both to the inherited traditions of the three participating denominations and to the Australian dislike of hierarchical authority. As now established the Uniting Church is governed by a series

of inter-related councils rather than a hierarchy of courts or
bishops and that is more appealing to the egalitarian consciousness
that still persists.

The seventy-five years of negotiation required to bring
the Uniting Church into being reflects the Australian tendency
to be wary of innovations and enthusiam in religion. Evangelistic
crusades provided some interesting diversions in religion in the
1950's and 60's; but despite the churches' plans to fight the drift
from organized Christianity by harnessing the interest engendered
by overseas evangelists, revivalism has not become a strong feature
of religious life. [43] It was an emphasis on a theology of the
Church and the ministry in the Presbyterian General Assembly
that led to the renewal of negotiations in 1954. The first report,
The Faith of the Church, setting out a theology for the Uniting
Church, provoked little critical response, especially amongst the
laity, revealing that careful theological statement in traditional
terms was not of great moment to the average church goer. [44]
It was accepted because it promised to facilitate the merging
of the three denominations. The second report, dealing with the
practical, institutional structures for the new church brought
forth much more critical comment. [45] When a theology of
ministry was expressed as meaning the placement of bishops in
the Church it was in this more pragmatic form that a decisive
response was evoked. Even although it was the Presbyterians
who first emphatically rejected the proposal for episcopacy in
the new Church, the subsequent experience of the Uniting Church
since 1977 has revealed how strongly attached the congregations
are to their denominational traditions and how loathe to accept
new ones.

While it may justly claim to represent a significant attempt to realize and express an Australian spiritual identity,
the Uniting Church is the beginning of the process rather than
its fulfillment, because it has brought to the fore some of the
important issues which Christians face as society rejects old
symbols of meaning and searches for new ones. Like the scribe
"instructed unto the kingdom of God" Uniting Church members
are called to bring forth from their treasure things both new
and old. [46] They value the treasures inherent in their British
traditions but they also sense the need for new styles of spirituality.
Now they must acknowledge that "home" for Australians is a
community where those whose first language is English are a
decreasing proportion of the population. The desire to visit Britain
persists but even the older generation no longer speaks of "going
home" to Britain. Similarly while the mateship legend once celebrated the Australian response to the vast open spaces, the citizens
of the most urbanized country in today's world seek different
symbols of identity. [47] Choosing to live in their places of leisure
rather than in proximity to their work Australians in fact invented

modern suburbia. Such a social context both threatens and challenges the churches. They are threatened by increasing materialism and hedonism; they are challenged in a leisure-loving society to embody what the **Shorter Westminster Catechism** once said was the chief purpose of humanity--to glorify God and enjoy him forever. What follows then is an attempt to discern some necessary elements in an Australian spirituality.

First, Australia's so-called secularized consciousness needs to be reconsidered. It has been too readily assumed that impatience with imposed authority and easy dismissal of traditional theology were signs that Australia had rejected the religious interpretation of life. If the bushranger, Ned Kelly, hanged in the last century for armed holdups, has taken on something of the aura of a Robin Hood, it is because as yet no other folk hero has captured the minds of those who delight in the liberation of the poor from the oppression of the rich. Australians make their sportsmen heroes because their liturgies are performed by life-savers on the beaches or players on the cricket pitch and the football field. The Rev. John Flynn is perhaps one of the few Australians who has touched the springs of the religious imagination and significantly his fame relates to practical service in the founding of the flying doctor service in the inland.

Robert Paul has argued that the strength of the Puritan position was its practical theological integrity. [48] Doctrine in Australia, it has been remarked, "is of interest only in so far as it erupts in political forms, as the long standing argument over state aid to denominational schools." [49] Australians for the most part are strangers to Puritan introspection but their hunch that the only theology that matters must be concerned with practical community affairs may not be wide of the Puritan tradition. Within the churches themselves theology has sometimes erupted, for example, in the case of the Presbyterian professor of New Testament accused of heresy in the 1930's by the New South Wales assembly of his church. [50] Yet on the whole the Australian laity in particular has reflected an ethos of skepticism in matters of formal theology.

Viewed negatively such skepticism may be seen as part of the "cultural cringe", a feeling of inferiority in the presence of more sophisticated and articulate traditions of theology. Yet Australians are beginning to recognize that the qualities which gave rise to skepticism, to egalitarianism and a secular way of life are the positive, not the negative, material of their identity. [51] Accustomed, of course, to find their cultural norms by reference to Britain, Europe and America, a certain wistfulness for traditional forms of religious experience and expression persists; but when the sense of freedom from such traditions is accepted, it is apparent that the Australian response to life can be judged in its own context. In the land down south comparisons with the Northern hemisphere may not always be appropriate. The reappraisal of convict beginnings is evidence of this conviction. The first settlers were criminals and their gaolers often corrupt and inept and yet they were founders of a nation. When theology is done from the grass roots rather than from the top, when styles of piety are related not to imposed theologies but to an historical awareness of the context in which the human spirit struggled to survive, then the pejorative connotations of "down under" disappear. We do not despise Jesus because he was born in a stable, indeed the stable becomes the proper symbol of humility. So what needs to be lifted up in the story of Australia's search for identity is the element of human struggle and suffering. There is no need to romanticize it, to adapt it to jingoistic notions of British military enterprise, nor to make denigrating comparisons with the more fortunate beginnings of America. With such a revised perspective it is likely that reflection on the Australian experience will reveal new sources of the Australian spirit.

Secondly, the characteristic sense of freedom in Australia's life-style promises a flexibility and tolerance often lacking in the traditions that nurtured it. As an anti-authoritarian attitude the churches have not found this easy to accept, nor conducive to their notions of the spiritual life. Yet over the years they have learned the wisdom of adapting. At first they sought to reproduce structures they knew and appreciated at home. The Church of England was to be the established church. Yet despite its acknowledged official status it was eventually to become a voluntary denomination like the other churches. The period of the Enlightenment also taught the churches the folly of refusing to change. Not the least impact of enlightenment thought was against the Bible, an impact accentuated by Charles Darwin in the middle of the nineteenth century. When the miners came in their thousands in the 1850's and sank their shafts in search of gold, they believed they could see the fossil evidence to support the popular notion that Darwin had disproved the Bible. So it is not surprising that Australian coins have never borne the imprint of American coins--"In God We Trust." The churches adapted to new patterns of thought and in time revised their arguments for the authority of the Bible maintaining, nevertheless, the conviction that they had the responsibility for making and keeping Australia Christian. [52]

Since the 1960's the difficult responsibility for encouraging a Christian society has been accentuated. A great variety of ethnic groups resulting from migration policies has made its presence felt. Reluctant to forego the freedoms they believe to be their right Australians are bound to grant the same freedoms to Catholic Italians, Orthodox Greeks, [53] Muslims from the Middle East, and to Australians themselves who, dissatisfied with their inherited traditions, have embraced the teachings of oriental religions. Refugees from South East Asia have added to the cosmopolitan character of the nation especially in the cities. Nurtured in the days of the White Australia Policy which excluded all colored peoples from settling permanently in the country, the older generation is not free of racial prejudice; but pluralism is the new fact of life in society. The negotiators for the Uniting Church in an early proposal tried to break through racial and cultural barriers by advocating a concordat with the Church of South India. [54] Too radical for church people mostly nurtured in denominations of British origin, it was rejected. Still there are indications that where Christian ethnic groups sense that their culture is not threatened by the Australian context, but rather can contribute to the national search for identity, it is to the Uniting Church that they are looking. [55] Within the Uniting Church itself the old polemical restraints are falling away especially in relationships with the Roman Catholic Church. Ecumenical relationships in the wider sphere are not without difficulty, however, because the continuing Congregational and Presbyterian denominations have withdrawn their support for the Australian Council of Churches. The resilience of these denominations and that of the Baptists, who have always maintained a sense of independence in the ecumenical sense, bears witness to the Australian disposition that on matters of religion the people will in no wise be coerced.

Thirdly, spirituality is seen to relate with more subtlety than earlier times to the spacious nature of the land. The population clings to the narrow strip of land along the coast, mostly to the East and the South, contributing to the urbanized character of the nation. Yet the legends which hitherto have created a sense of identity arose in the attempt to tame the wilderness and populate the dead heart of the interior. This shaped the image of the "little aussie battler", fighting a battle he can never win; the vast Australian loneliness always triumphs, fire and drought bring his best efforts to naught. Romanticizing the bushmen and the sturdy pioneers the legends concentrated too much on one human response and not enough on the variety of human adaptation to the subtle qualities of the context. Until the advent of environmental consciousness Australians celebrated only the taming of the land. Even their attitude to the first inhabitants, the aborigines, has emphasized submission. The qualities of muscular strength, of endurance and courage were praised. Now there is a new recognition that the land has its own character, its strange spaciousness, wide horizons and sunburnt colors, indeed a mysterious timelessness, which the aborigines in their wisdom understand and which Western Europeans initially could not recognize. [56] The sense of space and time is described by the novelist, David Malouf, in the words of an Australian returning from England:

> He liked its mixture of powdery blues and greens,
> its ragged edges, its sprawls, the sense it gave
> of being unfinished and of offering no prospect
> of being finished. These things spoke of space,
> and of a time in which nature might be left to
> go its own way and still yield up what it had to
> yield, there was that sort of abundance. [57]

Such an appreciation of the landscape makes the qualities of battle less appropriate and indicates the gentler qualities of patience and love. Australians are recognizing that they have a covenant to be cherished with the land of the Holy Spirit, not a score to be settled.

It is with the help of the aborigines that Australians are learning to accept a new relationship with the land. Where Christians have become involved in the land rights for aborigines question their primary concern is human justice; but it is also a recognition that spirituality for aborigines is vitally linked with the land, its trees and its animals. Aborigines cannot conceive of their worth and their identity as people apart from a close relationship to the land. The first British settlers could not understand this. The second chaplain to arrive in Sydney, Samuel Marsden, believed the first thing to do with the aborigines was to civilize them, educate them, westernize them and then they could be Christianized. [58] Marsden failed because the black culture was entirely adapted to a close collaboration with nature and had no place nor need for agriculture and industry such as Marsden thought essential. He eventually satisfied his missionary ambition by visiting the New Zealand Maoris whom he considered much more civilized and amenable to the Gospel. Lack of understanding and a savage sense of superiority effectually short circuited a recognition of the deeply spiritual relationship of the aborigines to the land. The land rights question is political, related, for example, to the right of a multi-national organization to mine an aboriginal sacred site. Yet new perspectives on spirituality are opening up for those who work for justice for the aborigines because they experience a sense of community with a people, who though deprived by two centuries of white settlement, have not forgotten the roots which nourish their self esteem. [59]

The controversy as to the origins of the mateship legend and its dominant note of maleness lead to a fourth element in contemporary Australian spirituality--a recognition of the role of the feminine. Indeed the attitude of covenant with the land implicit in aboriginal religion corresponds with emphases made by feminists. Like the original traditions of life and thought which helped to shape Australia, feminism derives from the overseas movement but its raison d'être is clearly evident in a nation where male domination has prevailed. In the late 1970's **My Brilliant**

Career [60] became one of Australia's most successful films appealing to a society now more attuned to women's need for liberation. Yet the male dominated mateship legend dies hard; a seventeen year old youth reflects the masculine ethos against which Stella Miles Franklin rebelled when he declares:

> Girls can be friends but never mates. Friendships die, especially friendships with girls. You stick to your mates for life. If you fight with your girl it may be all over; but a fight with your mate never ends things. After all he's your mate. [61]

It is not simply a matter of equality; there is a recognition that spirituality will always be stultified without an authentic acceptance of the feminine. A sense of fair play makes Australians willing to grant positions of influence equal to men in many spheres including some churches; though some reluctance appears in the trades unions. [62] It is the acceptance and celebration of feminine qualities as belonging to the very heart of reality which Australian congregations find difficult, perhaps because in the wider community sexual mores are either old fashioned and conservative or hedonistic and permissive. Appreciation of sexuality also tends to lack sophistication and finesse. The accordingly rough and ready Australian male whose conversation is limited to sport and crude jokes, the "ocker image", is not easily effaced, except in the cities where cultural and artistic events draw a higher proportion of men than hitherto. The acceptance of the feminine promises a deeper appreciation of sexuality and of the arts, and therefore will enrich the Australian spirit.

Finally the search for a spiritual identity in Australia underlines the question of suffering. Australians tend to be happy-go-lucky and pleasure-loving, perhaps because after the initial trauma of convict settlement they experienced no violent revolutions and their country has never been the site of great military battles. The first settlers came with few utopian dreams and later seekers after a new Eldorado were soon accustomed to something much less exciting than a golden age. Such experience of high tragedy as their twentieth century descendants knew was derived from the battle fields of Europe or far to the North in Papua New Guinea and the islands. The affluence and freedom of "the lucky country" are not then the result of an agonized triumph of the human spirit in circumstances of revolution and national disaster. [63] Rewarding markets for wheat and wool and mineral discoveries in return for normal human effort were readily found overseas. Human freedoms have been guaranteed by a geographical isolation which enables a certain political independence in the context of Western diplomacy and which, at the same time, provides a strategic democratic presence in the South East Asian and Pacific region, a presence unlikely to be ignored by Britain and America. Assured thus of security and yet in search of an identity Australians have until recently made much of the exploits of the Anzacs at Gallipoli as the birth of the nation and its baptism of fire. It is the belief that the essence of nationality must be mixed with past military glory before it satisfies the soul; it is perhaps the guilt reaction that good fortune must have its human price.

The notion that suffering plays a part in molding corporate memory and refining the sense of destiny is not altogether misguided. It is the thesis of this chapter, however, that in Australia it is an idea that is too much influenced by romanticized and imperialistic versions of history. Australia needs now to look at the experience of human suffering from a different perspective, from "down under", from within its Asian and Pacific context rather than its European beginnings. [64] This recognition emerges from the breaking down of the old mateship legends and the dehumanizing possibilities of a society for which the old rituals and symbols have ceased to refresh the human spirit. Revitalized symbols of meaning must be found in Australia's own history, in the issues of human justice close at hand like the treatment of aborigines. If suffering is a constituent part of the pursuit of holiness then Australia's cross is "down under" in the context of its own southern skies. [65]

A concern to come to terms with society's developed secular consciousness, the virtues of the sense of tolerance in human relationships, a growing new respect for the spacious land and the recognition that mateship denigrates the feminine contribution to life are the issues which call for reflection. Penal colonists, persevering pioneers and enlightened seekers of a new society have contributed to the Australian ethos. Inevitably the cultural traditions of the settlers' homeland continued to influence their manner of life; but the new context, often alien and terrifying, carrying its own ingredients of suffering, shaped their thinking and acting in ways which deserve more historical analysis and reflection. Indeed it is crucial for Australia's well being, where for example, mateship is readily replaced by a "me-first" mentality because of high unemployment, that a relevant spirituality be discerned and visibly embodied. The acquisitive spirit could all too easily triumph, and the Holy Spirit could all too easily be confused with the rewards of material success, in an unthinking life-style unworthy of God's gifts to the Australian nation.

NOTES

1. Manning Clark, **A History of Australia** Vol. 1 (Melbourne, 1971) 16.

2. Ibid., 24.

3. "The Accidence and the Essence of Puritan Piety," Austin Seminary Bulletin, 93/8 (1978) 6.

4. R. White, **Inventing Australia** (Sydney, 1981) 16.

5. J. D. Bollen, **Religion in Australian Society** (Sydney, 1973) 3-4.

6. Russell Ward, **Australia Since the Coming of Man?** (Sydney, 1982) 31.

7. Clark, op. cit., Vol. 1, ch. 3.

8. Before his ordination Marsden had almost certainly been influenced by Methodism. A. T. Yarwood, **Samuel Marsden** (Melbourne, 1977) 5-7.

9. A. Grocott, **Convicts, Clergymen and Churches** (Sydney, 1980) 28.

10. Yarwood, op. cit., 35.

11. There is no equivalent in Australia as yet of S. Ahlstrom, **A Religious History of the American People**, cf. J. D. Bollen, et. al., "Australian Religious History, 1960-1980," The Journal of Religious History, 11/1 (1980) 8-44.

12. E.g. R. Broome, **Treasure in Earthen Vessels** (St. Lucia, 1980); Grocott, op. cit.; W. Phillips, **Defending a Christian Country** (St. Lucia, 1981).

13. Cf. D. Millikan, **The Gospel in Australia** (Canberra, 1982) 8.

14. Yarwood, op. cit.

15. J. Carroll, ed., **Intruders in the Bush** (1982) 5.

16. White, op. cit., chs. 2 and 3.

17. Grocott, op. cit., 5-6.

18. Ibid., 5.

19. Melbourne, 1966.

20. Quoted Carroll, op. cit., 3-4. (Underlining mine).

21. Clark, op. cit., Vol. 5 (1981) 97.

22. Ibid.

23. Ibid., 136.

24. Carroll, op. cit., Ch. 2.

25. Ibid., 123.

26. White, op. cit., 83.

27. Clark, op. cit., Vol. 5, 224-5.

28. The word "digger" came to be used during the Gold Rush of the 1850's and acquired a new meaning during the First World War when Australians were heavily involved in trench warfare in Europe.

29. Quoted White, op. cit., 126.

30. The Returned Servicemen's League opposes any diminution of the importance of Anzac Day. Groups representing homosexuals and demonstrators against the rape of women in war were in 1981 refused permission to take part in the Anzac Day Parade in the national capital.

31. C. Wallace-Crabbe, **Melbourne or the Bush** (Sydney, 1974) 6.

32. White, op. cit., 159-161.

33. Quoted Patrick Morgan, "Hard Work and Idle Dissipation: the Dual Australian Personality," Meanjin, 41/1 (1982) 134.

34. Cf. an unpublished lecture delivered in 1982 by Prof. K. Cable of the University of Sydney entitled, "The Future of Australia's Religious Past."

35. Quoted Bollen, et al., op. cit., 43-44.

36. Ibid., 44; cf. the comment by the Australian novelist, Christopher Koch, "We are European people marooned on the other side of the world." The Weekend Australian Magazine, (Jan 8 & 9, 1983) 2.

37. Phillips, op. cit.

38. J. D. Bollen, **Religion in Australian Society** (Sydney, 1973).

39. Broome, op. cit., Ch. 4.

40. K. R. Campbell, "Presbyterian Conflicts in New South Wales, 1837-1865," The Journal of Religious History, 5/3 (1969) 233-247.

41. Congregationalist laymen took an early initiative in establishing a theological college in 1864. See **Camden College, A Centenary History** by J. Garrett and L. W. Farr (Sydney, 1964) 1-7.

42. G. L. Barnes, "A United Church is Born in Australia," Midstream, 16 (1977) 412-418.

43. The first Billy Graham Crusade in Australia in 1959 was perhaps the most successful.

44. Joint Board of Graded Lessons (Melbourne, 1959).

45. **The Church--Its Nature, Function and Ordering** (Aldergate Press: Melbourne, 1963).

46. Matthew 13:52.

47. The Charismatic Movement in Australia is evidence of the search for spiritual experience and symbols of meaning.

48. Op. cit., 14-21.

49. Wallace-Crabbe, op. cit., 11.

50. Lee, **The Australian Dictionary of Biography.**

51. Cf. Wallace-Crabbe, op. cit., 67.

52. Phillips, op. cit.

53. Melbourne has one of the largest Greek populations outside of Athens.

54. **The Church--Its Nature, Function and Ordering,** 52-57.

55. Applications for the ordained ministry in the Uniting Church in Australia have been received from Orthodox priests now living in Australia.

56. The mysterious quality of time is captured in Lindsay's novel, **Picnic at Hanging Rock** and effectively captured in the Australian film version.

57. **Fly Away Peter** (London, 1982).

58. Yarwood, op. cit.

59. Representatives of the Uniting Church have stood by aborigines in recent confrontations with the state governments of Western Australia and Queensland. See "Noonkanbah Reflections" <u>Trinity Occasional Papers</u> 2/1, (Brisbane, 1983) 3-12.

60. See p. 7.

61. See p. 7. Interesting illustrations of sexism appear in **They Dreamt of a School,** the centenary history of the Methodist Ladies College in Melbourne, by Ailsa G. Thomsen Zainu'ddin, (Hyland House: Melbourne, 1982). See especially p. 12.

62. The Uniting Church in Australia ordains women and some moves have been made in the Anglican church to ordain women priests.

63. The only real threat of invasion was by the Japanese in 1942. Donald Horne has popularized the phrase the lucky country in his book with that title, 2nd rev. ed. (Sydney, 1966).

64. Cf. H. Perkins, "Issues of Contextual Theology--an Australian Perspective," <u>Ecumenical Review</u> 28/3 (1976) 286-295.

65. Use of the constellation of the Southern Cross had its beginnings in the Anti-Transportation League flag of 1851 and the Eureka Stockade flag of 1854. Lee M. Cozzolino, **Symbols of Australia** (Harmondsworth [Penguin], 1980) 30.

THE DEVELOPMENT OF A PROGRAMME
OF CHRISTIAN NURTURE

John I. Morgans

INTRODUCTION

Study Seventeenth Century Puritanism in America, and at the "Insurance Capital of the United States"! This was surely to take Tawney's thesis on the relationship between Calvinism and Capitalism to ludicrous lengths. If it seemed ironic to a Welsh Nonconformist that he would need to pursue his studies at Hartford, it was only because of his ignorance of the New England of Cotton, Hooker and Norton. In 1965 the Hartford Seminary Foundation provided an accessible and well-catalogued specialist library of Puritan works and a rare combination of two exemplars of classical scholarship and imaginative flair in Ford Lewis Battles and Robert Paul.

Ford Battles enabled my contemporaries to discover, through an intensive study of **The Institutes,** the strength and flexibility of the Reformed tradition when it was faithful to Calvin. To travel a century later to the Mid-Atlantic Puritanism of the Seventeenth Century with Robert Paul as our guide opened up an encounter which demanded that religion and politics should inter-relate in our understanding of the working out of God's purposes. Calvin's Geneva and Cromwell's England flourished at Thomas Hooker's Hartford and together inspired a response not only of the pursuit of historical scholarship but also of serving the Living God in today's world. The God of Calvin, Cromwell and Hooker reached out to Battles, Paul and their students.

This background created the recognition that the Christian belongs to a community which exists to serve the Kingdom. The Church is a sign and foretaste of the reign of God. The Christian is under discipline: the "faith" is to be loved, understood and lived. This basis for a process of "Christian Nurture" was one of the foundations of the Hartford training. The heritage of the Puritan fathers and of Horace Bushnell is that the whole Church is involved in a continuing process of nurture, worship and mission.

Of course the questions of the practicality of this vision of Christian Nurture waited for me when I recrossed the Atlantic to return to my Welsh homeland. How was the vision of nurturing the whole of God's People to be translated into the life of a small rural congregation? My background was wider than that of Hartford: my upbringing in a Welsh-speaking chapel in the declining coal-mining valleys of South Wales; my studies in Arts and Theology at Swansea; my taste of the more "catholic" but less "Puritan" Oxford where I first met Robert Paul through the friendship of Horton Davies. The Welsh and Oxford years had helped to shape me before my arrival at Hartford but it was there at the Seminary, and particularly through Paul and Battles, that I discovered that intellectual rigor and emotional warmth needed to be combined before there could be genuine communication of the Gospel. The two years of "small-group" common study and sharing showed the way towards effective styles of communication. It was then with experience and hope that I began my ministry towards the end of 1967. Yet, despite all my preparation, a year later I was to record the following expression of my experience as a minister.

EXPERIENTIAL BACKGROUND

A. Llanidloes 1967-1974.

> This is certainly a "low" point in my ministry; this is the time when frustrations come to the surface and when it is extremely hard to contain them. Now is the time when I have to be prepared to walk patiently with God and yet not lose the vision and become lethargic. How easy it is to let the calling slide into the sinecure--to allow oneself to become so bogged down by the lack of progress and lack of vision and simply allow church-life to continue in its inevitable decline: but to get out before disaster occurs and leave for another church.

This extract from my diary for February 23rd, 1969, is an expression of my doubts regarding life of both congregation and minister (myself) after just fifteen months at my first pastorate. I had come to Llanidloes, a small town in rural mid-Wales

in December 1967, a town which seemed to present special opportunities for the expansion of the Church. Ecumenical relations
were at least tolerable and there were seven ministers (two Presbyterians, Methodist, Baptist, Congregationalist, Anglican and Roman
Catholic), all of whom met monthly in fraternity. Probably 40%
of the population (about 2,500 souls) were on various Church
rolls and 15% were regular worshippers. The town had strong
roots and most people knew each other well--perhaps at times,
too well.

I served the Congregational Church. Its membership
in 1967 was 102; and although this would seem to present reasonable
scope, statistics did not say the whole truth. Of the 102, 35 attended at the most once a year (the Annual Harvest Thanksgiving),
14 no longer lived in the area and 8 attended perhaps 20 times
a year. This left 41 regular worshippers. As in most Churches,
the majority of members were women (68) and over 55 years
of age. There was little concept of mission, either home or overseas. Youth activities did not exist and the Sunday School had
one teacher and eight children. It was clear that fresh channels
were needed to let new life into the Christian community. Neither
worship pattern nor buildings were fulfilling the needs of most
people. There was no outreach. If any impact was to be made
in the area, it would have to be in a different form. I suggested
to the Council of Churches in 1969 that we should experiment
with house groups, but at that time the Council felt that the
idea was impractical and unnecessary.

Formation of House Groups.

In October 1969, the first group was started. It consisted
of seven ladies whose age averaged 70. We met in one of their
homes (the lady was a Church member) and decided that we would
meet every two weeks to discuss the Gospel of Mark. A month
later, a second group, mostly middle-aged and middle-class, began
to meet. They were a very diverse group, ranging from the local
Catholic priest to an agnostic garage-owner. We began by looking
at the "state of the Church today", also met fortnightly and gradually moved into more theological questions as we sought the
reasons for the breakdown in belief and Church practice. Having
established these two groups, a Youth Group, which was already
meeting weekly, now developed into a discussion group, looking
at different topics each week. During the following year, five
other groups came into existence, through developing personal
relationships. The normal way was by my asking two or three
to begin a group, and allow it to snowball. This always happened
and thus by May, 1971 there were seven adult groups, one youth
group and a group for students at various colleges. The obvious
problem now lay in the direction of leadership and in the creation
of common material. Everyone felt that meetings should be held

regularly and in fact each group met at least twenty times a year from their formation in 1969/1970 to late 1974 when I left the area. Since I was group-leader, this meant attending all the groups every two weeks, and I felt it necessary to forge a common material.

In order to cope with all the work, I linked my preaching material with the house-group discussions. This would obviously serve several purposes, in that it would save time in preparation and also ultimately link worship with discussion. I changed my preaching-style and content to fit this purpose, and sought to preach "an approach to theology." I began by making my own way through John Macquarrie's **Principles of Christian Theology** (S.C.M., 1966) and this provided me with a framework for the creation of 130 sermons--which obviously became less dependent upon the original material as time wore on since the sermons were written over a period of four years. The first sermon was preached on Sunday evening, September 20th, 1970 and the final one on Sunday evening, September 29th, 1974. Each sermon was approximately 1000 words in length and 100 copies of each sermon was made. These were then distributed to each group member and were the basis of their discussions.

Each group session met for about two hours and everyone took part in reading the script, looking up Biblical references and in a discussion which was always vigorous, searching and tolerant. Almost half of those who attended had not been in contact with the Church for many years or had never been to Church and thus it was the first time they had grappled with the basics of faith. This would also be true for many who were regular worshippers.

Effects.

(1) There was a remarkable growth in theological awareness. All major life-issues were shared.

(2) Growth in relationships and the breakdown of barriers. All generations shared a desire to discover answers to the major problems of life. There were 15 year-olds and 80 year-olds, all handling the same material and all capable of discussing these issues with each other. Age barriers disappeared. The same was true of other barriers: educational, political, social and not least, denominational. Conservative Catholics and conservative Baptists shared the same material with the most liberal and all were confronted by the Gospel. As a result, those within the groups cared for and pastored each other. There was a real koinonia.

(3) Growth in Numbers. At its peak there were

over 100 people closely involved in the work (in a community of 2,500). Eight were full-time theology students at various universities and theological colleges. Five entered the Ministry: two women and three men. It is probable that none of them would have studied theology but for their house-group background. Approximately 40 new members were received into the United Reformed Church during the period and two young men were ordained as elders of the Church.

(4) I left the area in October 1974 and 9 years later some of the groups still meet with their own indigenous leadership. For several years there were five adult groups and two youth groups (led by people who had been trained in earlier groups). During the last year a young minister has been inducted to the U.R.C. pastorate and he reports that he finds his greatest support from the house groups.

(5) Social Concerns. In 1974 the groups formed a Social Action Committee and during the years have sustained care for the elderly and at the same time raised considerable amounts of money for various charitable concerns.

(6) Wider Concerns. During 1971-4, large numbers of Llandiloes were taken on "retreat" for 3 day courses to the Cistercian monastery at Caldey (in Dyfed in South-West Wales) and the numbers were so great that we increased the visits from once a year to three times a year (24 people each time, of all ages). More will be said of this connection later.

B. Manselton 1974-1977.

The situation here was completely different from Llanidloes. Manselton is an old-established terraced housing area of Swansea with a population of about 5 thousand, although the surrounding districts would multiply this many times. The United Reformed Church was also a complete contrast from that in Llanidloes. In 1974 it had a membership of 370 but of this number there was a worshipping congregation of about 210 (of these 94 were over 60 years old; 69 between 40 and 60; 38 between 15 and 40; 147 were women). The Church had a very strong, although traditional, weekly programme of separate Men's and Women's Fellowships, a Sisterhood, a Band of Hope (to encourage total abstinence), a Mid-Week devotional service, a Youth Club and uniformed organizations. Its greatest asset was a concerned Eldership which recognized the strengths and weaknesses of the congregation. The Church's mission overseas was imaginative and powerful; its local concern real and effective. House groups in this area would have a new dimension and role. The Manselton Council of Churches took groups under its wing in September 1975 and there has always been the closest cooperation. Our Elders and Church Meeting accepted the scheme at the same time and the Church Magazine included the following article.

The U.R.C. at Manselton is a busy Church. From September until May, there is something going on either in the church or in the hall almost every evening--and often during the afternoons. All ages are catered for with a great variety of activities.. Why then is there the suggestion to have a new structure of activity--and in homes rather than in church buildings?

1. We must deepen our faith in the God who has come to us in Christ and who comes now through the Holy Spirit. To do this often involves thinking, reading and sharing ideas about Christianity. This is no intellectual enterprise; it is to seek to share our Christian experience with the experience of the Bible and the church. Every member of the church has a valid contribution to make--simply because we are all different.

2. We must evangelize. Throughout Wales, at the present time, the church is declining very rapidly and the trend shows no likelihood of stopping. Often, we are complacent about the vast majority in our country who do not know the Gospel. Often, we are simply not interested--or we have given up trying. The development of the house group is an attempt to reach out into the community and ultimately to bring some of the non-churched to knowledge of God.

3. We must know each other. One of the great problems of a large church is that so many do not know others in the church. This creates unnecessary barriers, not the least of which is an age-barrier. It is important to recognize the different needs of people, but at the same time I am convinced that the same basic things concern us all. By coming into groups, which do not segregate according to age, we shall discover people within the church whom we have not met properly, and indeed we shall discover depths about people whom we think we have known for a long time.

What is the programme? The Manselton Council of Churches is setting up three house-groups and in addition, our church is creating a further four. There will be at least seven groups by Christmas. Each group will meet for about an hour and a half every two weeks and will receive a copy of one of the sermons. This will be discussed in each group. The actual organizing will be done when we discover the number of people who would like to be involved this year.

A few practical points.

1. There is no need for each group to visit each home. It may be inconvenient for some families--children, aged parents, sickness, small rooms, etc.

2. Refreshments are strictly limited to tea/coffee and at the most, biscuits.

3. Meetings will be limited to an hour and a half.

Effects.

The material used in house groups was closely linked with Morning Family Worship (which increased from an average of 70 to 130 worshippers, with many younger families attending regularly) and was based upon a system of twenty theological themes. [1] Between 1975 and 1977, I was responsible for leading 1 ecumenical group, 4 U.R.C. groups and a Sunday School class of young mothers. The local Baptist minister led 1 ecumenical group and 3 Baptist groups and the Methodist and Presbyterian ministers led a group each. In all during 1976-1977 about 140 people were involved. The visits to Caldey continued and 170 people visited between 1974 and 1977. Four men trained for the Ministry: three into the U.R.C. and one into the Welsh-speaking Baptist denomination. Sixteen new Sunday-School teachers were appointed and far more people became concerned about the life of the Church and its service to the community.

C. Moderator for Wales of the United Reformed Church 1977-present.

During the past six years I have been separated from local pastoral charge in order to exercise a wider ministry within the United Reformed Church. [2] These years have given me the opportunity to relate intimately to the majority of the 160 local congregations of the U.R.C. in Wales and also to work closely with the Councils of the Church at the local and wider level:

> attending Church and Elders' meetings
> leading house groups in local congregations
> presiding at worship in almost all our congregations
> counselling ministers and Church members
> leading "Day-Schools" for ministers, lay-preachers, elders, church-teachers, women, young people
> leading over 30 half-week retreats at the Cistercian Abbey at Caldey
> working with pastorate and District Councils as they seek new ministry

232

attending District Councils in their over-view of the life and mission of the Church

presiding at Synod and working with Synod Committees in the service of Church and Community

meeting candidates for Ministry within Wales and counselling those recently ordained to Ministry

cooperating at Assembly level with fellow Moderators

serving on an Assembly Committee advising on Ministerial Training within the U.R.C.

representing the U.R.C. on many ecumenical councils at national (Welsh) level

My convictions after 15 years of experience at local and wider Church level is that the basic concerns which confronted me as a young minister of a small-town congregation in 1967 are the ones which the Church faces at every level.

D. Summary of the Experience 1967-1983.

My experiment in Christian Nurture developed pragmatically. I had been able to convince (by personal contact) over one hundred people to commit themselves to meeting in small groups for six sessions in which we would discuss together major questions of "life and death." Within the total number involved there were represented most Christian denominations, all ages, people of "no faith" and many who had little confidence or respect for the Church. They were from all kinds of social, economic and cultural backgrounds. Where was I to begin? How could their interest be captured and sustained? Would they all come to a second meeting? The common denominator soon became clear: has life any purpose? Is there meaning to existence and to my own life? The quest might have been motivated by curiosity, a search for security or the need for a more friendly and open companionship, but it was soon recognized and acknowledged that the individual quest was at the same time a common enterprise. The agenda had various ingredients: I was responsible for introducing "the faith": quite as significant were the issues and responses raised by my fellow participants. There was a tripartite conversation between myself as "leader", the objective material and the rest of the group. Soon the group members were confident enough to be setting their own agenda, creating their own shape to theology and producing their own leadership.

At first my normative material was Macquarrie's **Principles of Christian Theology** but it was not long before that material, under the scrutiny of one hundred people meeting in ten groups week after week, led us into many theological worlds: that of classical writers like Augustine and Calvin and Twentieth Century theologians like Barth and Tillich. At the same time I was constantly being pressed to "open up the Scriptures." How was the Bible to be interpreted? What was the nature of its authority? Did it have any authority at all? Once a basic confidence had been established amongst members of the groups, then the questions came thick and fast: the relevance of "theology" for actual living; the place of worship; the Church, its ministry and structure. During the course of five years, each group of about ten people met at least eighty times and it was through their discussion that the body of material developed.

By the time I had left my first pastorate, my first approach to "communicating the faith" was complete. It was the result of four years of preaching in the local congregation and comprised 130 sermons forming a kind of "systematic theology." Each sermon had been preached, discussed, amended and reshaped by the searching comments of so many people who represented such a wide variety of experience. When I moved to my second pastorate and was eager to begin again, I realized that I needed to develop the approach in two directions: (1) There was the need to discover the Scriptures in the same way as we had been confronted by theological dimensions. How was this to be done in such a way that people who had never read the Bible, could do so without becoming "literalists" or without spending all their time reading commentaries rather than the Scriptures? What was the relationship between the Biblical text and the commentary? It was then that I discovered the work of Alan T. Dale. [3] (2) There was also the need to reveal that the contemporary search for the truth of the Gospel was part and parcel of a discovery that had been going on for centuries. This led to a re-evaluation of the classic writers of the faith and I had a burning desire to share this treasury with my fellow disciples. My basic source was **The Library of Christian Classics** [4] from which I was able to draw several hundred extracts which were related to major theological themes.

During the second year of my second pastorate I began my second approach to "communicating the faith." It was a different challenge. Instead of the original 130 themes, I now shaped an approach of twenty theological themes. Each theme was still used as the basis for an act of worship as it had been in my previous pastorate, but I was now faced by a further issue. How could "theologically-based material" become the shape of "family worship" and of the nurture of children as well as being suitable as a source for more adult discussion. Could it serve as a foundation for the worshipping life of the whole family of the Church, as well as being appropriate for the work of mission where churched and unchurched were meeting each other in the open-style and flexible discussion groups?

The following year saw the third experiment. By this time the new approach had been used in family worship for a year and in discussion by six house groups. The material had also been reshaped and developed by church members responsible for the nurture of children in the Church. In the light of this experience the twenty major themes were now rewritten and subdivided into 38 sections. This was followed by a further year of worshipping and discussing within the Church and the wider community and resulted in the fourth experiment in which the basic twenty themes were now shaped into 54 sections in order to link the series more closely with the traditional Christian Year.

This final experiment was published as **Discovering Together** (First Edition 1977; Second Edition 1978) and has been used widely during the past six years in Sunday family-worship, in day-retreats, half-week courses as well as in discussion groups in many parts of Wales--for which of course the material was originally intended. As a result of that long and rich experience I wish to make several observations about Christian Nurture and Mission.

INGREDIENTS FOR A PROGRAMME OF CHRISTIAN NURTURE

A. The Sweep of Theology

A privilege and responsibility open to all people is that of searching for, discovering, sharing and communicating faith. The theological question and answer must be open to the whole People of God and must never be the preserve of the so-called academic. At the same time the pursuit of theology should be liberated from both the clutches of anti-intellectual conservatives and from those "liberals" whose only norm is their own experience.

It is also important that a shape to theology should respond to the demand for mission. How is "faith" to be communicated? The believer's pilgrimage of discovery towards a deeper faith and a greater understanding of his convictions should enable him to reach a greater understanding of his "neighbor" and to a development of the art of communicating. Theology must never stray from apologetics. **Discovering Together** is centered upon the death and resurrection of Christ and in its twenty themes seeks to introduce the reader to the sweep of theology, to the alpha and omega of Christian conviction. It is crucial for the ordinary Christian to have confidence in his faith and to be assured of its validity in every situation. While a book of this type cannot deal with every human problem, it attempts to introduce a Christian standpoint to the broad spectrum of issues.

There are twenty major themes, subdivided into 54 sections. The series begins with an evaluation of human experience and the awareness of mystery, religious experience and the accommodating presence and action of God. The Bible is then evaluated as a record of the divine/human encounter. The center of the approach is the Person and Work of Christ, and from this foundation, progresses to questions of God, humanity, creation, eschatology and the role of the Church in the fulfillment of God's purposes. Each of the 54 sections is linked into a concise theological system and yet all have separate identities in terms of worship and discussion.

B. The Sweep of the Bible.

A major contemporary problem is that many Church members (let alone those outside the Church) do not know how to approach the Bible. They may mistrust it completely and regard it as irrelevant, or they may read it in a literalist and private fashion. Most ordinary readers (and many ministers) separate their reading of the Bible from the insights and discoveries of Biblical scholars. A critical awareness should be developed by all who seek to understand the Bible. The fruits of Biblical scholarship should be made known to all.

There is much evidence within the Church that the Bible is treated as no more than a source-book or a commentary on "modern" problems. This indirect or thematic approach is of course valid but it ought not to be confused with discovering the message of the Bible. The Scriptures contain an intrinsic message and it is this message which is to be shared by the people. There must be a consistency of approach of teaching for ministers and laity. [5]

1. Literature.

Like all literature, the Bible must be understood within its own background. We must seek to enter into the thought-forms and experiences of the writers and compilers of Scripture and discover their motivations. This means (a) noting the different types of literature, e.g. historical writing, biography, prophecy, poetry, letters, etc. (b) discovering the geographical and historical backgrounds of the Old and New Testaments.

2. Insights and Convictions.

The Bible is to be read as a record of the insights and convictions of real people. Learn to appreciate these great men and women and see how they responded to actual situations, e.g. Moses, David, Amos, Jeremiah, Jesus, Paul.

3. Debate and Clue.

What is distinctive about the Bible? It can be a confusing book because of the variety of its backgrounds and the length of its literary history. It is not a literature of easy questions or easy answers. But, it provides ultimate questions and answers about the nature of human existence--about God and man, life and death. There is a sense in which the Bible reveals what it is to be really human in a world which is God's world. The writers of the New Testament believe that the issues raised in the Old Testament have received their fulfillment in the person and work of Jesus Christ. In Him and in His followers there is a new experience of the love and power of God.

There are of course various ways in which the "heart" of the Biblical message can be discovered, interpreted and represented, e.g. Promise and Fulfillment, Salvation History; Covenant Theology; Exodus and Deliverance; the Death of Two Cities and the Death of Jesus; Prophet, Priest and King. Despite the variety of ways, it is always possible and necessary to share the Good News uniquely encompassed in the writings of Scripture.

4. Foundation Documents.

The Old Testament is the foundation document of the Jewish People and the Old and New Testaments are the foundation documents of the Christian People. By comfort and challenge, they nourish these communities. They present the standards by which these communities judge themselves and are prepared to be judged by others. It is therefore important to discover, evaluate and "live in and with" the communities of the Book.

5. "My History".

The Bible is a document about life which speaks directly to everyman. God communicates to us in our contemporary situations but we do not know how to listen for or respond to the revelation of God. What the Bible does is to show us how to listen and respond, and how to "hear him" through individuals and communities.

> The Bible says to us: this is what the world is
> really like; this is what God is like; this is the kind
> of person you are. This is the direction in which
> to look; if you walk in this direction you will find
> your way. [6]

Bible study involves a conversation in which people ask questions of the Bible and of each other. A miraculous alchemy takes place when we discover that the Bible is asking questions of us as persons and communities.

I advocate the use of Dale's **Winding Quest** and **New World** for a first reading of the Bible. This is not only because of the author's ability to communicate the research of the soundest scholarship into a language and an approach which can speak to all ages, but also because he has successfully introduced his readers to the sweep of the Biblical story and to its climax in the Good News of Jesus Christ. His books are not only translations of sections of the Bible but they are also introductions to understanding the Scripture and discovering its constant relevance. Mr. Dale's work was not intended to take the place of the full text, but it offers an introduction to the "heart of the Bible."

C. The Sweep of History.

The majority of Church members are unaware of both the "sweep of theology" and the "sweep of the Bible." Even more clear is the fact that few have been introduced to the wealth of Christian experience, particularly to the major Classic writers of the Church. In **Discovering Together** I have referred to the major writers from the Apostolic Period to the close of the Sixteenth Century because they, along with the Bible, provide the foundations for contemporary understanding of the faith. As already stated, my source was **The Library of Christian Classics,** an authoritative approach to these seminal areas of Christian living. [7]

In my earlier work in Llanidloes I had made particular reference to more contemporary theology and thus in my later experiments I was able to draw upon that experience. I now decided to introduce the Church members to three important theological statements which would represent different ecclesiological traditions within the mainstream of contemporary Christian thinking. The three statements reflect how "modern" Christians can express the faith, based upon personal experience, the Bible and the thought of the Church throughout the centuries. I used **A Declaration of Faith** of Congregationalists (1967), **A New Catechism** (1970) from the Roman Catholic Church in Holland and **The Common Catechism** (1975) which claims to be the first "statement of religious belief produced by theologians of the Protestant and Roman Catholic Churches as they have developed since the Reformation of the Sixteenth Century." [8]

The references are chosen to whet the appetite and to stimulate thought and discussion. In their use in various churches, they have encouraged lay people to discover for themselves the original sources. The aim is not to "provide all the answers" but to help the enquirer to discover answers with the help of the Bible and the classic writers.

238

D. The Sweep of Today.

It is also crucial that our approach to faith be related to and respond to our world of today. There is an important inter-action between the Bible, history and contemporary experience which goes into the creation of an approach to theology. This involves understanding our experience of self, family, locality, national and global issues and to do this demands careful appraisal of many resources of information. We must seek to understand our world from a Christian standpoint.

Although the Christian and the non-Christian may share a similar stance towards many issues of life and death, at the same time the Christian has a viewing-point which is motivated by his God-experience. How is a specifically Christian approach to be discovered and developed amongst the plethora and variety of media information? The Christian needs to respond intelligently and sensitively to the secular media, but at the same time must be alert to the approach of "Churched-media," particularly from the ecumenical context of the Church and notably the communica-tions of the various National and International Councils of Churches. In contemporary Britain, the Christian is molded by secular media and is often completely unaware that the Church has sources of information and opinion which may not conform to the prevalent social mood. An urgent challenge facing the Church is the creation of a more open and discriminating Christian community which is motivated by a Christ-view and is open to the opinion of the world-Church. Probably this will be achieved more through personal contact than through the dissemination of information, however sophisticated the media. With the world discovering its common humanity in a remarkable way as a result of mobility and trans-national media and yet with divisions between nations and systems reaching such dangerous proportions that an appreciation of the work of the Church ecumenically is urgent and exciting and open to the most local congregation.

E. Nurture and Worship.

What is the place of worship in Christian Nurture? Possi-bly, the emphasis already made on the need for the Christian to understand and articulate the faith could give the impression that Christianity is the preserve of an intellectualist élitism. How far that would be from the experience of the Church. The center of our Christian experience is in the worshipping life of the community. Worship is the indispensable element of a Chris-tian's life. It is the means by which the faithful are met by the Living God. There we are nurtured in discipline and comfort and we respond in penitence and praise. Through the act of worship we are enabled by the power of the Holy Spirit to continue the journey towards God and towards the service of our fellow humans. Worship has a centrality in the Christian's life, a centrality which is not an end in itself but is a means towards the furthering of the Kingdom of God.

The initiative in worship lies with God. He is the primary subject in the divine-human encounter. Worship is a celebration of what God has done for his people, a reaffirmation that he is now meeting and serving them and a hopeful and triumphant anticipation that God is leading them into the future climax in time and beyond time.

The people respond to the miraculous action of God for the world in their penitence and thanksgiving. God has redeemed his people. In worship we cry "Amen" to the great affirming action of God. We answer the acts of God in Christ. As well as being a hymn of praise, worship maintains faith and equips the People of God for its service to the community. Through worship the gifts of the Holy Spirit are deepened in the lives of the individual and the community of Christians. Faith, hope and love are nurtured. Response must be complete: worship is the most effective way of creating, sustaining and completing this response.

This supreme activity enables us to become what we were created for: the Children of God. Life's purpose is focused in acts of worship where we are confronted by the realities of existence: that we are sinners redeemed by God in Christ, and now we are empowered by the Holy Spirit to respond to God and to serve the world in gratitude.

I have struggled to hold together the "theological" and "liturgical" areas of Christian experience in the "Sunday worship" of Word and Sacrament with the whole family of the Church; in group worship in "retreat" situations; in worship in house-groups and in family and individual prayer. An important aid in this context has been my work in creating a lectionary of Scripture Readings which integrates the theological and apologetic norms, the "sweep of the Bible" and the rhythm of the liturgical year.

CONCLUSION

Prayer must be rooted in the thinking and acting life of the Christian and the Christian community. It always relates to what we believe about God. Christian Prayer is distinctive in that it stems from faith in the God of creation and redemption, the God who acts in Christ and who comes now by the Holy Spirit. Prayer translates theology into action. The power of its prayer-life determines the effectiveness of the ministry of God's People. Theology is barren without the fruit of prayer, and prayer becomes egocentric and superstitious without the discipline of fidelity to the acts of God. Thus prayer is offered in the name of Christ, in accordance with the will of God as we have received it in the Biblical and community's witness. To pray for the fulfillment of God's purposes is to subordinate our will to the will of God. It is Christ's Kingdom and not man's kingdom which is the goal of the praying Christian.

Prayer must be associated with the search to discover the acts and the meaning of the acts, of God, and this is the task of theology. Like theology, prayer is a form of conversation between God and man, and as in theology, the initiative rests with God. Prayer may be a natural phenomenon, but for prayer to be in accordance with the will of God there must be an awareness of and subjection to Christ. That may come only after honest, patient and disciplined search. To cry "Abba" with any kind of assurance demands the qualities of perseverance and confidence.

The Christian is assured that in Christ, God's purposes will be fulfilled (indeed, already "it is accomplished") but there is the hope that these purposes will be manifested in the human sphere as they are in the divine sphere. We seek to respond to the will of God, and to bend our will to his will. This striving is gruelling and is as long as life lasts, but prayer is the means by which increasingly we conform to the purposes of God.

The Church has discovered throughout its long tradition that there are channels which enable the individual and the community to discover the presence and action of God. A programme of Christian Nurture should seek to present the sweep of theology, the drama of the Bible story, a recognition of the rhythm of the Christian Year, and at the same time be open to the contemporary situation. The key to any such programme must be its affirmation of the centrality of Christ who is the heart of theology, Lord of Scripture, pivot of the Church's Year and our living contemporary. A Nurture which will enable us to walk courageously and graciously in the Way of the Lord will produce a discipleship conformable to the vision of the Calvin of Geneva, Cromwell of England and Hooker of Hartford. We seek to be faithful, hopeful and loving in our common discipleship.

NOTES

1. See below p. 235.

2. "There shall be a Moderator for each Provincial Synod being a minister appointed from time to time by the General Assembly to which he shall be responsible . . . The Moderator shall be separated from any local pastoral charge; he shall stimulate and encourage the work of the United Reformed Church within the Province; he shall preside over the meetings of the Synod and exercise a pastoral office towards the ministers and Churches within the Province." **The Scheme of Union of the United Reformed Church** 25.

3. See below p. 235ff.

4. Baillie, McNeill, Van Dusen, eds. **The Library of Christian Classics,** 26 Volumes (S.C.M./Westminster).

5. A possible approach is that suggested by Alan Dale in his **Bible in the Classroom** (Oxford University Press, 1972).

6. Ibid., 14f.

7. The twenty-six volumes in this series contain extracts from the major thinkers of the Church down to 1600 and I used my personal file to enable me to share their thoughts on the major theological themes.

8. **A Declaration of Faith of the Congregational Church in England and Wales** (Independent Press, 1967). **A New Catechism,** Catholic Faith for Adults (Search Press, 1970). **The Common Catechism,** A Christian Book of Faith (Search Press, 1975).

FORSYTH, FORSOOTH

John Garrett

O LORD, bid us come forth. We are in our graves.
Lord, raise us up! We are bound in grave-clothes;
loose us and let us go. We are tied up in our habits,
our views, our pursuits, our prejudices, our egotisms,
our politics, our interests, our fears, our passions,
our fashions, our friends, our sects, our creeds. And
our life is stale, our bones are dry, and we are weary,
our little souls are easily weary of so great a world.
It presses on us like a weight and frost of earth.
All we often seem able to do is to turn in our coffin.
Lord, open unto us! [1]

The disturbing prophetic voice behind this prayer belonged to the son of a maidservant who married a postman, Peter Taylor Forsyth, born in Aberdeen on May 12, 1848, the year of European revolutions. Forsyth was the most profound and biting British theologian of the last years of Queen Victoria and the over-ripe imperial autumn leading up to the first world war. The words of his prayer, based on Ezekiel 37, closed his sermon Holy Christian Empire, preached before the Wesleyan Methodist Missionary Society and published in 1908 as part of **Missions in State and Church.**

Much has been written about Forsyth as theologian, less about the stinging critic of suburban Christianity who bewildered genteel publics in Britain and America. Many who praised his Celtic eloquence never understood him. His wit flayed their weak assumptions. He summoned them to accept the bitterness of the cross as a necessary pathway out of triviality into God-given holiness. He pleaded with the captives of a soft and cosy Christendom. Markus Barth, who understood the affinity between Forsyth's cry of alarm and his father's is said to have declared Karl Barth's work would not have been necessary if everyone who read Barth had read Forsyth. But Forsyth is no pre-echo of Barth; he was no systematizer; his books have no index. Though learned and brilliant, he gave few footnotes or bibliographies. He renounced the bouquets and delights of academia for a career as preacher, guide and pastor. He came out of the groves of calm study on to the cold heaths of prophecy and prayer. Edwardian Nonconformity found him piquant and baffling. His own Congregational churches knew he was a phenomenon but mostly missed the painful points he made.

To account for Forsyth's Jeremiah-like vocation it is necessary to re-trace the life-crisis that led him out of a religion of reassurance and comfort into faith in the tragedy of the cross and the transformation of the resurrection.

In boyhood Forsyth attended Aberdeen Grammar School. His Scots ancestry gave his speech the savor of epithet and paradox. He also shared the Scotsman's fascination with what lay to be discovered across the oceans. He could never settle into the genial reasonableness of much English theology south of the border. The continental rather than the English Reformation first attracted his attention.

At the University of Aberdeen he studied classics and philosophy and resolved to be a Congregational minister. He spent a semester at Göttingen under Ritschl, becoming a Ritschlian in his understanding of the distinctiveness of justification by faith, the importance of the Church as community, and the atonement as a moral and ethical crisis. It is doubtful whether Forsyth was ever the kind of liberal who thinks of Christ's work only as supreme example of an ideal love. On his return to England, still a young man, he seemed to his contemporaries to be a radical. The brand of liberalism they found increasingly acceptable was an ecclesiastical version of Matthew Arnold's "culture" as "sweetness and light". Forsyth's combination of biblical higher criticism and a new-found taste for Wagner's operas and German phrases went against their grain.

A young man with these preferences found re-entry into the strongholds of victorian English Congregationalism uninspiring. After three years' training for the ministry at New College, London, his first two pastorates were served at Shipley in Yorkshire and back in London at Hackney. His daughter described him at Hackney: "My baby memories begin during this period, and I see him in the pulpit, wearing a short black coat, shepherd's plaid trousers, turndown collar and a brilliant tie. (He first began to preach in an academic gown to hide a sling, after breaking his collar-bone in a collision when he was figure-skating on the Serpentine.) London was like wine to him. He was in touch with so many sides of its life--politics, literature, art, music, and even the theatre, taboo to so many Victorian saints." [2]

Up to this time Forsyth's affinity in England had been with the thought of the Anglican Frederick Denison Maurice's vision of Christ's Kingdom made more manifest through renewal in church and state. His interest in socialism was compatible with his personal attachment to the Liberal Party in English politics and derived partly from his wide reading in German and French books and periodicals. Forsyth, who spoke good German, kept in touch with intellectual currents on the continent. "It was one of his few naïve vanities," his daughter recalled, "that when travelling in later years he was always mistaken for a German." [3]

In 1877 Forsyth had married an intelligent, vivacious and discerning woman, an Anglican turned by his influence to Dissent. Her influence gave him spiritual and physical strength in his successive pastorates at Manchester, Leicester, and finally Emmanuel Church, Cambridge, where she died a week after he arrived. Up to this time he had published little--a book of graphic sermons for children, **Religion in Recent Art** on the pre-Raphaelite painters and on Wagner, not much else. He was forty-six. At Cambridge with his young daughter, among a people who loved him, he went through three years of loneliness, poor health and a searching of the depths.

When he emerged from this shadow he began to publish his books, generally at least one each year. In 1890 he remarried. His second wife, younger than he, was lively and wise. She helped him in his periods of ill health and strain. Forsyth said he could not "remember since boyhood passing a day without pain." [4] This did not prevent his living productively until his death in 1921 aged 73.

The death of his first wife and the centrality in his thought of unmerited grace are bound together. The mid-1890's brought about Forsyth's "conversion". Though he was reticent about the details, the words he used to describe the change are reminiscent of Calvin's reference to his own in the preface of his Commentary on the Psalms. "It pleased God," wrote Forsyth, "by the revelation of His holiness and grace, which the great theologians taught me to find in the Bible, to bring home to me my sin in a way that submerged all the school questions in weight, urgency, and poignancy. I was turned from a Christian to a believer, from a lover of love to an object of grace." [5]

The words appear in Forsyth's Yale Lectures on preaching, delivered in 1907. There is a more reserved autobiographical reference to the background of this experience in Forsyth's **Marriage, Its Ethic and Religion,** published in 1912. This speaks with recollected anguish of his own deliverance through pain:

> Of all social institutions in the natural realm the family is that which has the most deep and unconscious effect on us. How else is it that death and loss reveal to us in heart agony the depth of a relation which was growing up, we know not how, amid all the routines and trifles of day after day, and closing in upon our heart, as it were, with strong but transparent walls, which were for us as if they were not, till we found ourselves cut to the bone among their splinters. Amid all the happy give-and-take of common life, and common joys, and common cares, we were being subtly bound with a network of ties which, when they are torn out, take our hearts in bleeding pieces with them. [6]

After the death of his first wife Forsyth's writing took on evangelical grandeur--an exploration of the greatest themes of theology. His medium became the lecture or the sermon. He wrote with emotionally taxing intensity in prose that played on words, often with ironic classical asides. The illustrative material is what Von Hügel, commenting on the Fourth Gospel, called "dark with excessive bright." In his Yale Lectures Forsyth answered the charge that he was obscure:

> I am long accustomed to being called obscure by many whose mental habits and interests are only literary, who have felt but a languid interest in the final questions of the soul as the New Testament stirs them, who treat sin but as lapse, God's grace as if it were but love, and His love as if it were but paternal kindness. At first I believed I was obscure, and I took pains to be short in the sentence and unadorned in style. But I found my critics still puzzled. And I have come to think that the obscurity is at least in some degree due to the fact that while I am attracted by such matters beyond all else, I am often dealing with people to whom they are not only strange, but irritating. [7]

The new Forsyth emerged in five great sermons bound together in a single book, **God, the Holy Father.** The collision that developed with R. J. Campbell's New Theology was brewing. In these sermons Forsyth struck the tragic note, regarded by upholders of refined sentiment and cheerful progress as unjustified pessimism. Here he engaged fully his long battle with bland bourgeois religious complacency.

In 1901 Forsyth became Principal of Hackney College, London. His photograph shows his deep and mischievous gaze. His hair was brushed back from a high and broad forehead, his moustache full and drooping in the manner of Lloyd George or Kipling. His wit, like Puck's could be barbed. Against dilute immanentism he insisted on God's infinite qualitative difference from spoiled humanity, His holiness. In all faith he asserted the primacy of grace. God's love lay in the unbelievable compassion of his holiness, shown in Christ's death. This became the content of positive preaching. The posited is the given; all is grace. Forsyth fenced mercilessly with culture religion, the sweet effusiveness of much Edwardian church life. He detested the replacement of judgment and mercy by the exaltation of natural sentiment. He called the congregations where all this was ripe and flourishing "religious clubland", scathing its affability and compromise:

> We forget that we are an apostolic Church, and that for an apostle the friendship of the world is enmity with God. Multitudes of the good care nothing for principles compared with pieties, schemes, funds and numbers. They are not interested in freedom, but in conventional philanthropies. Recently I read a complaint from a large County Union that they were not getting the young into the Churches, and that, too, while the Churches were going to unheard of lengths in providing cricket, football, draughts and dominoes, dancing classes and pierrot troupes. I agree with the protests made on the occasion, and should say that that was just the way not to fill churches, except with burdens. Speak to a suburban church, for instance, about the nature of the Free Church or its ministry as founded in the principle of the Gospel, and you are met by mute bewilderment. There was nothing touching in the address, forsooth! These people live on religious tea. [8]

Forsyth spoke those words in an address published in 1908, a year after the New Theology controversy reached its height. The source of the conflict was R. J. Campbell, the minister of London's City Temple, a person of eloquence and considerable charm. His book **The New Theology** defends immanentism, appearing at about the same time as the condemnation of Loisy, Tyrrell and the Roman Catholic Modernists. Forsyth did not advance into either of these controversial crises; he was dragged in by followers of Campbell's general line of thought. On one occasion Forsyth was reported to have been present at a meeting of London ministers who were discussing Campbell's thought. When asked if he would join in the discussion Forsyth declined on the grounds that what was being dealt with was "not new, not Campbell's and not theology." [9]

Forsyth's distaste, in this and similar comments about some of his contemporaries, is reminiscent of Kierkegaard's critique of a similar phenomenon in Copenhagen of the 1840's. Forsyth was one of the first English theologians to be aware of Kierkegaard's warnings against the collapse of a Protestantism that degenerated into a decoration for the lives of the effete. He called Kierkegaard "that searching Christian genius . . . in whom Hamlet was mastered by Christ." [10] Forsyth himself was a largely unheeded watchman on the walls, praised for wrong reasons—his personality, massive pulpit style, social eminence. He was, in fact, an unheeded herald of the decline of British and American liberal Protestant bourgeois optimism.

Before the turn of the century, Forsyth, possibly under the partial influence of Schopenhauer, to whom he does not directly allude, criticized this frame of mind:

> The Englishman is an optimist. He has little sympathy with the pessimistic systems which lay such hold of other lands. He puts them down to disordered digestion; he is like an ancient haruspice; he is too much influenced by the viscera, and too ready to read events in the state of the liver. His optimism is based quite as much upon ignorance as upon faith; he succeeds, so far as success is attainable by underrating what he has to contend with. In the spiritual region this is especially so. [11]

Forsyth's Pauline awareness of sin and death appears in his powerful sermon <u>The Taste of Death and the Life of Grace</u>. Its purple passages look rhetorical in print, but would have been gripping when spoken:

> What is the <u>taste</u> of death? That is something horrible-- below the power of any art to convey. Art may try expression by sight or sound. But taste! No art speaks to the sense of taste. So the horror of the deathliest death cannot be mitigated or dignified by the treatment of art. Death in its lees is bitter and ashy. It is nauseous and sordid when we really taste its last touch on life. The more we live and the greater our vitality the more acrid and squalid is that subtle, stealthy death which thwarts, poisons, corrodes and erases life. It is grey, leprous and slow. [12]

In his last and best book, **The Church and the Sacraments,** Forsyth described the forms of church life that flourished when these depths of evil and the scale of grace seemed shut out of awareness by what the age, though not the Bible, called prosperity: "The social, not to say convivial, element is getting the upper hand of the sacramental. The tea meeting is much more welcome to many Christians than the Communion, more remembered, more felt as a church bond. The Christmas food, festivities, and charities hide from us the child Who was born to die, and thus give us the gospel according to Dickens." [13]

His remarks at Yale no doubt caused a few scalds in America. "A bustling institution," he said, "may cover spiritual destitution, just as Christian work may be taken up as a narcotic to spiritual doubt and emptiness. The minister's study becomes more of an office than an oratory. Committees suck away the breath of power. Socialities become the only welcome sacraments. The tea-meeting draws people together as the communion table does not. The minister may talk the silliest platitudes without resentment, but he may not smoke a cigar in some places without causing an explosion. And religion becomes an ambulance, not a pioneer." [14]

Thus Peter Taylor Forsyth prophetically pursued "the triviality which is our mildew." [15] He indicated that resurrection life is possible only for those who acknowledge they are spiritually defunct. "We can be much too kind to human nature for the gospel it needs," one of his sermons said. "Give George MacDonald a well-earned rest, and take up your Pascal. The gospel can be ineffective because it is not incisive enough, not unsparing enough, not real enough to face us, not deep enough to trawl the foul bed of the soul." Then, with characteristic flourish, he continued: "Is this theology? Then theology it must be. It only means that it is upon some kind of theology that a Church must live. An individual may get on with mere religion, but a Church must have dogma." [16]

Not surprisingly R. W. Dale, the eminent nineteenth century Congregational preacher-historian, said of Forsyth, who was his friend for only a short time before Dale's death: "Who is this P. T. Forsyth? He has recovered for us a word we had all but lost--the word grace." [17]

D. R. Davies gave another testimony to the quality of Forsyth's mind. "Away back in 1909," he recalled, "I was a student at Owen's College, Manchester, which, as it happened, was the year of Lord Morley's Chancellorship of the University. It fell to his duty to open the new Student Union buildings . . . I was an intense admirer of Morley in those days . . . I determined to have a word with him . . . He noted a book I was holding under my arm. 'Ah,' said he, 'I like to see a student carrying a book. What have you got there?' Trembling with excitement I handed him the book. He looked at it. 'Socialism, The Church and the Poor,' he read. 'Ah!' By Forsyth. One of the most brilliant minds in Europe.' " [18]

What influences were assimilated to form Forsyth's mind?

The legitimacy of the historical-critical method is assumed. A strong post-Kantian emphasis on a transcendental moral authority in the being of God remained with him to the end. He read and pondered Goethe and the philosophy of the Word as act. He is respectful toward the early Christian fathers, but suspicious of Gnostic elements in them and in the classical creeds. He refers seldom to medieval philosophers and theologians and is disparaging about the ceremonial apparatus of post-Tridentine Catholicism. His sympathy with the seventeenth century theologians of English classical Independency, their soteriology and ecclesiology, is prominent always. He shared with John Robinson, John Owen and John Goodwin a passion for Christian liberty, approving their respect for great systems of thought and, familiar, as they were, with ancient languages. Like them he revelled in being a citizen and a churchman without becoming a captive to any place-seeking establishment mentality. Of the Puritans of Shakespeare's age he wrote that "they were more than Shakespearean; they were Dantesque." [19] The observation reveals Forsyth's love of the arts and artists--and his joy in the redemption lying beyond hell and purgatory.

In dealing with the continental Reformation and its sequel in Britain Forsyth was ahead of his time. His **Faith, Freedom and the Future**, published in 1912, embarks on rehabilitation of the "radical co-Reformation, the persecuted and despised movement of the peasants and Anabaptists." [20] Troeltsch's major work demonstrating the contribution of the Radicals to modern secularity and liberty appeared in the original in 1911, one year earlier.

The inner clue to Forsyth the prophet lies, however, in prayer. Among his most revealing writings are **The Cruciality of the Cross, The Soul of Prayer** and **This Life and the Next.** The first affirms that God suffers fully with man and dies. Forsyth wanted to preserve the mystery of suffering in God at the risk of being thought subordinationist and patripassian. He was not impressed by what he considered the over-refinement of the doctrine of the Two Natures. [21] He published his first writings on prayer in company with Dora Greenwell, an Anglican lady widely read in the classics of the spiritual life, who influenced him deeply. [22] Dora Greenwell's emblem, displayed on her books, shows a hand grasping the cross and bears the Latin words Et teneo et teneor. "She is a great expositor of the cross and its poignancy," Forsyth wrote of her, "and her vision is as delicate as it is deep." [23]

For Forsyth Christian life meant prayer. Though he expressed sympathy for the mystical experiences of Jacob Boehme, he was no follower of the via negativa and of absorption into the divine stillness. "Cast yourself into His arms not to be caressed but to wrestle with Him," he wrote. "He loves that holy war." [24]

One aspect of his thought about prayer is unexpected. He believed in purgatory and prayer for the dead:

> We threw away too much when we threw purgatory clean out of doors. We threw out the baby with the dirty water of its bath. There are more conversions on the other side than on this, if the crisis of death opens the eyes as I have said . . . If a man does not at once receive the prodigal's robe, at least he has the entrée to the father's domain. How natural in this connection to turn to prayer for the dead. Prayer for the dead is healthier than tampering with them [Forsyth was averse to spiritualism]. Prayer is our supreme link with the unseen--with which otherwise we have no practical relations. We should resume prayer for the dead, were it only to realize the unity of the Church and our fellowship with its invisible part. In Christ we cannot be cut off from our dead nor they from us wherever they be. And the contact is in prayer." [25]

Many other aspects of Forsyth the theologian fascinate by the free converse he holds with living and dead. His exposition of the atonement as an objective work, with its Augustinian accent on the solidary sinfulness and solidary redemption of humanity, is a central example. Historians and biographers find Forsyth the man, within the setting of his period and his personal drama, equally fascinating. To an Anglo-Saxon religiosity bound fast in the grave-clothes of its prejudices he spoke his word of outrage-- forsooth! In his salutary protest we recognize a prophet and allow ourselves a certain awe at the sound of the name, Forsyth.

NOTES

1. **Missions in State and Church** 342.

2. Jessie Forsyth Andrews' memoir of Forsyth in new edition of P. T. Forsyth, **The Work of Christ** (London, 1938) xiii.

3. Ibid., xi.

4. **Missions in State and Church** 41.

5. **Positive Preaching and Modern Mind** (London, 1907) 282-3. [The same is reprinted in P. T. Forsyth, The Man, The Preacher's Theologian, Prophet

for the 20th Century. A contemporary assessment by Donald G. Miller, Browne Barr, Robert S. Paul (Pittsburgh: The Pickwick Press, 1981)].

6. Op. cit., 112–13.

7. Positive Preaching and Modern Mind 34.

8. Faith, Freedom and the Future, (London, 1912) 122; Missions in State and Church 92.

9. Personal communication of the late Dr. E. S. Kiek, (Adelaide, South Australia, 1945).

10. The Work of Christ, new edn., (London, 1938) Preface, xxxii.

11. God the Holy Father, new edn., (London, 1957) 47–8.

12. Ibid., 50.

13. The Church and the Sacraments, 5th impression, (London, 1955) 259.

14. Positive Preaching and Modern Mind 171–2.

15. Missions in State and Church 154.

16. Ibid., 76.

17. Ibid.

18. In Jessie Forsyth Andrews memoir in new edn., The Work of Christ xv.

19. The Grace of God as the Moral Authority in the Church cited in Harry Escott, Peter Taylor Forsyth (1848–1921), Director of Souls (London, 1948) 128.

20. Faith, Freedom and the Future 45.

21. Missions in State and Church 28–9; The Work of Christ, new edn., 227 and n.

22. Dora Greenwell and P. T. Forsyth, The Power of Prayer (London, 1910).

23. Ibid., 55.

24. The Soul of Prayer, new edn., (London, 1949) 92.

25. This Life and the Next, reissued (Boston, 1948) 37.

A PLEA FOR CONTINUITY

Donald G. Miller

In honoring one who has given his life to the study of history, it is fitting that a plea should be made for continuity with the past in our approach to the Christian faith. The necessity for the plea may be dramatized by recalling an examination for ordination to the Christian ministry of four recent graduates of several well-known theological seminaries. The first question of the examiner in theology was: Who was the major opponent of Athanasius, and what was the central issue between them? This drew a total blank from all four. The second question was: Who was the major opponent of Augustine, and what was the major issue between them? Again, a total blank from all four. The questioner then moved closer to our time, and asked: What was the central organizing focus of Schleiermacher's theology? Again, a total blank. These young men were not stupid. They could likely have given a pretty good account of themselves on psychological, social and economic issues. Yet they apparently had no grounding in any theologians prior to Barth, Bultmann, Tillich and Thielicke. And, needless to say, had they been thoroughly grounded in any one of them, they would have heard of Athanasius, Augustine and Schleiermacher! They had no grasp of the history of doctrine, nor any understanding of the major theological turning points in the church's past. They had a today--but no yesterday. And without a yesterday, what of a tomorrow?

In examining the issue, I should like to look at two aspects of it: first, a mood; and second, a method.

I

The mood of the current scene poses a sharp contrast between the new and the old, with a bias toward the new. The old is branded as obsolete. The new is heralded with enthusiasm, as though novelty in itself had saving virtue. We have accumulated scientific and technical knowledge so rapidly in the past few decades that our generation tends to think that those who lived from our grandparents back to Adam were stupid, benighted souls who are at worst to be ridiculed, and at best to be pitied, but most certainly not to be looked to for guidance. Since we can go faster, farther and higher than our forebears, can make better tin cans more rapidly than they could, can install glamorous inside plumbing to enhance our privacy, comfort and dignity in a way unknown to them, and can grace our lives with a thousand new products which even our parents never knew, we have subconsciously, at least, decided that the old is suspect, the new is sacred.

Granted that we can do so many things our ancestors could not, are we any the better for doing them? Do we really think more profoundly? Are our appreciations more refined? Do we, casting about to carve out an existence on the moon and other planets, have more wisdom than did our fathers scratching out a living on a New England farm or languishing in a Bedford jail? It could well be that if Socrates, Augustine, Aquinas and Calvin showed up at a modern university as candidates for doctor's degrees, they would create an embarrassing situation. They might be in the position of the famous Shakespeare scholar at Harvard, the late Professor Kittredge, who never took a doctorate. When asked why he had never taken a degree, he replied: "Who would examine me?" Granted that they likely all used outdoor plumbing, and would likely ride a horse to the gathering, and had never used a stainless steel double-edge safety razor blade, and had never dulled their taste for seasonal fruits by eating frozen ones twelve months a year--would the range of their minds, the power of their thought, the force of their reasoning, their grasp of profound realities transcending the mechanical and the measurable-- would these be matched by us? Could the experiment be carried out of actually having them present, I suspect it might--if that is at all possible for our generation--produce in us a little humility in our stance toward the past. In a recent article James H. Smylie pointed out how Philip Schaff, as early as 1845, "poked fun at Protestant pride in labelling [the Middle Ages] the 'Dark Ages.' He described the nineteenth century, bathing in its presumptuous light, calling out for the poor children of darkness--Anselm, Aquinas, Da Vinci, Francis, etc. But Schaff mused 'they have no desire to come back, the mighty dead!' 'With a compassionate smile,' he continued, 'they point our dwarfish race to their own imperishable giant works, and exclaim, Be humble, and learn that nothing becomes you so well.' " [1] Our generation may be like children playing in a modern library, who can push elevator buttons to go from floor to floor, or operate IBM computers, or reproduce pages of books on Xerox duplicators, but who know little or nothing of the wisdom locked up in the treasured horde of volumes. We are pushing the buttons which operate the machinery of the universe, but what do we know of its mystery, or of ourselves, that outranks our fathers?

Whence came the view that seems to be almost axiomatic with many, that a thing is supect just because it is old? Breathing is old, and unglamorous, and unexciting, but is nevertheless indispensable. The sky, on clear days, has been blue for at least as long as there have been human eyes to see it, but it does not therefore lose its beauty. The stars and planets have been flaming and circling in their ordered freedom for longer than the human mind can grasp, yet the sense of wonder they evoke is undimmed, nor do we improve the scenery by removing them from sight by our dazzling artificial lights, which are new. The view that novelty, by its very nature as novelty, is always an improvement, is a lie.

Biblically, it may be well to remind ourselves that the word "old" is in the Scriptures at least twice as often as the word "new." And, lest one be accused of building a case on inconsequential arithmetical figures, it is useful to note that the Bible's use of the word "old" is found in some very significant relationships. Among the last words attributed to Moses by the Deuteronomic editor were: "Remember the days of old, consider the years of many generations: ask thy father, and he will show thee; thine elders, and they will tell thee" (Deut 32:7). A few lines later the problem of the wandering Israelites was diagnosed as this: "They sacrificed . . . to new gods that came up of late, which your fathers dreaded not" (Deut 32:17). This analysis is furthered in Judges: "They chose new gods" (Judg 5:8). One of the most tragic events in the life of the developing nation Israel--the shattering of their unity into two rival kingdoms--came about, we are told, because Rehoboam "forsook the counsel of the old men . . . and took counsel with the young men" of his own generation (I Kgs 12:8). Jeremiah complained that his people's troubles lay in that "they've stumbled from their way, the ancient trails, to journey on bypaths, an ungraded road" (Jer 18:15). [2] He counselled them: "Stop where you are, and look; ask for the ancient paths, where the good way lies. That take, and find for yourselves repose" (Jer 6:16). [3] In addition to such counsel to realign themselves with the continuities of history, the Bible abounds in the admonition to God's people to "remember." Their tragedy was described as that they "did not remember the Lord their God" (Judg 8:34). John Bright, dealing with the entire prophetic movement in Israel, some years ago wrote an article entitled "The Prophets Were Protestants," in which he insisted that the prophets were not so much innovators as reformers calling the nation back to its Mosaic heritage. [4] The biblical evidence championing the continuities of history against the recent and the untested could be multiplied tenfold. This should caution us against falling into the trap of uncritically blessing the novel.

Worthy though many new things may be, do they automatically cancel out the old? Does not authentic newness build on the authentic old? Nuclear science, for example, has called into question what many of us were taught in college, that the atom was the basic unit of all matter beyond which there could be no further reduction, and that the elements which were composed of various combinations of atoms were the elemental structures of the material order. The atom has now been split, and the talk is of nuclei, electrons, protons, etc., with the hypothesis that the basic elements are merely different combinations of energy. This is undoubtedly something new, which goes quite beyond past understanding. But the newness does not lack continuity with the past. It is built on past understanding and is still significant only in the light of that. The new is not the abandonment of the history of former scientific study, but is that history brought up to date. A technical writer says of this: "Although it has been shown that an element is not an ultimate constituent of matter, it still has a real chemical existence and a true order of chemical magnitude. The term, then, retains the same meaning, but our physical conception of the element has been altered." [5] In spite of the incomparable advances in modern scientific knowledge, the elements are still listed with their symbols, their atomic numbers, and atomic weights. Here is a combination of the new and the old; the acceptance of the new as an advance growing out of the old but not detached from it; the continued use of the old as an instrument of the new.

There is another meaning to the word "new" than something "novel" or something "not formerly known." "New" may mean, according to Webster, "the recurrence, resumption, or repetition of some previous act or thing; as a new year; also, renovated or recreated; as, rest had made him a new man." [6] In this sense, "newness" does not mean the appearance of something which had never been heard of, but rather the recurrence at a new level of a former phenomenon; or the renewal of something which has long been in existence but has wasted its powers or lost its vitality; or the consummation at a higher level of something which has been long in the making. A man made new by rest is not a totally new entity which has just come into being. He is one in continuity with a long past who has recaptured the energies and the freshness of vision which were his before, but who, in the recapturing, discovers new depths of meaning in the old which he little dreamed were there.

It is this use of the word "new" which is frequently found in the Bible. Even the "new covenant" of Jeremiah, for example, repeats the same formula as that of the old covenant: "I will be their God, and they shall be my people" (Jer 31:33; cf. Exod 6:7, Heb 8:10), a formula which, says John Skinner, "is capable of no enlargement, but only of a fuller realisation" [7]--not something novel, but the emancipation and consummation of what has been there in essence all the time, the final realization of the fullness of what it means for God to be our God, for us to be His people. The same is true of our Lord's words in Mark 14:25: "I shall not drink again of the fruit of the vine until that day when I drink it new in the kingdom of God." The "new" here means "afresh," a heightened and perfected recurrence of an earlier fellowship, "a reassembling round another board," a reconstituting at a higher level of an earlier reality.

This is not, of course, to deny to the new covenant the element of freshness, and surprise and superiority. But it is to suggest that the "new" speaks more of continuity than of novelty, more of consummation than of recency, more of metamorphosis than of originality.

The way into the future will be more fruitful as we recover a sense of history and move toward our destiny out of a fuller understanding of the way we have come in the past. Where we are now, and where the future may take us, must be set in the light of where we have come from. Actuality and hope must never be severed from memory. We have ancestors; we are what we are because of our membership in a family of faith. To know who we are, and to face the future with either courage or wisdom, requires that we know who our ancestors were. And we must strive not only to know them, but to appreciate them. The study of theology, therefore, should be deeply rooted in church history and the history of doctrine. To do this, we must correct the current mood of patronizing our forebears and humbly allow them to be our teachers. This was voiced recently by Felix Adler who, although he is a philosopher, has made a plea for saturating the modern student mind with history as the way out of our present academic chaos. [8]

T. F. Torrance challenged the Bultmann school at this point. He argued that their outlook "appears to kill interest in the past . . . This emphasis is accentuated by Bultmann's . . . thesis that the meaning of past events is only disclosed in the future, and that it is only as we make them understandable to ourselves within our own situation that they can be given any reality at all . . . But nothing can be more disastrous than a refusal to take stock of one's position through historical inquiry, for then one's thinking is apt to be quite rudderless, and one is at the mercy of all the winds that may blow from this or that direction. The immense value of church history and of the history of doctrine is the dimension of historical depth it gives to one's understanding of the faith, and the balance it brings into one's judgments." [9]

If we knew the history of the past, it would be apparent that much that is called new today is but old errors dressed out in new garb. Furthermore, attention to the total pathway by which we have come would be a savory corrective to the tendency to think we have made new discoveries when we are only succumbing to the spirit of the time and reflecting the current temper. To listen to our ancestors might save us from excitedly telling people what they already know, and calling it the Christian faith. To quote Torrance again: "True thinking takes place within a frame of continuous historical development in which progress in understanding is being made . . . no constructive thinking that is worth while can be undertaken that sets at nought the intellectual labours of the centuries that are enshrined in tradition, or is undertaken on the arrogant assumption that everything must be thought through de novo as if nothing true had already been done or said. He who undertakes that kind of work will inevitably be determined unconsciously by the assumptions of popular piety which have already been built into his mind." [10]

I am not proposing that our fathers knew all that there is to be known, that there is no more "light to break upon the sacred page" than that which they saw, that we should be "cabin'd and cribbed" by their modes of thinking or their results, or that any one of them or group of them should be the sole orientation point around which all theological thinking revolves. Historicism of this type has often been a handicap to theology, substituting a survey of other men's thought for the vigorous process of doing our own thinking. I am suggesting, however, that we stand in a stream of continuity with them and that the meaning of the span of this stream where our own generation stands will be obscure without tracing the stream to its source, and that the theological objects which come floating down the stream will be confusing and valueless unless we explore the banks of the entire stream and look at these objects in their original setting. We need a mood which seeks to understand our own time in the light of the past, and is willing to root our exploration of the banks of the stream of history in a clearer knowledge of the full course of that stream. Our "now" needs a "then." Our "henceforth" must be guided by a "hitherto." I am not arguing for a binding "historicism" but for a liberating "historical perspective" which will break the pattern of our contemporaneity and free us from the bondage of the moment.

II

This leads quite naturally into the second stage of our theme--a look at the method which seems to control much current theological effort. Methodology should be determined by the nature of the object of investigation. To begin with a methodology inappropriate to the field of study vitiates the results. We seem today to be caught between the Scylla of positivism and the Charybdis of existentialism; between a false objectivity and a false subjectivity, or a false objectivity which leads to a false subjectivity, for a positivistic approach in science seems to lead to subjectivity when applied to theology. Positivism, based on the experimental method of the physical sciences, reduces reality to that which can be observed and controlled. Since the God of the Bible, by His very nature, is not subject to scientific investigation or control, He is therefore ruled out of bounds. Religion, then, if it exists at all, becomes almost the worship of humanity, the reverent appreciation of the marvels of human culture. Are there echoes of this in the rejection by many of the so-called God "out there" who is transcendently independent of us? Does not a religion deduced from the verifiable facts of our experience, and related only to our inner states of mind and the subjective struggles of our own lives, become almost identified with man's maturing and his technological control of nature, so that God becomes the imminent spirit informing our present secularization? And does not the tendency to identify God with man's enforcing of his own will upon nature through technological science, and thus trying to create his own future through so-called "responsible decision," sound very much like an ancient story where men sought to create their own destiny without God, by saying: "Come, let us build us a city, and a tower, whose top may reach unto heaven, and let us make us a name; lest we be scattered abroad upon the face of the whole earth" (Gen 11:4)? There may be little more future in the current approach than there was in that enshrined in the story of the Tower of Babel. The God "out there," we are told, "came down to see the city and the tower, which the children of men builded" (Gen 11:5), confounded their language, and scattered them. The interesting remark of the writer that "they left off building the city" (Gen 11:9), may suggest that the sooner we are done with an exclusively Christian imminence the better.

It is interesting that the existentialist's reaction against positivism as the sole approach to truth leads to a subjectivism which often seems to come out very near the position just described. The insistence that there is a realm of knowledge not verifiable by the scientific method, but dependent solely upon inward awareness "through involvement in the actual business of living," [11] although true in itself as a corrective of the limitations of positivism, tends in the thought of many to eliminate the objective, rather than to supplement it. In theology this ends in ruling out the objective study of God and focusing on man's experience of God. The gospel, then, becomes <u>my experience of the gospel</u>. The <u>kerygma</u> does not declare what God has done "for us men and our salvation"; it is rather a summons to us to make an existential decision whereby we pass from "inauthentic existence" to "authentic existence," whereby we are set free to realize our true humanity in the midst of all that would deny it. According to this view, the forms in which the New Testament writers cast the kerygma were time-conditioned and now outmoded, so that we may view the theology of the New Testament as "a first century envelope" which not only may, but must, be discarded by modern man. In Bultmann the one authentic historical fact which does not need to be "demythologized" is the cross. At least one American scholar, however, has gone beyond him and "demythologized" even that. He suggests that a fully "demythologized" theology will no longer speak of "authentic existence based upon Jesus of Nazareth or an encounter with him. There is . . . no saving work performed by Christ; Jesus Christ is but a manifestation of that primordial love which makes possible authentic life." [12] My former colleague, Markus Barth, has described this view as "obviously a Christianity (or rather, "authentic existence") without Christ, without . . . any necessary referent in history." [13] It is obvious that this is an extreme form of subjectivism which places the knower in such a central position in theology that there is scarcely any object of knowledge beyond himself. No "saving work" by Christ--just the believer and the idea of primordial love!

But does not the focus on the experience of the Christian to such an exclusive extent in the long run vitiate the gospel, leaving nothing but a story or an illustration to achieve our salvation? And if salvation can thus come subjectively through hearing a story, does this not suggest that man is bound by nothing beyond his own ignorance and fears, and that he essentially can save himself when he is enlightened about his true situation? At least one psychologically oriented theologian, when pressed in a discussion for a definition of salvation, described it as "the ability to cope with life." This is hardly the act of a Savior, but the ability of the saved.

Does such a view involve a sufficiently profound analysis of man's predicament? Does it rest on an adequate conception of sin? One wonders whether a Jew, imprisoned in Auschwitz during the Nazi regime, who heard or read a story about an ancient person who was the manifestation of primordial freedom, would thereby have his problem solved. His enslavement is quite objective. He is victim not merely of his ignorance, nor of his folly; and his deliverance cannot be a subjective thing. The powers which hold him in thrall must be quite objectively broken in order for him to be freed. Someone from the outside must act in his behalf. If there is no objective reality to the story of release, there can be no objective reality to the release. Hence, to focus exclusively on the subjective experience of the Christian, denying anything objective to produce the experience, would, it seems to me, vitiate the experience itself and turn it, at best, into autosuggestion, or, at worst, into some form of neuroticism.

As Alan Richardson has put it: "The biblical symbols are founded on fact. . . . The biblical images . . . were formed upon the matrix of history; they arose, as . . . mythology did not, as a means of expressing the significance of the historical. Without the history there would have been no symbols, . . . they are as different from the mythical expression of general religious truth . . . as the news of a victory is from a general assurance that all will turn out well . . . The events precede the faith and account for its rise; it cannot be the faith which gave rise to myths and legends about fictitious events; a cause can explain an effect, but an effect will not explain a cause." [14]

Eduard Schweizer, in a public address, used what to me was a telling illustration. He said: "I did not get to the theatre last Friday night. Tell me what happened there." If the one questioned should reply: "Oh, it was wonderful. I was deeply moved. Tears flowed down my cheeks. My heart beat faster. I was so excited I could not sleep!", Schweizer said he would have to reply: "You have not answered my question. I did not ask what happened to you, but what happened at the theatre." What happened to the person was important, and cannot be wholly separated from the objective event, but what happened at the theatre to produce the response in the person was more important. A like response cannot be produced in me merely by a rehearsal of the other person's response. I must know what he was responding to before I can likewise respond. And if it should turn out that nothing happened at the theatre, that there was no play at all, yet the one who replied made the above response, psychiatric treatment would be in order. Schweizer remarked in his lecture that two emphases of the apocalyptic literature of the Bible must be recovered in our day: 1) That God is free to act entirely outside our experience; and 2) that God creates an entirely new world, and does not only give us a new understanding of our individual existence.

The proper subject of theology is God, not man. And this subject is the living God, not the idea of "godness," as though the God of the Bible could be lumped together with all the other gods which are no gods and studied in a bundle with them. The living God is unique, and has uniquely revealed Himself in His Son, Jesus Christ. Obviously what happens to us through that revelation of Himself is important, but the God revealed is more important, and nothing authentic will happen to us unless it happens to us through His action and not our own subjectivity. The proper study of theology is the living God manifested in Jesus Christ in history, through the biblical witness to that event.

The real question, then, is whether the living God actually was incarnated in Jesus Christ in history; whether the homoousion of the Fathers was expressing ontological reality. Modern existentially oriented theology would seem to be nearer to Arius than Athanasius at this point. Arius believed that the Word of God through which He communicated Himself was "not grounded in the eternal Being of God . . . This means that the imagery and conceptuality of God mediated to us through the Word or Son of God is correlated to man's own powers of conceiving . . . and not to the nature . . . and reality . . . of God in himself. . . . the conceptions we form have no objective truth corresponding to them . . . They express the view taken by the human mind in its own understanding of divine things." [15] How much this sounds like modern thought which "rejects ab initio any attempt to interpret the events recorded by the New Testament writers as 'objective' and 'really factual,' . . . and insists on interpreting them as modes in which the creative nature of the early Church was at work making 'history through its responsible decisions.' " [16]

T. F. Torrance, who has described Arius' thought as indicated, suggests that "The formulation of the homoousion in the Early Church taught that the self-communication of God to us in Jesus Christ is identical with God himself in his own eternal Being, that the Gift and the Giver are one. What God is in his act toward us in Christ he is antecedently and eternally in himself . . . " [17] It is this One who is the proper subject of theological study. With our focus on Him things will happen to us, we will discover "authentic existence," but this will be not a self-discovery, nor an existential affirmation on our part, but rather the receiving of the gift of His grace--the gift of Himself. He will do for us what needs to be done. We shall find "authentic existence" not so much in self-understanding as in the response of gratitude, devotion, and service.

Perhaps it is not the "envelope" in which the truth of the Bible is carried that bothers modern man so much as our refusal to believe that truth itself. When the Ptolemaic understanding of the universe gave way to the Copernican, and when the earlier view of the process of creation gave way to an evolutionary view, the church, after some struggle and adjustment and restatement, came through with essentially the same faith as that of the New Testament writers and of the Fathers who framed the classic creeds, so far as the role of Jesus Christ in redemption is concerned. The fact that the new science in our day, particularly the social sciences, has led many in the church to renounce the theology of the New Testament and the creeds raises the question whether this is a process of adjustment and restatement, or whether it is an abandonment of the historic faith for "another gospel" of our own making.

Oscar Cullmann has written: "It must be stressed again and again that the difficulty in believing . . . does not lie in the Bible's outdated 'mythological cosmology.' The technical progress of our time with its electricity, radio and atom bomb has not made faith in Jesus Christ as the center of the divine redemptive history one bit more difficult than it was for the ancients. Rather, the skandalon, the foolishness, lies in the fact that historically datable events ('under Pontius Pilate') are supposed to represent the very center of God's revelation and to be connected with all his revelations. That was just as hard for men of that time to accept as for us today." [18] Multitudes of people who shared the "world view" of Jesus and the apostles and who knew Him "in the days of his flesh" and thus had no historical problem, rejected Him and all that the Church believed about Him. So maybe it is not the ancient "world view" of the Bible that is really the problem of modern man. Alan Richardson has stated: "This is the 'scandal' of the biblical witness, as it is the scandal of the Incarnation: that the Eternal should have become historical and that therefore the historical should become the bearer of the eternal Word." [19]

Was the living, creating, judging, redeeming, sustaining, ruling God actually present in the historic man Jesus, acting "for us men and for our salvation" quite apart from our experience, and offering us the gift of His redemptive achievement as sheer grace? This seems to me to be the real issue. And it cannot be evaded or transmuted into something else by a changed "world view" or by man's "coming of age" through great advances in his scientific understanding of the material order. The question may be put squarely in this way: "When was I saved?" In my judgment, the Christian answer to this is that given by a German scholar many years ago: "Somewhere between the years A.D. 27 and 33!"

Whether modern man will "hear" this or not does not determine its truth, nor should it determine the methodology of theology. P. T. Forsyth was once told that "the man in the street" would not hear what he had to say. He replied, perhaps with little grace but with a good deal of theological insight, "The man in the street may have to come in off the street if he is to hear the gospel." Some years ago I heard a speaker at an Interseminary Conference use the symbols of Adam and Prometheus to characterize biblical man and modern man. Adam was biblical man, Prometheus was modern man. He insisted that since Prometheus did not understand Hebrew, Adam would have to speak Greek if he were to communicate with him. The thought occurred to me, however, that there are some things which are untranslatable, and that if Prometheus were to understand all that Adam had to say, he might have to learn Hebrew. Communication is a two-way affair. If one seeks to understand motors, we do not adapt to his lack of knowledge or to his customary terminology. He must be willing, through examination and study, to discover what pistons and bearings and wrist pins and crankshafts are. If men today are to understand the Christian faith it may be that it cannot be put precisely in their terminology or adapted to their modes of thought. They may have to adjust their ways of thinking to the faith, and accept that which to the natural man is unbelievable and scandalous. "For my thoughts are not your thoughts, neither are your ways my ways, says the Lord." (Isa 55:8).

Our attempts to be relevant to modern man may be self-defeating. The basic meaning of the word "relevant" is now listed in the dictionary as "obsolete" or "rare." I believe, however, that it comes closest to the highest meaning of the word. Our English word "relevance" comes from the Old French, which was in turn derived from the past participle of the Latin word reléváre meaning to "lift up again, lighten, relieve." Hence, it came to mean "help, assist." That which is really relevant, therefore, is not what the one to whom we are trying to be relevant determines it to be, but that which really lifts up the true meaning of the situation and offers help in it, in terms not of the apparent but of the actual realities of the situation. Hence, true relevance cannot be limited to that which men will at the moment accept as significant, or that which speaks to the thought forms which are axiomatic in any generation.

The danger in the current quest for relevance in theology may lie here. Either the biblical word, understood in the light of the church's long wrestling with it, is bypassed for a quick word of our own which seems to speak immediately to "where the action is," or we are tempted to shape the biblical word to a mold which our generation has decided beforehand is relevant. But as James Barr has pointed out, relevance "cannot work as a guide to interpretation before the interpretation is done. Only after we have worked on the meaning of the Bible [and the same could be said for theology] can we tell in what way it is relevant. . . . Any attempt to judge relevance at the beginning of our study must only perpetuate the value systems we previously accepted. Where this is so, the relevance conception works like tradition in the negative sense." [20] If the church is to be truly relevant, it must keep vigorously bound to the biblical, theological, and historical disciplines which themselves help to determine what is relevant, and at the same time give a depth and solidity which lift up the true meaning of the human situation and kindle the undying hope that the God who has committed Himself to us in the history of Israel and in the Incarnation of Jesus Christ will never withdraw that commitment.

It seems to me that the subjective methodology of theology

today, which takes man and his needs as the starting point, and tailors itself to what modern man will accept, or to what will answer the questions modern man is asking, or to what will sanctify his technological and secular development, needs to be thoroughly reexamined. Theology has its own proper sphere, its own proper subject matter, its own proper demands. It has a rich heritage from the past which, if ignored, results in a theological amnesia which destroys any real understanding of the present. If we do not recognize this, it may well be that in spite of our modernity of communication, we shall be speaking not _to_ our generation but _out_ of it, giving it its own word back in pseudo-theological dress. It may also be that we shall be open to the charge of Jeremiah:

> " . . . they treat my people's fracture
> With nostrums, and cry,
> 'It is well! It is well!'
> But it is not well!
> (Jer 6:14) [21]

NOTES

1. "Philip Schaff: Ecumenist," _Encounter,_ 28 (Winter, 1967) 8.

2. John Bright's translation in **Jeremiah** [The Anchor Bible, 21] (Garden City, New York: Doubleday & Company, Inc., 1965) 122.

3. _Ibid.,_ 45. The first four words are a paraphrase made by Bright in a note on page 48.

4. _Interpretation,_ I, (April, 1947) 153-182.

5. **Webster's New International Dictionary of the English Language,** Second Edition, unabridged (Springfield, Mass: G. and C. Merriam Company, 1947), number 9 under the word "element."

6. _Ibid.,_ number 4 under the word "new."

7. **Prophecy and Religion** (Cambridge: Cambridge University Press, 1922) 329.

8. Adler's statement was made in a television interview.

9. **Theology in Reconstruction** (London: SCM Press Ltd., 1965) 22f.

10. Ibid., 24.

11. Cf. Alan Richardson, **The Bible in the Age of Science** (Philadelphia: The Westminster Press, 1961) 102.

12. Schubert N. Ogden, described by Markus Barth in **Acquittal by Resurrection,** co-authored with Verne H. Fletcher (New York: Holt, Rinehart and Winston, 1964) 155.

13. Ibid.

14. Op. cit., 157, 173.

15. Torrance, op. cit., 48.

16. Ibid.

17. Ibid., 182.

18. **Christology of the New Testament** (Philadelphia: The Westminster Press, 1959) 327.

19. Op. cit., 141.

20. **Old and New in Interpretation** (London: SCM Press Ltd., 1966) 192ff.

21. John Bright, op. cit., 45.

ANTHROPOCENTRIC TO THEOCENTRIC

Worship in American Churches in the 20th Century

Dikran Y. Hadidian

In the sixth Congregational Union Lecture in London, James Guinness Rogers states: "America inherited systems from us, but in the very process of being transplanted they were freed from traditions which restrained and regulated their development here, and it was only to be expected that in the freer atmosphere of the New World, and amid less conventional surroundings, they should exhibit many varieties from the old type." [1]

One hundred years later the American Church in the Protestant tradition finds herself proliferating in spite of the ecumenical efforts for church unity. There is no major transplantation of systems and thought from the United Kingdom to the U.S.A. now, but what was transplanted a century ago and on, and developed by the thirties of this century seems to have left an indelible impression on the laity and the clergy in spite of the theological training of the latter group.

Bishop Creighton has said that the supreme mistake of Laud's career was the mistake of fighting for great principles on small issues. This is a mistake not limited to one person at one time in history. It is an ever-recurring experience and the history of the Church--on the local, national and international level--abounds in many such instances where Christians have fought and are fighting for great principles on small issues or even worse on non-issues. But each generation finds itself struggling with its immediate past and rallying at some point to raise the Church from her present quagmire into the future of better understanding of what the Christian faith and life are all about.

What we are and think do now depends on what happened in the early decades of the twentieth century. The American Church was integrally related to British theological thought (any

German influence came primarily via Great Britain,) and when it reached the shores of our country, it underwent developments which made both evangelicalism and liberalism authentically different from its parent thoughts.

In Great Britain, at the very threshold of the twentieth century (1902), six Oxford tutors were responsible for a work entitled **Contentio Veritatis.** The tutors--H. Rashdall, W. R. Inge, H. L. Wild, C. F. Burney, W. C. Allen and A. J. Carlyle--were in their thirties and forties, and having experienced "the rapid progress in certain departments of human knowledge which has made the Victorian age the most revolutionary epoch (in these matters) since the Reformation" felt that a "very considerable restatement and even reconstruction of parts of our religious teaching is inevitable and at the same time they agreed that 'other foundation can no man lay than that which is laid even Jesus Christ.' " Being Anglicans, they found "the Church of England face to face with some very urgent problems. Of these the most clamorous, and perhaps the least important is the controversy which rages around the ornament Rubric and kindred topics--the problem which the daily press has dignified by the title of 'Crisis in the Church.' " [2]

Whereas in England "the acrimonious dispute between Natural science and the old orthodoxy which agitated the last generation [was] happily a thing of the past . . . [and] a great many of the clergy [had] accepted the principle of criticism . . ." [3] In America "another problem which affected the churches directly was America's belated and hence unusually harsh confrontation with many revolutionary forms of modern thought, most notably historical criticism of the Bible, and Darwinian evolutionary theory." [4] Ahlstrom goes on to state in the next chapter: "The long epoch from the Second Awakening to the war with Spain was also a century of great tribulation and 'ordeal of faith' for church going Americans." [5] The response of American Christianity is known as the liberal movement in theology, which made Alfred North Whitehead remark: "Liberal theology . . . confines itself to the suggestion of minor, vapid reasons why people should go to church in the traditional way." [6] A full record of American Christianity's response may be found in H. Shelton Smith, Robert T. Handy and Lefferts A. Loetscher, **American Christianity, an historical interpretation with representative documents,** vol. 2, 1820-1960, (New York, 1963).

The American Church in 1936 through her young leaders who happened to be former students of William Adams Brown, looked back at half a century of the Church's life with no attempt to 'restate or reconstruct' the teaching of the Church but to present a useful survey. These younger men were: John C. Bennett, J. Seelye Bixler, B. Harvey Branscomb, A. T. Case, Henry Sloan

Coffin, Charles W. Gilkey, Walter M. Horton, A. C. McGiffert, Jr., and others who honored their teacher by a collection of essays entitled, **The Church Through Half a Century.** [7] This, in the perspective of our decade, was an impressive list of scholars looking at a half century of American Church life.

Two aspects of American Church life need to be looked at: The Church at worship, and preaching in the Church. My interest was roused by reading the article, "Name tags and the theocentric focus" which appeared in Christian Century (Nov. 26, 1980). It was the result of an extensive visitation by Dean and Mrs. Browne Barr of San Francisco Theological Seminary, of the main-line Protestant churches in twenty-three states of the Union from coast to coast. He stated: "With a half-dozen reassuring exceptions, the services were centered on the glorification of human life, human potential, the human community. They often began with a 'Good morning, friends,' as though we had come primarily for human conversation . . . If the theocentric focus be lost or obscured or compromised in the worship of God, how can we expect its support and correction and energy to be kept in the work of the agencies of the church; if it be dimmed in the being of the church, will it not be incongruous in the doing of the church." [8]

The doing of the church is where the action is now in our decade, even though the Church is seemingly concerned about the purity of doctrine, with a great deal of energy and time spent on defending the inerrancy of the Scriptures, or ordination of women or preoccupation with the sexist English language used in the Scripture and hymns of the church. In the Catholic Church, in the words of Hans Küng, "Catholics are tearing themselves apart in the struggle about orthodoxy, formulations of faith and infallibility, while the world around them is threatening to fall to pieces." [9] Seldom does one see any concern for the being of the Church in the act of worship where the loss of theocentric focus is the central issue.

The focal point of our faith is our public worship. So we look at Henry Sloan Coffin's article on that topic to see if for some reason one can find an explanation for Dean Barr's observations. Coffin stated: "The most noteworthy changes in the mode and spirit of worship have been due mainly to alterations not in theology but in taste." [10] The search for the roots of the American church at worship is found in Coffin's chapter on "Public Worship." His description of nineteenth-century church architecture and its implications for the function of Christian worship should give us a long pause to reconsider the phenomenon of worship in our own days.

> . . . the church architects of the nineteenth century were oppressed by building committees who demanded utility rather than beauty. Thousands of churches were erected, larger and smaller, with an "auditorium" of the lecture or concert-hall variety, often rendered more unsightly by series of sliding or folding doors which gave access to Sunday School rooms . . . The more pretentious both in their exteriors and interiors these buildings were, the more ugly they became . . . Walls were decorated with complicated tracery. Sometimes they were filled with symbolic patterns, which were occasionally grotesque, like a huge all-seeing Eye, or (a favorite device in Baptist churches) a meandering river (the Jordan) which began somewhere near the ceiling of the wall behind the pulpit, and gradually widened until it emptied into the Baptistry . . . At the entrance of the church there was a large lobby, where before and after the services members of the congregation could be introduced to one another and talk together. Sociability was emphasized and an effort made to produce friendly atmosphere. [11]

Coffin describes some aspects of the ritual in the non-liturgical churches and he comments: "Churches with an architecture and ritual of this sort and a home-like atmosphere were designed to foster an impression of the 'humanness' of God. The element of awe was absent from the worship. The attitude towards Deity was familiar. At its best the service mediated the friendliness of God . . . it always ran the risk of becoming so human that it ceased to suggest the Divine." [12]

When the change came (due to wealth) with the introduction of Gothic architecture, then its concomitant demands for more formal worship were introduced: robed clergy (how they love to be robed and hooded!) and choir, chancel replacing platform, prepared prayers, stained glass windows, the use of Gloria in every conceivable place in the order of worship. The emphasis on 'enrichment' by all sorts of additions to the order of worship, brought no theological reasons for their adoption. On the other hand, there were "attacks upon the garrulity of Christian worship, and place for silence in which a congregation can face God, and listen for His inward voice, utter the needs each individual worshipper feels, and together adore the ineffable Most High." [13]

The focal point of our worship is the preaching and therefore we look at Charles W. Gilkey's essay on "Protestant Preaching" in the same half century. He points out that "The 'rediscovery of the social gospel' has often been called the most significant happening in American Protestantism during the last half century--

more important perhaps in its bearing on the future than even the intellectual reorientation to the results of scholarship and science." [14]

Of the many scholars who had a share in the 'rediscovery of the social gospel', the name of Walter Rauschenbusch, professor of Church History at Rochester Seminary, stands out as its chief exponent. It is worth signaling the fact that the year his **Christianity and Social Crisis** (1907) appeared, P. T. Forsyth delivered the Yale Lyman Beecher Lecture on Preaching: **Positive Preaching and Modern Mind,** reminding his audience that "Christianity rises and falls by its preaching," [15] a series at Yale which a year before had heard Charles R. Brown on **The Social Message of the Modern Pulpit** (1906).

A return to the sense of God's sovereignty and righteousness, as Coffin had observed, was more of a return to the social righteousness than to God's sovereignty, which P. T. Forsyth in Great Britain and young Karl Barth in Europe were preaching and writing about. The social gospel that had preceded the onslaught of the First World War had not prepared the American pulpit for the devastation that came about with the conflict. "Its confusing and disillusioning influences have carried American preaching, along with all our religious life and thought, into a markedly realistic swing of the pendulum during the post-war years, moving away from easy-going optimism and sentimentality of pre-war liberalism toward a franker facing of the powerful forces making for evil in human nature and in our present social order, and of the inertia and ignorance which so often reinforce them." [16]

It is one of those inexplicable happenings to find a young Congregational clergyman, Douglas Horton, who in the late twenties of our century had the urge in the English-speaking world (five years before Edwyn Hoskyns' translation of Barth's **Romans** appeared) to make Barth's **The Word of God and the Word of Man** (1928) available in translation. In the translator's note, Douglas Horton states: "People in general have heard Professor Barth gladly because he seems to understand their inner needs." [17] In England Sir Edwyn Hoskyns, in his sermon on "Sin and the Remission of Sin" preached at Cambridge during the academic year 1927-28, spoke about being "engulfed in ideas about God, about Christ, about the Bible and the Church and we listen attentively, sometimes in agreement, sometimes in disagreement . . . to what Mr. Bertrand Russell, and what other distinguished men think about God or about the Sacraments of the Church." [18] Hoskyns ends his sermon with these haunting words: "We all need a thorough and radical purgation from the egocentrism, anthropomorphism, which is invading our whole conception of life, and which if it proceeds far, renders the Christian religion powerless and insignificant, since it is not what we think about God and Christ and the Church

272

and the Scriptures, which in the end matters very much; but rather what God thinks about us, how we are judged by the Christ and by the living Word of God, made manifest in the Scriptures and in the Church." [19] In our country the voice of Reinhold Niebuhr was also being heard, with its full impact culminating in his Gifford Lectures for 1939 on **Nature and Destiny of Man,** a work which had been written prior to experiences of the Second World War!

The great Depression, and eventually the Second World War, had their temporary sobering effects on worship and preaching, but the rank and file of American preachers continued to remain under the spell of the early nineteenth century frame of mind described by Charles W. Gilkey as follows: "Modern preaching in America has been profoundly affected by the far-reaching results of their innovations." [20] The same frame of mind still lingers on. Innovations introduced in the early decades of this century are still with us: children's sermons, constant relocation of the various components of "worship" such as the "Gloria", the offertory, prayers of all kinds, soft background music preceding pastoral prayers and continuing throughout (in larger churches the blasting of the pipe organ drowning congregational singing), use of candles, altars, and crucifixes with altar boys and girls and most important of all the legacy that the pulpit is a "disseminator of contemporary culture and a molder of public opinion." [21]

The Christian Gospel which should determine the nature, content and form of our worship of God, has given way to the dictates of our technological culture and contemporary 'business' precepts and concepts of growth and success retaining also the legacy of the early nineteenth century innovations. The "downward mobility" which is at the heart of the Gospel has been overshadowed by the ideal of "upward mobility" of the secular world. [22]

Public relations take precedence over the Creator-Redeemer relation to the creature-sinner. All our alterations are followed by so-called theological apologias and we are back in the barren land of worshiping God made in the image of man. A lackadaisical approach to the study of theology (in its broader and 'professional' context) where the outcome is an intimacy and informality in our God-talk and worship of God, has not generated the sense of "awe, wonder and reverence before the sovereign holy God" [23] which Arnold Come spoke about (quoted by Browne Barr in his Christian Century article cited above).

What are the options before us? We could continue to remain under the spell of secular culture and let the precepts of the business world control our faith and life in the church, OR make a conscious effort to rediscover the primary meaning of the word 'profession' both by clergy (and the institutions that train the clergy) and by the laity, namely, to mean "that which one professes . . . spec., Christian or religious faith and purpose openly avowed." [24] So to be professional means 'pertaining to a call.' Will it be acceptable to quote from the Shorter Westminster Confession: "What is the chief end of Man? Man's chief end is to glorify God and to enjoy Him forever." And we let a contemporary British Methodist theologian, Geoffrey Wainwright, who is presently teaching at Union Theological Seminary in New York City, give us the much needed word about Christian worship: "The function of Christian worship within the world is to bear symbolic witness to the Christ-pattern. In so far as the Christ pattern impresses itself upon human life, the kingdom of God is being established; consequently, the witness which authentic Christian worship makes before the world is itself doxological." [25]

Within the doxological context all attitudes are human responses to God in Christ. The Lordship of Christ with its implications for worship, doctrine and life is our distinctive profession, confession and proclamation to the world. All else in our personal and institutional life looks like "a poor player that struts and frets his hour upon the stage and then is heard no more, it is a tale told by an idiot, full of sound and fury, signifying nothing."

Christian worship affirms life but gives God the glory, for the Christian has seen "the light of the knowledge of the Glory of God in the face of Christ."

NOTES

1. **The Church Systems of England in the Nineteenth Century** (London: Hodder and Stoughton, 1881) 8.

2. **Contentio Veritatis; essays in constructive theology** (New York: E. P. Dutton, 1902) v.

3. Ibid.

4. Sidney E. Ahlstrom, **A Religious History of the American People** (New Haven: Yale University Press, 1972) 733.

5. Ibid., 763.

6. **Adventure in Ideas** (New York: Macmillan, 1933) 174.

7. **The Church Through Half a Century; essays in honor of William**

274

Adams Brown. By former students. (New York: Scribners, 1936).

8. Christian Century 97 (Nov. 26, 1980) 1160-1161.

9. "Where I Stand," PSR Bulletin 59 (1981) [8].

10. "Public Worship," in The Church Through Half a Century 188.

11. Ibid., 186.

12. Ibid., 187-188.

13. Ibid., 203.

14. Ibid., 214.

15. Positive Preaching and Modern Mind (New York: Armstrong, 1907) 3. [The same is reprinted in P. T. Forsyth, The Man, The Preacher's Theologian, Prophet for the 20th Century. A contemporary assessment by Donald G. Miller, Browne Barr, Robert S. Paul (Pittsburgh: The Pickwick Press, 1981)].

16. The Church Through Half a Century 216.

17. The Word of God and the Word of Man (Boston: Pilgrim Press, 1928) iii.

18. Edwyn C. Hoskyns, Cambridge Sermons (London: S.P.C.K., 1938) 42.

19. Ibid., 45.

20. The Church Through Half a Century 221.

21. Ibid., 210.

22. Cf. Henri J. M. Nouwen, "Downward Mobility; vocation, temptations and foundation of ministry. The Virginia Seminary Journal 23 (January, 1981) 3-17.

23. Christian Century 97 (Nov. 26, 1980) 1160.

24. Webster's Third New International Dictionary (Springfield: G. & C. Merriam Co., 1967) 1811.

25. Doxology: the praise of God in worship, doctrine and life (New York: Oxford University Press, 1980) 69.

CONGRATULATORY LIST

Clifford E. Barbour Library Staff, Pittsburgh, PA
Bunty Bates, Isle of Wight, England
Marion D. Battles, Grand Rapids, MI
Robert and Ann Benedetto, Honolulu, Hawaii

Sir David and Lady Cairns, Ashtead, Surrey, England
Marion Childress-Usher, Lockhart, TX
Jon Clifton, Pittsburgh, PA
Garry Cole, Austin, TX
James S. and Mary M. Currie, Whiteside, MO

Ernest S. and Shirley Dean, Weimar, TX

Robert and Marilyn Eichenlaub, Waynesburg, PA
Barry and Valerie Ekins, Downton, Salisbury, England
Mary D. English, Austin, TX

David M. Gill, Sydney, Australia
James B. Gooch, Santa Anna, TX

Jean W. Hadidian, Allison Park, PA
Donald A. Hagner, Pasadena, CA
Donna Knight Harder, Austin, TX
Col. J. E. Harrell, Austin, TX
Herman A. Harren, Austin, TX
Catherine R. Harrison, Tacoma, WA
Justin J. and Margaret Hartman, Acton, MA
Richard A. Hasler, Belpre, OH
Rachel Henderlite, Austin, TX
George S. Heyer, Jr., Austin, TX
Catherine Hubbs, Austin, TX

Institute of Youth Ministries
    Darrell L. Guder, Dir., Colorado Springs, CO
M. Bruce Irwin, Pottstown, PA

Melancthon W. Jacobus, Hartford, CT
Tom and Hiltje Jamieson, Southampton, MA
Edward Dixon Junkin, Austin, TX

The Tom Kites, Austin, TX

Laura B. Lewis, Austin, TX

Sandra Maxwell, Austin, TX
William L. McClelland, New Concord, OH
Betty Meadows, New Orleans, LA
Brett P. and Mary Doyle Morgan, Louisville, KY

David Robert O'Neal, Honey Grove, TX
Ronald E. Osborn, Seaside, OR

Martin O. K. Paul, New York, NY
Timothy and Ann Paul, Pittsburgh, PA
Tommie Pinkard, Austin, TX

Dale Ratheal, Austin, TX
Rollin O. Russell, Burlington, NC

Mark E. Salmon, Belton, TX
David K. Schaller, Lake Village, AR
Harold and Mary Ellen Scott, Pittsburgh, PA
John C. Shetler, Collegeville, PA
Basil and Barbara Sims, Weston-super-Mare, England
Samuel Wayne and Sara Steele, Austin, TX
Mark A. Stoddard, Denison, TX

Dean and Lydia Tapley, Burnham-on-Crouch, Essex,
    England
James Tomasek, Jr., Austin, TX
John C. Towery, Austin, TX

Joanne Windbigler, Austin, TX

૨